BAMSO

OTHER WORKS BY ASANARO

The Secret Art of Seamm Jasani: 58 Movements for
Eternal Youth from Ancient Tibet

The Secret Art of Boabom: Awaken Inner Power Through
Defense-Meditation from Ancient Tibet

Bamso II: The Legend of the Mmulmmat

JEREMY P. TARCHER/PENGUIN

a member of Penguin Group (USA) Inc.

New York

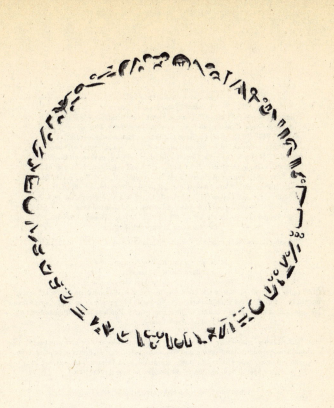

BAMSO

THE ART OF DREAMS

ASANARO

TRANSLATED BY AMLOM AND YEMADO

JEREMY P. TARCHER/PENGUIN
Published by the Penguin Group
Penguin Group (USA) Inc., 375 Hudson Street, New York, New York 10014, USA •
Penguin Group (Canada), 90 Eglinton Avenue East, Suite 700, Toronto, Ontario
M4P 2Y3, Canada (a division of Pearson Penguin Canada Inc.) •
Penguin Books Ltd, 80 Strand, London WC2R 0RL, England • Penguin
Ireland, 25 St Stephen's Green, Dublin 2, Ireland (a division of Penguin Books Ltd) •
Penguin Group (Australia), 250 Camberwell Road, Camberwell, Victoria 3124,
Australia (a division of Pearson Australia Group Pty Ltd) • Penguin Books
India Pvt Ltd, 11 Community Centre, Panchsheel Park, New Delhi–110 017,
India • Penguin Group (NZ), 67 Apollo Drive, Rosedale, North Shore 0632,
New Zealand (a division of Pearson New Zealand Ltd) •
Penguin Books (South Africa) (Pty) Ltd, 24 Sturdee Avenue, Rosebank,
Johannesburg 2196, South Africa

Penguin Books Ltd, Registered Offices: 80 Strand, London WC2R 0RL, England

Most Tarcher/Penguin books are available at special quantity discounts for bulk purchase for sales
promotions, premiums, fund-raising, and educational needs. Special books or book excerpts
also can be created to fit specific needs. For details, write Penguin Group (USA) Inc.
Special Markets, 375 Hudson Street, New York, NY 10014.

Library of Congress Cataloging-in-Publication Data

Asanaro, date.
Bamso : the art of dreams / Asanaro.
p.   cm.
ISBN 978-1-58542-752-9
1. Dreams.   2. Fantasy.   I. Title.
BF1078.A83   2009   2009031568
135'.3—dc22

Printed in the United States of America
1   3   5   7   9   10   8   6   4   2

Book design by Meighan Cavanaugh

Dedicated to those who search,

to those who imagine,

to those who dream . . .

to all the Teachers and Students of Boabom

who have defended this dream . . .

JA

ACKNOWLEDGMENTS

My sincerest thanks to Joel Fotinos and the entire staff at Tarcher for their dedication and perseverance, and for all the books they have helped to bring into this world.

I would also like to thank all of the Teachers and Students of the Boabom Arts who have taken the time to read the manuscript of *Bamso*. I am very grateful for all of their comments and positive energy.

CONTENTS

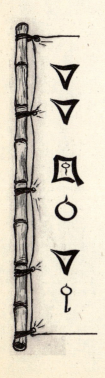

TIME OF GROWTH

TIME OF BIRTH

The time after dreams
being the dream of time.
Awake . . . ! Go where there will not be
and when will not be . . .
go tranquil, go confident,
you will not lose your way
in the path of the Moon-Sun:
the lucid road of Dawn.

Remember that one life marks the other;
one thought knits another.
Think of what you do not need to take
and rest, before the final rest.
Being the time of dreams, the time of awakening.

Today you must fly;
today you must be free;
what here disturbs, there comforts;
what here you long for, there it happens.
Go, Apprentice of Dreams,
simply wish, and you will be there . . .

Preface

The world of dreams is real. Though at first you may think it impossible, all you have seen and felt in the dream state, all of it, is as true as anything you have ever experienced in your waking life. Furthermore, just as two neighboring countries eventually influence each other's culture, the lucid and Astral lives have influenced each other since the beginning of time. For those of you who search for a place beyond imagination, where dreams become more solid yet still more fluid, you will find this volume a good fit.

In the beginning I contemplated writing this book in the form of a course. But that would have been almost impossible, as the delicate processes of mind and energy are not rigid or prescribed and, to get to their core, perhaps the least appropriate thing would be a list of rules and determined practices. No, to teach you what I have learned I must tell you about my own journey to discover what has been called Astral Projection, but which is more adequately described as the awareness and control of consciousness. If you are excited about discovering what dreams truly are and how to begin controlling them, read this work carefully; you will find forms developed that will help you to find lucidity where others see only confusion and diffuse shadows. Though this is a memoir, I have written these experiences in the third person because of the particular nature of this story. In dreams, the dreamer is often simultaneously himself and an observer; with time this effect is amplified as all things seem more distant and one's past life in turn becomes like a dream.

The simplicity of listening to a gentle song calms us with its tranquil sensations; I hope that the story I am about to tell will give you incentive enough to begin cultivating the Art of Dreams. But before we begin I will ask this of you: Open your mind. The road to the awareness and control of consciousness in dreams is the road by which we let go of our prejudices. If the mind is limited in conscious life, so will the unconscious life be limited—its capacities will be solely dedicated to making up for the chains imposed by daily life. However, if the mind is liberated when awake, that same liberation will come immediately into dreams, as a rapid and inevitable consequence.

Asanaro
In the year of the Bamsei

TIME OF AWAKENING

I.

Apprentice of Dreams

Haa ... saa ... naa ...

"Who am I?" he wondered. He raised his eyes toward the pale green sky while, in the west, slowly and in some strange order, eight Star-Suns were setting. There was a white beach ... soft ... warm ... perfect ... all matched with the great silver sea that caressed it with gentle waves.

The visitor stood and looked around him. He could see three buildings, apparently made of wood, though if they were wood it was a very odd kind. They were perfectly circular, and on the side of each there was a round platform on the ground, of the same size as the building. There were no streets, only half-hidden paths camouflaged by the grassy fields that began where the sands appeared to sigh.

Slowly, without really paying attention, he came to a small promontory made of smooth rocks that seemed to form a natural

jetty. The view from there was grandiose and beautiful. The mild glow of the sea and the suns distracted him from his thoughts, and the tranquillity he was feeling was beyond description. Even though he could not see anyone as he looked toward the forest or the sea, it seemed that he was well accompanied. As the suns set, the sands pulsed strangely, as one's chest expands and contracts with slow, deep breaths. In this same way the sea, too, breathed, the waves exhaling upon the beach in a counterpoint to the sea's inhalation, pulling itself back before the next wave broke. Suddenly he felt a soft, unseen hand touch his left shoulder. Even without seeing it, he knew that it was the hand of a girl. He felt compelled to turn to see her, though he did not want to. He turned . . . and there was no one there.

The suns now patiently disappeared as the sky and water became one, the suns setting in a line from small to large. They were not so bright as to hurt his eyes; instead their soft light was calming, as if they intended to match the light of the land and sea. At that moment he wished to fly, to move up and away from the natural jetty where he stood.

He did so, and began to fly steadily, gently. He flew higher, and as he did he looked more curiously on the shining sea,

the white beaches, the grass, and those three circular buildings that so perfectly matched their environment. He thought
about how it would feel to live there. Why weren't there any
roads? Maybe the people did not need them anymore, maybe
they could fly as easily as he was flying right now. All of a sudden he thought about flying itself . . . how could he be flying?
The moment that doubt came into his mind he began to drop
quickly, falling fast until his feet nearly touched the ground. In
an instant he took up the impulse again, and running just an
inch above the grass, he began to fly again. Soaring again, it no
longer distressed him, because now all he could think about was
wanting to see someone, anyone who lived in that strange place,
though he could not see anyone or anything. He could see neither animal nor bird, no living being, although he felt strongly
some presence; it was just that he could not see them . . . he
could not . . .

Suddenly he felt an emptiness, a sensation of cold, and he felt
a pull that caused him to fall backward, not toward the ground
but up into the sky. Everything became dark.

"Where am I?" he said to himself, still asleep. He tried to
look around, and for a moment he seemed to recognize a room
between the shadows. He closed his eyes again, still sleeping.

The cold feeling returned, along with an uncomfortable
dampness and a tickling feeling, soft, through what seemed to
be his body. After a while he began to notice the sounds from
far off: tremors that could be the humming of cars . . . a clod
of indecipherable noise. And then the sensation of the body's
weight, immovable and dominant. He could not move, he could
only feel that inevitable weight. With another moment came
some sense of touch, and then vision, first opaque then slowly

translucent, accepting light bit by bit through his half-opened eyelids.

He began to move, with only clumsy control of his body. For a fraction of a second his mind wandered in no idiom: Where was he? What was he doing there? Who was he? These questions of the unconsciousness of consciousness repeated themselves several times until . . . Wham! Quick as a whip he recovered his link with time and space, and with that link his consciousness came snapping back—work, habits, responsibilities . . . He covered his head with his pillow.

Like a bucket of cold water came that spine-chilling RINNNNNNNGGGGGGG! of the alarm clock. He thought . . . "Mmmm . . . Now I know it's inevitable . . . I'm awake!!!"

"Come on! Up, man!" was how our Dreamer gave himself a bit of courage and at the same time welcomed himself to the world. Especially the world of responsibilities. He sat, still a little sleepy, on the corner of his bed, and began a new day. In those days he always had something to do. The first thing was waking up, and next, looking at the clock he despised yet needed desperately, he would say the same thing:

"What the . . . I'm already late!" He jumped out of bed, washed his face and brushed his teeth, combed his hair a bit. "I'm ready, but for what . . . Ah, University!"

Despite the fact that he lived on the coast, the mornings were not too cold. Just a little cool, but running from home to catch the bus to make it in time for his first class always warmed him up quite a bit. Then came city traffic, with its typical pulse and routine. That was the time when he would finish tying his shoes and fix himself up a bit. Almost every day the same people, same sleepy faces and same weak smiles, sat on the bus. This time of year everyone was just waiting to go on vacation, and this day in particular was the last day of classes. He wasn't quite awake enough to realize it, so he sat and counted traffic lights, streets, a church, a supermarket. He played his occasional game of trying to recognize the same cars, even entertaining himself with his favorite silly little game of following the telephone wires.

And then—University. Who ever thought up such a thing? Wasting half a day of the best years of your life sitting in that witness stand of a seat, waiting to face the teacher's questions, all on a whim. One really has to have character for that. In those days our Dreamer just told himself that it was all for the degree ... But then he would wonder ... who gave the first degree to the first university?

While everyone made an effort to look serious for the morning professor, our Dreamer would often draw. His classmates' books were full of letters and words, while his were full of worlds, figures, and strange characters. On more than one occasion he was discovered.

"Let's see Mr. . . . . What can you tell me about the case of . . . blah blah blah?" To tell the truth, he never could say much, and even if there were some times when he could jumble a few thoughts together to get out of trouble, there were plenty of others when all he could say was "Sorry!"

Those long mornings of "study" were endless. Really, there are things that you are born for, and to be honest, though he didn't know why, he knew he wasn't born for that. But he persevered, armed on one hand with the question "What else would I do?" and on the other with a sharp pencil to draw away the time while the others wrote down every word the professor said.

But now our story has gotten sidetracked ... how did we get here? Ah ... we were exploring this world of dreams. Actually, this is where the interesting part began.

Our Dreamer had been impatient with the common facts of everyday life since he was a little boy, perhaps even before. For some, as they grow, impatience turns to restlessness, and this restlessness into searching. With this kind of search comes investigation and adventure, which had led our Dreamer into some surprising situations.

In those days our Dreamer had already known Alsam for a while. Alsam was one of those strange beings who do not fit so well with the norms of the city. He had formed a small, unique school in that coastal city; his teachings possessed a certain mystery, and his students were not at all stereotypical. Alsam's school taught arts for the body called Seamm-Jasani and Boabom; to the beginner's eye these arts looked something like a cross between yoga and an unusual form of defense. Over time, a few of the students began to encounter some unexpected and surprising aspects of Alsam's teaching, which, as we shall learn, is precisely what happened to our Dreamer.

That afternoon our Dreamer would go to visit Alsam and the school. It was the moment he always waited for, the day of his class! But this class was different. It was nothing like those university classes that bored him—it was a class he never wanted to miss. He always ran faster than anyone else, away from the routine of the university, and toward his lessons in the Old Arts.

It was a hot but breezy afternoon, and the ride on the bus seemed interminable. As soon as he got to Alsam's school, our Dreamer knocked on the door three times and Hernan, who had also been a student for some time, opened it almost immediately.

Hernan smiled and told our Dreamer that there was a group of new students and that Alsam was describing the different courses offered at the school. Entering the main room, our Dreamer saw many people: some regular students he recognized, as well as eight people he had never met before. They all greeted him with a bit of curiosity, as did Alsam. A man of average height with a long beard and a smiling but enigmatic expression, Alsam was nearly finished addressing the attentive new students.

"So, to summarize, in these teachings, which comprise Boabom and Seamm-Jasani, we learn and then execute simple movements; these progress from the most basic steps and projections to the most complex coordinations, with the goal of achieving tranquillity and fundamental balance. The beginning course in which you could participate consists of three subjects, or courses, essential to the development of body, mind, and relaxation, as each physical movement taught here has a direct link within the mind. These three courses are: the Art of Awakening, or Jass-U; the Art of Active Relaxation, also known as Seamm-Jasani; and the Osseous Art, also referred to as Boabom. The Art of Awakening is a fundamental beginning to these classes: in it we move the body in order to awaken our physical-psychical energy. Seamm-Jasani, the Art of Active Relaxation, combines gentle movements and breathing to promote quietude, vitality, and health. Finally, Boabom, or the Osseous Art, is an art of defense and energy united in meditation. Together they comprise an Art we call the Path of Eternal Youth. If you consider the practices you will learn here as exercises for relaxation, they will help you relax. If you see them as ways to improve your health, they will also bring you health benefits, and . . .

"... if you look at them as a way to awaken in dreams, they will be a key ..." This last seemed a whisper, and our Dreamer looked around, wondering if anyone else had noticed.

Alsam continued, "If you see Boabom as an Art of Gentle Defense, it will improve your personal harmony, security, and vitality. Basically, it's a bit like dancing: You have to feel it, dance it, in order to understand what it is! Now ... do you have any questions?"

Some of the new faces asked a few questions about the classes, about the days and times and some other details. Our Dreamer, meanwhile, wondered why Alsam had said that about dreams. Our Dreamer had never heard him speak of that before, and, besides, no one at the school even seemed to have noticed Alsam's whispered comment—they had come because they had heard that Boabom and Seamm-Jasani were an excellent combination of relaxation and physical exercise. Dreams had nothing to do with it. Why had Alsam said that?

While our Dreamer was agonizing over that question, most of the new students left, saying that they would come back later that week to begin their classes. A few of them stayed to speak with some of the more advanced students like Juan Carlos and Eduardo, who were waiting for their own class to begin.

Our Dreamer, however, was still intrigued. That morning's dream, as well as others before, had piqued his curiosity, and though he had been wondering about his dreams for a while, now he wanted to know: What did these classes have to do with all of it? He would wait for just the right moment to ask Alsam, for our Dreamer was sure that Alsam had some knowledge, knew something about dreams, though this was the first time he had ever heard him mention it.

As Hernan's class was about to start, all the students were comfortably dressed and ready for their new lesson. There was always a feeling of expectation among the students before their classes; every class was different from the previous, always enriched with a surprise, some new movement or coordination to learn. They all came respectfully and silently into the room where the classes were held. Our Dreamer quietly followed, finding a place where he could sit and watch without distracting or interrupting. But he *was* distracted; he couldn't stop thinking about dreams. While he wondered, the students followed Alsam's directions in rhythm, beginning low and long, progressing to breathing techniques, exercises for the eyes, the neck, and balance, then through the midlevel techniques. It was always interesting to watch the students link these peculiar movements, from the very simple to the most complex, and the hours flew by.

Once the lesson was finished the class was completed with a special greeting made with both hands gathered in a gesture of respect. The still-perspiring students began to leave for the waiting room, and our Dreamer felt that it was his chance to find out a bit more about the subject, to find out just how much this mysterious teacher knew about dreams. He stood close by him and asked, "Alsam, what is your opinion of dreams?"

"Whaaaaaat?" Alsam sounded amazed, but our Dreamer wasn't sure if he was just pretending to be. The others who were nearby came closer.

"Well . . . I mean . . . to tell the truth, I wanted to, uh, ask you . . . about dreams. I've read somewhere that there are people who can, um . . . leave their bodies and . . . I don't know if you know . . ."

"Eh? I can't hear so well through this ear. People who breathe? We all do!" He scratched his ear, inhaling theatrically. The rest of the students began to laugh. Our Dreamer was a bit angered by Alsam's answer; if he didn't want to say anything, why had he mentioned dreams when he was speaking with the new students?

Just then someone entered the room. It was Marilyn. She was flushed and, before anyone could greet her, she was already speaking. "I've got everything ready!" No pause. "Well, what are we doing? I bet no one's remembered to figure out the food and everything else we need for the trip! There are only three and a half weeks left!" She took a breath and added enthusiastically, "Don't forget that we're going to be lost in the mountains for a long time! Have you forgotten already?" Alsam just smiled and watched.

With his mind on dreams, our Dreamer had completely forgotten about the trip. That year the students who had been in the school the longest had gotten together and asked Alsam to take them to the Osi Mountains. A lonely place between beautiful peaks, the Osi Mountains were ideal for relaxing and developing the teachings. He couldn't yet fathom what he would learn there.

Angelina, Vanessa, and Marcelo, three of the most energetic students, arrived just then to interrupt his wanderings and interject their opinions on how to best organize every tiny detail, and the students broke out in loud enthusiasm over the trip.

While they were making noisy arrangements to organize the trip, our Dreamer quietly approached Alsam. He was still full of questions, so without being noticed this time, he interrogated him directly.

"Excuse me, Alsam, but while you were speaking to the new students, why did you say that the Art you teach is also useful for . . . 'waking up in dreams,' or something like that? I really didn't understand what you were trying to say. How can you wake up in dreams?"

"I haven't said anything." Alsam smiled strangely. His answer was emphatic, and the way he spoke made it seem true.

Alsam was by no means a common teacher. He was always open and willing to show his teachings, but only the ones related to the classes and their movements; it was very difficult to get answers out of him on any other topic. His students knew that the Arts that he taught were far from ordinary, that they weren't the kinds of techniques taught in any institution, and that they were old, very old, from an ancient Tibetan school, and from long before most other teachings they had heard of. Though people sometimes were skeptical when they first heard about the school, after they started taking classes it didn't take long to convince them of the depth and age of the teachings. Yet beyond this Alsam remained mysterious, and more than a few students had been left talking to themselves when they asked Alsam about how and with whom he had learned what he knew. Despite this difficulty, our Dreamer was always trying to learn more, and he sensed that, in one way or another, Alsam could help.

A couple of hours later, after another class, almost all of the students had gone home to get some rest. That day, as on many others, our Dreamer stayed until the very last minute; he wasn't going to leave without an answer! Once everyone else had gone Alsam arranged the room for the next day. They left together, and as they were walking down the street our Dreamer gathered the nerve to ask all the questions that had been occupying him that day. He didn't really know how to begin, but after a few steps he did, though with a certain anxiety.

"Excuse me, Alsam, but, you know, I had a very strange dream today. It was as if I was on another planet, totally different from this one. It had many suns and a big silver sea. What do you think? Could there be a place like that? Or was it just my imagination, and am I just exaggerating . . . ?"

Alsam answered quietly, still walking. "What is imagination to you, Asanaro?"

Our Dreamer was happy that Alsam had addressed him so; he knew that that name held a special meaning in the Boabom Arts, and in truth, it had taken him time and dedication to earn it. After thinking for a moment, he answered.

"Well . . . I don't really know." Our Dreamer felt insecure. "Maybe it's what you want to see but doesn't actually exist."

"Why have you asked me about dreams?"

"Because I want an answer . . . actually, I just want to know what you know about it."

"That means you want to know if I know about dreams. Well, tell me something first. Have you imagined that I know something about dreams?"

"Um . . . I don't know . . . actually, yes!"

"You see, if you think so, it's just what you want me to know. But that doesn't exist," he added, smiling.

"Come on!" our Dreamer said, caught. "I didn't mean to say that. I know you know something, I know, I know!"

Alsam laughed. "Well, who knows it, you or your imagination?"

"Aaahhh . . . I'm positive that you know something about it, but you refuse to teach it!"

Alsam looked at our Dreamer more seriously and said, "Imagination is a powerful strength, Asanaro; do not ignore its value. This isn't the first time you've spoken about your dreams. I've heard you. I know that you're curious and that you want to learn, but most people are not ready to listen. They just follow the road, the current trend, and they don't want to hear anything that might change their way. And if they do hear something, they misunderstand it and, therefore, I prefer silence."

"But if you know about it, why don't you teach it as you teach Boabom and Seamm-Jasani? Why don't you have a school dedicated to dreaming?"

He answered quietly. "No, Asanaro, it's not so simple. What you see as Boabom is not only the development of many external movements, but of internal ones as well. For most of my students it's a path to relax, to learn a unique form of defense, and to gain security and health—nothing more. But for a few, such as yourself, it has an intense and profound effect. Even so, certain stages of the Art are forbidden . . . I mean, forbidden by their own requirements, because they require too much dedication, not just a few hours of exercise each week. Speaking about dreams is a delicate subject—people are not prepared."

"I would like to learn, to know what really happens when you dream, and to control that whole stage." Enthusiastically he added, "I know you can teach me!"

"Well, you want everything. Wanting is easy, but proving it with facts is hard."

"I'm willing to prove it. But tell me what I have to do to start. I've always been intrigued by the world of dreams, and lately they've gotten a bit strange."

"Well . . . if so, I can help you, but you are going to need a discipline and dedication much stronger than what you've had in your classes in Seamm-Jasani and Boabom."

"I understand, and I'm willing. Just tell me what I have to do. I'm all ears!"

"Well, Asanaro, first, from now on, pay attention to every detail that you hear." He continued, "Because your dreams are your window to another world, look at them no longer as dreams but as concrete realities. I know it's difficult to understand, but if you are disciplined and follow certain exercises, you'll soon see results. In about three weeks we're going on our trip with the rest of the students . . . you already know the Osi Mountains, so get ready, because it's a great place to begin."

Our Dreamer couldn't contain his excitement, so he blurted out, messily, "That's great! I knew it, I knew it, I knew you'd help me! I mean . . . I knew you knew . . . you know . . . as soon as I see my classmates, I'm so excited to tell them about it!"

"I said pay attention, Asanaro! Not call everyone's attention . . . The Art has many paths, and not everyone is prepared for all of them. Perhaps for the basic ones, but not beyond. The remainder of the way can be difficult . . . very difficult. You are the one who wants to learn, not your classmates, so let each one find their own path. That task is for each individual, so don't start imposing your desires on them, do not even insinuate. Dreams will bring you many surprises—you might learn from them, but you must also learn how to keep to yourself many of the things that you'll see. You will have to center your mind and learn how to control it."

Alsam's words left our Dreamer a little dazed, though in time he would discover why Alsam said the things that he did. At that moment, however, our Dreamer could only ask, timidly, "Is there a special exercise that I should do now?"

"Nothing special, Asanaro—you are a good student of Seamm-Jasani and Boabom. As I said before, most of the students see the classes simply as exercise, but each movement has a reflection in the mind. In each coordination, in each projection, what moves is the mind, not just your hand, your arm, or your leg. Thus as the Art becomes more and more complicated, it becomes more deeply rooted in the infinite webs that are woven through your body, your brain, and the electric sparks that awaken the areas that had been sleeping ... you begin to see what you couldn't before. But that isn't for everyone, since not everyone can sense it, not everyone has the same conditions, the same amount of imagination. For now, what you've learned as breathing exercises in the Art of Active Relaxation will be the best exercise for you to prepare for the Astral Journey. Do them every morning and before going to sleep."

Our Dreamer asked immediately, "Astral Journey? What do you mean?"

"Step by step, you will learn, all in its moment ... I can tell you that from a higher point of view, dreaming is a synonym for traveling, for consciously separating from the body, and that 'Astral' is merely a reference to the universal, because dreaming can open doors for you so you can see the infinite. In time you will learn the true words and more appropriate ideas. For now, dedicate yourself to your exercises in the Art, and cultivate your imagination, as I've already said ... every night and every morning. It's the first step on a long road."

"Okay! Alsam, thank you very much for your explanations.

I've only got one question, about the breathing exercises. How long do I have to work on them every night? An hour?"

"No, no, no . . . this is simple," he said quietly. "Take it easy. Do you remember the breathing technique of the Great Circle from your Seamm-Jasani classes? Well, every morning, when you wake up, sit on your bed and do it three times, no more, which won't take you more than a couple of minutes. It will be a great help, though, because the more oxygen entering your blood the better. The oxygen is one part of the food of your mind, where you must store the memory of your dreams. In you that memory is still a little unstable . . . on the other hand, it barely exists in most other people. Later, at night before going to sleep, do the same thing. It will calm you from your daily activities while bringing more food into the blood and brain. This is fundamental— understand that the first hours after you fall asleep are when you fall into the greatest unconsciousness, but that doesn't mean that you stop dreaming. Have you understood?"

"Completely. But . . . in terms of imagination, what special things do I have to do?"

"Well . . . this is a bit more complicated . . . for now, keep in mind the fact that the Earth is moved by two great forces, and one of them is imagination. From now on you shall grow your imagination, adore your imagination . . . take care of it as if it were a newborn child, and do not expose it to those who are not willing to respect it. Believe firmly in it, for it is the door to the world of dreams and it is the link that carries us from the inconsistency that we are accustomed to in dreams to something more real, strong, and solid even than what your imagination sees as physical reality.

"The mind is projected in imagination, creates in imagination, forms in imagination. You move your arms because of it, you walk, you even speak because of imagination ... each movement is anticipated by imagination. Actually, the act of speaking in a particular language is a powerful act of imagination. If you ever hear an ignorant person say that dreams don't exist, just think to yourself, 'Therefore, words do not either ...' "

"Well, Alsam ... I must say I'm intrigued ..."

Alsam laughed hard and slapped our Dreamer on the back. "You'll make a good Apprentice of Dreams!"

"What?"

"You have been a student and apprentice of Boabom ... from now on, you can also consider yourself an Apprentice of Dreams. Remember, too, that in every dream there is some reality."

He liked the sound of that—Apprentice of Dreams; it reverberated like his name in the Boabom Arts, Asanaro. Both sounded great, and he felt happy. Distracted by those thoughts, by the time he turned to ask Alsam another question, the teacher had already crossed the street. He could barely see his teacher, up through the old stairs between two poorly lit streets. In the distance Alsam raised his hands to say good-bye, saying, "See you on the trip to the Osi Mountains! When you're there, you will have time to awaken!"

Asanaro, our Apprentice of Dreams, could only raise his arms and say good-bye without words. That moment and its lessons had been important, and left him with the feeling that there would be great surprises to come.

II.

Artisans of Mind

The city looks so strange from here, up on my roof," Asanaro said to himself. He thought, "What would happen . . . if I threw myself from here? Come on, come on . . ." he repeated to himself, "if I jump from here I'll wind up splattered on the pavement, my hot, red, real blood everywhere . . . or no?"

He mulled it over in his mind as he sat on the roof's corner, dangling his legs and propping his chin up with one hand like a pouting, spoiled child who wants to run away. He repeated his thoughts: "Can I jump? Will I fly or fall flat on the pavement . . . I'm sure I'll fall on my face . . . or am I dreaming? If so, then nothing can happen to me. I can do anything! Can I?

"I could fly high up, the night is so beautiful and the sky seems, well, too clear . . . what am I doing here on the roof, anyway, in my pajamas, dangling my feet? This really is a dream, now I remember ... Alsam said, 'Use your imagination, your imagination, your imagination ...'" he repeated, trying to convince himself, when all of a sudden he felt himself levitate just a tiny bit.

He came back down, saying, "Wow! This really does seem to work! I'll jump!" and he stood up on the roof of the two-story building built high into the side of a hill. He hesitated, thinking, "No ... I can't take this risk! What if I'm really awake! Or maybe I'm really sleepwalking, and if I do jump, I'll really be jumping! And tomorrow I'd just be a headline in some sensationalist newspaper: 'Poor Fool Jumps from His Roof in His Pajamas' ... and he laughed to himself, trying to relax.

"I'll jump, that's it, since I'm certain I'm sleeping ... it's just that this is so real! I guess Alsam was right ... But if this is a dream, is it just a product of my imagination? Is it real, or what? Oh, now I'm just talking myself in circles ... here I go! Waaahhh!!!"

Just like that, Asanaro jumped from his roof and, just before nearly crashing on the ground he began to float, to move upward; he knew then that it *was* a dream and smiled to himself. He was flying, higher and higher!!!

"But ... but ... is this a dream?" at which thought he immediately started falling, again nearly belly flopping onto the pavement. He propelled himself with his hands and feet as if crawling, trying to move himself higher. Then he jumped, first little hops, then larger and larger, until he could fly again, though he wasn't as high up as before, and he looked quite like a kite on a windless day. He had been in the middle of a city street and was lucky there weren't any cars around. In an instant he flew up several feet and, looking to his right he saw a white horse far off, behind a street, nearly impossible to follow. Surprised, he looked ahead and saw that he was headed straight for some power lines.

"I wonder if I can fly through them?" and before he could answer he was caught in their midst, all tangled up as if they were gigantic, sticky rubber bands. All he could say was, "I hstaaaatttttteeeeeee these lines!"

RIINNNNNNNGGGGGGGGG!

The alarm clock rang. Asanaro woke up, agitated and rushed: He was going to be late. In the bathroom he saw himself in the mirror and remembered the dream, remembered that he should have done the breathing exercises before getting out of bed, thinking that he should have gotten up earlier. Then he thought, "Wait a minute! I'm on vacation! Why am I in such a hurry?" He continued, to himself:

"What a strange dream ... Well, it was just a dream, though Alsam said that in every dream there is a bit of reality ... nah, it can't be, he's probably exaggerating. What a shame that it's so long before our trip to the mountains! And the school is closed until then; no classes, and no one knows where Alsam lives. He's so secretive. What should I do?

"Well, he told me that I should let my imagination grow . . . so what if I imagine that I leave earlier for the Osi Mountains? Well, what about the rest of the group . . . they're not even considering it, so I'd be alone for three weeks, not to mention the long walk . . . but, imagination . . . That's it! I'm leaving now!"

That morning Asanaro packed his bags, carefully folded his special clothes for the classes, and quietly left for the last morning bus. He knew there was a long trip ahead of him, alone, but he didn't let that concern him; he simply followed what he felt.

Hours passed as his bus came slowly closer to the place where he would meet the other students in eighteen days, from where they would walk, ascending to the place where they would camp with Alsam. The sun was getting low and Asanaro felt a bit concerned. But he had made his decision and would have to climb on his own as it grew dark; there would be no one waiting for him. The bus stopped, only two or three country folk left on it, neighbors of those lonely landscapes. While taking his bags from the bus, he wondered at which exact moment he had chosen to come here before the rest—it was insane! The bus left him in a cloud of dust, alone in the dirt road, and though he knew that now he could not escape this adventure, he still felt quite overwhelmed. That part of the country was known for being rocky and isolated; he didn't want to enlarge the list of those who had gotten lost off the trail. In that moment, though, there was no solution other than taking the path that would lead him to the small valley in the mountaintops that Alsam and his students had long used as a gathering place.

The sun was setting, irremediably, accompanied by a cool evening breeze, the mountains closing slowly around him as his way became steeper and steeper. He had been walking for a few hours already and was tired. The breeze gently swayed the tops of the trees, the road was wearing him out, and his bag, full of food, was not cooperating. According to his calculations it couldn't have been much farther, but as it was quickly growing dark he became disoriented.

All of a sudden he saw the light of a distant fire clearly reflected in the towering mountains.

He began to think, "Who can that be? Some local probably camped where we usually do . . . No, that can't be right; no one likes this place! It's too far from everything; it's so isolated!

Maybe some hikers or people on vacation . . . ? No, it can't be, they're all on the beach, there's never anyone here!"

As he came closer he tried to distinguish something, but it was too dark already. At nightfall in the mountains, the curtain drops. Looking around, he kept trying to pick something out, but there was only that shining. He tripped several times, beginning to sweat. His mouth was dry. What was he thinking?

Soon he was close enough to see the fire, but no one was there. He dropped his bag and came closer when, not knowing from where, he heard a voice.

"You are late, Asanaro."

"Aaahhh!!!" the Apprentice shouted when he heard the disembodied voice. He turned his head and, a few feet from him, quietly sitting on a rock was Alsam, who added:

"I expected you earlier . . . you look like you had a difficult walk."

"ALSAM! It's you! I never expected you'd be here so long before the rest . . . it's such a long time before the gathering."

"I like solitude, too . . ." replied the teacher.

"Wow, that's great! Actually, I'm sorry, I probably interrupted you, since I was supposed to arrive with the rest of the group, three weeks from now. Am I disturbing you?" asked Asanaro, a bit concerned.

"No, not at all. In fact, I was waiting for you."

"Really? Actually, I followed my feelings, and my imagination told me that this would be a very interesting time . . ."

"It's fine," continued Alsam, "you have successfully completed a stage, and I see that you are understanding. Now, rest and warm yourself by the fire."

. . .

Asanaro began arranging his things, and Alsam helped him to set up the tent that he had brought to spend those nights. While they were working, the Apprentice spoke of the strange dream that he had at dawn. When they were finished they sat in the light of the fire and drank a tea made from medicinal herbs that Alsam had gathered nearby. They calmly continued their conversation, for the Apprentice had many questions on his mind.

"Tell me, Alsam. What precisely are dreams?"

"First, you must analyze what reality is to you, and then you can understand dreams. If you want an answer, I'll tell you that there is no answer, only a path to follow; if you believe that you're ready for it, take it, but if not, then you're better off not even trying, because you will encounter some unpleasant surprises.

"What?"

"Pay attention: The world of dreams is a science and an art, and like every science and art it requires constancy, dedication, and a big, open mind, since you can see too much. That is the 'dream,' and the difference between the 'dream' and 'traveling in dreams' is enormous. Every living being dreams; it is a way to rest and renew all of the physical and psychical energies, but at the same time it also is a very special state of consciousness and sensitivity."

"But . . . does what you see really exist?" Asanaro asked excitedly. "And where do you see it? Inside your mind, or outside of it?"

"You are trying to learn many things without having experienced them, Apprentice of Dreams."

"I like that you call me Apprentice of Dreams. If I am the Apprentice, then you'll be my Guide, right?" he added, excitedly.

Alsam laughed out loud. "If that is what you want, then, yes, I will be your Guide."

"Okay, Guide ... please tell me what I have to do to learn ..."

"I'll start you off with a tip: Begin with experience and come to your own conclusions. But I will tell you something— there is a state in dreams between total unconsciousness and semi-unconsciousness; this is the state that everyone experiences. Later on there comes a state of consciousness, and that is the state that you lived today, according to what you've told me. This state is the threshold at which you can begin to cultivate dreams as an Art. When the Internal Art is born the Astral Journey is born, and from that comes the Universal Journey: the Bamso."

The Apprentice was awed; he didn't know exactly where in the conversation he had gotten lost. Alsam continued.

"Pay attention. A common mind conforms to darkness in its time of sleep; unconsciousness is the price you pay for abusing mind and body with your daily obsessions. Only on rare occasions will the mind break into the second world, as you have today. In order to live the higher stages, to understand their essential nature and their real reach, one must be very well prepared, Asanaro ... very well prepared."

"Why is it so complicated to reach those stages? And why do you have to be so prepared?" asked the Apprentice. "I don't quite understand."

"You will understand, you will. The higher stages are far

too intense, and you will see things that mean you'll have to come face-to-face with many things, unravel many schemes from your world that have taken root inside of you, become something normal. The real Astral Journey is very different from normal reality, and it always brings with it a message ... Everyone likes the funny scenes but not the direct truth ... it only brings trouble. Truth is ugly, always in the minority, and discredited by newspapers."

The evening quiet had set in; off in the distance crickets were chirping their penetrating and harmonious melody. The sky was full of stars, and from where Apprentice and Guide sat they could almost grab a handful of them. The Apprentice became engrossed in his Guide's explanations, even if he couldn't understand them all of the time, in the manner or at the speed he would have liked, and without imagining the places where this teaching would bring him.

"What do you mean by Astral Journey?" asked Asanaro, perplexed. "I still don't quite understand . . ."

Alsam lowered his eyes for a moment, holding his hands nearer to the fire, and in a quiet, strong voice continued his explanations. "In order to truly understand, you will have to be patient and listen to many things you may believe have no relation at all to what you are asking. Both consciousness and experience in life are relative to a specific time and space and to a cultural how-when. Your desires, conscious and unconscious, are endless chains that are formed out of your actions, while, at the same time, they are interlaced with the actions of those who surround you, who create your environment in a given time.

You, together with them, form a cycle under the influence of passing thoughts that have themselves been influenced by life, with its own capricious changes and countless elements. You are the product of this, and another link in this chain, and your actions are a reflection of all of it . . . but do *you* act?"

Asanaro was nearly pouting. "But Alsam . . . I don't understand. How is this related to the Astral?"

"Be patient. Learning is a slow process. In one way or another, what I've been telling you is that, first of all, you need to let go of your prejudices, your overanalyzing, your ignorance . . . and then, only then, will your true Journey start."

"I don't know . . . I'm just getting more confused . . . instead of becoming clearer."

"Observe, and observe yourself . . . there are positive ways to feed consciousness in dreams, like the Art's breathing techniques and your imagination. There are also negative ways that retard the process, such as ignorance, intolerance, and prejudice. Ignorance is to know wrong yet to neither see nor want to be aware of it. Intolerance is not accepting reality or the truth, except through the filter of our conveniences and fears. Finally, prejudice is when you believe yourself wise and all-knowing but are incapable of coming closer to reality and the essence of things if those things do not accommodate you, your vanity, and your fear."

There was a pause in which Asanaro thought, attempting to make an effort to rid himself of the ideas rooted deep within him, yet what came to the surface was a feeling of defensiveness toward Alsam's words.

"What are you thinking, Asanaro?"

"Um . . . sometimes I am troubled by what you say, and I

don't want to ask, just listen . . . but then my mind switches, and it's as if I hadn't been listening at all."

"Don't worry . . . you have been listening. Nothing escapes you. Just because you don't understand immediately does not mean that it isn't there. In time it will come to the surface, and if you have advanced it will come in the right way. If you have taken the wrong road, it will surface as a feeling that seems to point at you with what people call guilt, which inevitably carries doubt, fear, and the desire to take refuge in the false, searching for the opposite to the truth that you could discover, placing yourself as far from it as you can. Have you ever wondered why there are so many errors, so much inconsiderateness, on Earth?"

"Yes, Guide, I have thought about that. There are too many cruel things, too many evil people who live in hatred and envy."

"Evil? Hatred?" the Guide asked. "I don't know what you're talking about."

"What . . . ?"

"Don't confuse your judgments . . . think, think . . ."

Asanaro was confused. "I don't understand you."

Alsam was silent for a few seconds as the Apprentice frowned, struggling to understand.

"There is only error . . ." the Guide said. "You must pay more attention to what I say. Everyone possesses the instinct of learning, but we haven't all had the chance to awaken it. It only comes for them in the way I mentioned before, pointing at them, in feelings of regret that make people run as far away as they can, or that make them lazy, drowsy, distracted, and incapable of listening to themselves. This is evil, hatred, and terror, no more and no less, just a terrible and profound mistake. From that mistake to envy and destruction there is only one step. This is a long discussion, but we must grasp it step by step. Further along you will see for yourself. Now, you have come for something special: your lesson in the Path of Dreams, and it is time for us to continue."

Asanaro, more enthusiastic, said, "Yes! Actually, I have been wondering and trying to figure out how all of this can help me to become conscious in my dreams, to help me understand what they really are."

"It is not necessary to think too much about it. Remember that if you leave the bread in the toaster too long, it will burn, and that is lost time. Just by talking about these subjects you are planting inside of you seeds that will open the passageway to a new dimension, what people have called 'consciousness in dreams.' You must realize that nothing is guaranteed. Forget your primitive beliefs. You are not buying a bus ticket with a money-back guarantee, insurance, and the like ... the Journey is something perfect, and it acts out of vibration, purity, likes, simplicity, fluidity, humility ... not on your personal wishes."

"I'm lost again ... because," the Apprentice exclaimed, "I really, truly want it!"

Alsam smiled, playing with his words. "Want ... want? Oh ... ambition!" Then, with more understanding, he added, "Asanaro, when you say that you want, you are saying ambition, and you imagine goals, and in your mind and upbringing goals mean triumph, which means material reward and fear of failure, which means vanity, which means needing the approval of others. That is the way your world works ... all for fame."

Asanaro thought a moment before quietly responding, "Yes ... it is."

"Now, put the pieces together. 'Wanting' in itself is a concept, a word in a language stored in your brain. However, every spot in your brain means thousands of connections that are all infinitely interrelated, and just as with an enormous spiderweb, when you move one of the threads you move all of the others. In order to move the correct threads you must remove every cultural concept; only that way will you discover the State of Astral Vibration. That is the first big step."

"I want that, I want to give it my strongest effort . . . but I still don't understand you."

"You'll have to learn how to knit, Asanaro, and you'll have to take care of your knitting. If you fight and struggle too hard to get away from those concepts of desire, you'll only get caught back in your own web—it won't be effective or possible to achieve it."

The Apprentice frowned again; it was still hard for him to follow Alsam. But the Guide continued.

"I know it may sound complicated to you, but one thing leads to another. You must also understand that if you want not to want, you are falling into a contradiction. Your system does not understand, it becomes stressed, and it dissolves your emanated energy in order to suppress this concept—which will keep you from traveling in the Astral. By not wanting it, you can't escape it. Denial is a part of affirmation, it is too close . . . do you understand? I know that what I am explaining is difficult, and I am missing words in your language . . . but once you feel, not understand, your journey will be closer, dreaming will transform its state, and you will be able to smell, see, and feel like never before. Think about this."

"That's when I'll be able to feel the true Astral Journey! The real Conscious Dream!"

"Well," murmured Alsam, "again you are closing a door. Learn how to open doors, not to close them."

"But what did I say now?" asked the perplexed Apprentice.

Smiling, the mysterious teacher replied, "Asanaro, if you say 'true,' it is because everything that you have felt and vibrated within the Astral Field so far has been false. To discipline and knit your mind in *that* way takes it away from the stage of vibration of which I have been speaking. You must begin by recognizing what you have lived, and there is only one thing: stages. A higher stage is more lucid, clearer, more complete, but this doesn't mean that the other stages are in any way false."

All of a sudden Alsam, who had become enthusiastic as he spoke, stood up, and as he continued to explain he used not only words but gestures with his hands and movements of his whole body that animated his explanations and drew the Apprentice's attention.

"If you are a child you want sweet things, your body needs them, and you reject strong or spicy foods." Alsam now imitated a child, putting on a face of rejection. "If you are a grown-up, you prefer stronger foods because your senses have been polished and your needs are different, you are satisfied by foods that shock your palate. This only means that everything must come in its own appropriate time, which doesn't mean that the other times are false or unreal, or that they don't exist. This mistake, this tiny error, has provoked so much persecution in your Earth, so much intolerance, so much hatred. No one wants to understand that each one of you has his or her own path of evolution. When someone says, 'Hey, you're wrong!' he is really saying, 'I am blind, I don't have the capacity to understand.' Everyone wants to be 'right,' they all want *me, me, me, me.* Behind this intolerance is the desire for power, for control, and behind that is not power but *fear*. On all of this you must meditate . . . as you clear your thoughts you will come closer to the Astral and its higher stages."

"You are right." After a pause, Asanaro added, "Now I've got many things to think about, to meditate on, as you've said. I feel in my mind what you were saying about knitting, as if I were gathering pieces . . . it has all come so fast!"

"You must be prepared—a big adventure is waiting for you. Even though it is complicated to reach the higher stages of Astral Consciousness, coming closer to the Universal Journey is much more complicated."

"I can't say much about it, since I've only achieved what you call the primary consciousness . . . I don't think I've gone any further."

"Don't think too much—you judge too quickly."

Asanaro looked at Alsam, surprised. "Why?"

"Primary, medium, and high consciousness stand together, holding hands—they are very nearly one, like the fine threads in embroidery. Better said, they are only one, all three together. Only time and your real evolution can tell you which one is which, and when that day comes you will see that they were only one."

The Apprentice sank into thought. "Now . . . now I'm lost . . ."

Alsam stopped speaking for a moment and gazed up at the wealth of stars. Then he began again: "Put simply, as we have been speaking about both Energy and Consciousness, let us unite them. Let's get rid of the rough, culturally imposed 'desire' and see things as a child, enjoy them, and not ask ourselves whether they belong to this or that state. When a child plays with his new truck he doesn't care if it's made of plastic or wood or if it was manufactured in a rich or poor country: He just plays. It is the adult who makes him dirty, telling him that it was done in this or that way, adding his dirty, adult, classist, racist, materialistic prejudices to an innocent game. Enjoy your Journey in a simple, innocent way, and don't think about superior stages—they will present themselves to you."

"In fact," replied the Apprentice, "the few experiences I've had with higher consciousness have all come with an immense feeling of joy . . . expansion . . . I don't know how to express it."

"It doesn't matter, I understand," said the Guide, smiling.

"Alsam, do you think I'll be able to come closer to what you've called the Universal Journey?"

"Yes, but in a way that you don't expect. The best always comes as a surprise. To where you'll be taken I can't tell you yet. It depends on many things, on your most unconscious inner world, on what is deepest inside of you and chained to your will, on the energy that has come to you and that you have emanated since you've occupied your body, and even beyond the fluid of time. It depends on what you knit inside of your mind."

"I can't help but be anxious . . . what is the fluid of time?"

"Patience . . . everything has its moment. For now, knit, only knit . . . be an Artisan of Mind."

Quiet, Alsam arose. The lesson of the first day had come to a close. After a few moments Apprentice and Guide respectfully said good night to each other and left for a well-deserved rest. The Apprentice was tired; many ideas revolved within his head, especially the last—becoming an Artisan of Mind.

III.

Three Movements
and a Log

The new day seemed to pass too quickly for Asanaro; after some early morning reviews of the Osseous Art they took a long walk through the area, Alsam explaining many things to Asanaro, "forming the knit," as he put it. His explanations were always entertaining, his hands full of gestures, laughing and making a variety of expressions—for every word he had a different face. Time flew.

Everything was new for the Apprentice, yet he felt as if he had always lived that way, in the mountains, away from the responsibilities and duties of the city. "Mind is free," he thought. "It need only feed on the open sky above, the sound of the river, the eagles' cry, and, of course, the lessons about other worlds." Nothing seemed strange. Sometimes he wondered why Alsam would say, "Out there in your world." Wasn't his Guide from it, as he was? But after a little while he didn't care about those details; they passed as quickly as they came.

Under the setting sun the Guide and Apprentice prepared the fire and a light dinner. During their conversation, Asanaro asked, "Alsam ... what is a dream, really? Why do you always speak of it as a Journey?"

The Guide answered quietly, "Well ... your entire body is always journeying, even when it seems still. Think that you are formed by an immense number of cells, and by an even greater number of atoms that never stop moving, each journeying along its own unique path. From this point of view the mind is like an antenna; at the same time it is a projector of energy. When you dream you are, in fact, projecting out from your body; you are going beyond it. The 'journey' might be short, you might find yourself projected to the corner of your bed, dangling your legs and pouting, like a spoiled child who's had his favorite toys taken away. But you might project yourself beyond, and that is the Astral Journey—going beyond yourself, beyond just you! A simple dream is the numbing of a consciousness that lacks discipline; however, the conscious journey of dreams, if you are prepared, can lead you lucidly out of the mountains and farther ... out of this continent, this planet ... even beyond this time!"

The Apprentice was stunned, wondering if that was what he had lived in his dreams, if it were really possible. He could only stammer, "B-b ... but ..."

"Asanaro! Live it! This is for fine minds. You must begin to split hairs."

There was a pause, after which the Apprentice asked, "I don't know ... is it real? ... But can someone double themselves, as

I've heard? I mean, leave their body behind and take a projected copy, in another plane?"

"You will experience the truth for yourself, but from a certain point of view that—the coming outside of one's body—does not exist. Mind and body remain one, only projected, or enlarged, in a different way."

"I've also heard somewhere that bad things can happen, like being captured by evil creatures, having your body stolen, or dying in your dreams . . ."

Alsam began laughing, hard, for long enough that the Apprentice became uncomfortable. "I'm sorry, Asanaro . . ." he said, still chuckling a little, "it's just that your question is quite amusing, though it's good for you to learn about it. Many people believe in the things that you have asked me about, and these beliefs simply become another foolish limitation on their abilities. I have already explained a little to you about the weight of culture, and soon you will come to know how and why it has prevented you from having conscious dreams. Nothing negative can happen to you in the Astral, and if you see something odd that you might believe to be an evil being, it is simply because you are not well enough prepared. The worst thing that can happen to you is to wake up believing that you've had a nightmare. On the contrary, you must be prepared to see things as they are, accept them, learn, and not be scared. Fear is the worst form of delay."

The Apprentice digested the information silently, analyzing what his Guide had said. After a while he spoke again. "When you teach the defense aspects of the Osseous Art, you begin by teaching simple movements of relaxation, then the basic hand and arm projections, the steps, and later the leg projections.

With time, bit by bit everything is gathered, everything becoming increasingly more complex until the student gains a certain amount of control over the movements and is able to give them harmony and meaning, forming a dance. I can understand this more or less, even though I know that there is much for me to learn. But please tell me one thing . . . what are the movements that allow a person to gain control, or at least come closer to what you call the Astral Journey?"

Alsam took his time. Sitting on a flat rock at one side of the fire, he began to draw some strange figures in the ground. His voice was calm and sure as he spoke. "There are three disciplines for the body, three disciplines for the mind, plus three techniques for meditation. On the other hand, there are four elements that must be avoided and, finally, there is an element from the air." He paused, then added, "I have already spoken to you about each of these, but I will explain them again in a different way, as they are important to anyone wishing to gain consciousness in dreams.

"The THREE DISCIPLINES OF MOVEMENTS FOR THE BODY are the following: First, Healthy Exercise, by which I mean the Art of Eternal Youth in its various forms, including the basic forms of relaxation, the Seamm-Jasani, alongside Boabom. This is the first vitamin you must take to awaken your mind, for each form of the Art brings tranquillity, equilibrium, trust in oneself, confidence, and the awakening of vital energies. The second discipline for the body is Balanced Food, because your body requires something from all of the elements of the Earth, each in its amount and in a middle state. If you overload, it causes unnecessary tensions and tiredness; if you don't eat well or enough, your energy will decay and you won't pay attention

41

must do. The third discipline is Absolute Respect
dy: You must not do anything to harm or intoxi-
npare your body to a vintage car—the more original
has the better. Maintain your integrity. These three
disciplines, apparently physical, will be the base from which you
can accomplish what you are looking for.

"The THREE DISCIPLINES OR MOVEMENTS FOR
THE MIND are: One, Grow Your Imagination; not only that,
adore your imagination, believe firmly in it—it's the door to
the world of dreams and it's the cord by which you can pull
your dreams out of inconsistency; it will also make them stronger, more real and more solid than what your imagination sees
as physical reality. The second discipline for the mind, which
is connected to the first, is to Think Positive. The mind is the
beginning of everything, so be strong, be humble, and always be
positive! Learn how to center your energy, to believe in yourself, no matter what other people say. Learn to enjoy everything,
the big and the small, the strong and the gentle, that which you
consider useless as well as useful. Always think positive—it will
bring you enormous surprises. Finally, the third discipline of the
mind is Constancy; meditate on this. Constancy has given shape
to the whole Universe, from the smallest atom to the largest star.
Constancy has given shape to every form of life that you know,
even your own. If you wish to trespass the frontiers of dreams,
you will have to know this last discipline."

Asanaro listened very carefully, being as silent as he could
be, trying to catch and distill the smallest details within Alsam's
words.

"You must take special care with the THREE EXERCISES
OR MOVEMENTS OF MEDITATION: They are an applied

form of the previous movements. The first of these is Breathing, which I have already explained to you—the Breathing Technique of the Great Circle and its inner processes, which you must practice in the morning as well as before you go to sleep. This will provide you with the tranquillity and oxygen necessary for your projection, as well as to nurture the links in your memory between this dimension and the other. The second exercise is Relaxation, particularly before sleep. You must learn how to relax your body, to release it from the day's tensions, as any sort of discomfort, either mental or physical, can interrupt your work with consciousness in dreams. The third exercise is the Path of the Imagination. As I explained to you before, you must focus your imagination, see it from a different perspective. To begin, just before you go to sleep, try this: Imagine yourself getting up from your bed, looking out the window, then flying out of it. Feel that and live it as real, with all of its details. You only need to do this for a couple of minutes—you won't need more than that.

"Once you have mastered these simple exercises, Eight Major Movements for Dreaming Projection will come, but everything in its time.

"From now on you must begin sleeping close to a log, a personal notebook, your 'pillow partner'; a vital tool in the Art of Dreams. Inside it you must record every detail of what you live during your practice, in your dreams, and during your conscious projections. These writings are essential—very, very important. This notebook will become your apprentice's log."

Asanaro continued to listen carefully. His Guide then solemnly added, "Last, Apprentice of Dreams, there is a final aspect, which is the FOUR ELEMENTS YOU MUST AVOID. Do not deny them, only avoid them. They are fear, doubt, rejection, and prejudices."

Alsam stopped speaking. After a moment Asanaro asked, "I am still uncertain about a few things, Guide. You also spoke of an element from the air, or something like that. What exactly did you mean?"

The Guide smiled. "For now I can only say that it means that you will never know everything; on the contrary, the more you learn, the more conscious of your own smallness you will be, of your own strength; and also that wisdom is simple."

The Apprentice sank further into thought. The truth was that it was too much for just a few days in the mountains. He only said, "Alsam, you have amazed me again. There are so many things to analyze, to consider. I have so many questions in my mind, but I can't digest one thing when just as quickly another comes into my head. I was thinking about what you said the other day, that there are two great forces on Earth, and that one was imagination. What is the other?"

"Take it easy, Apprentice of Dreams. You already know the second force. You haven't yet learned to recognize or grow it, but your time will come. Patience. For now, meditate and rest: Watch the fire, for it hides many secrets, and it will relax your sight and your mind."

The bonfire gently lit their faces as the flames trembled restlessly, their shining light hypnotizing the Apprentice. His eyes stared deep into the eternal dance of the flames; he was able to see figures in them, scenes from other times, people, animals. These images faded in and out amid the questions that passed through his mind. He wanted to be inside that yellow whiteness that shone in the center. Even though he felt certain that it would be difficult to accomplish this stage, Traveling with the Mind, he wanted to avoid thinking of difficulties, as they would take him further away from it, as his Guide had explained. From that thought he returned to the flames, and then on to wandering, rambling with his mind.

"It's late, young and humble Apprentice, and we must rest. You must also learn that tiredness is an enemy of the Astral. It's been a long day, and in the greater dimension we'll have an even longer day."

"Whatever you say," replied the Apprentice, recovering from his stupor. "But . . . can anyone sleep more time than they spend lucid?"

Alsam chuckled. "Sleeping takes up less of our time than being awake, that I know; the day has eight times, and you don't use more than three of them while asleep. If you see it in this way, then that's the way it is! But if you are trying to use the state of the body in rest to realize the Conscious Voyage, that's another thing. If you do it in an open manner, you will notice that you live more time in that dimension than in this one, even though you might be using less by the measure of Earth time."

"Until the end of the day I can learn from you! Now that you mention it, sometimes after I wake up I go back to sleep, become conscious within it, and feel that a few hours have passed, but when I wake up again only a few minutes have gone by! That few minutes of sleeping had been, or seemed to be, a lot longer."

Enthusiastic about the student's perception, the Guide responded, "That's what I meant when I spoke of the difference

between time in the day and time in the Astral. The measure of
the Earth's rotation is the turning of the planet, but that is not
necessarily related to the spin that each of your particles has, and
less related to the twenty-four hours that they speak of on Earth,
which aren't actually twenty-four! If you were on a spaceship
traveling faster than the speed of light, a watch would be useless.
When you slide through the Astral you can travel at the speed of
thought and the speed of light becomes irrelevant, as the speed
of a walk in the park compares to the speed of light. Now do
your exercises and go rest; tomorrow we'll analyze the results.
Have a good journey, Asanaro!"

"See you tomorrow, Guide," answered the Apprentice
happily.

"Be a good artisan," replied his Guide.

Each saluted the other with the same respect as in the lessons of the Osseous Art, then they went off to their shelters,
which were protected by the shrubs of the mountain. A gentle
breeze began to blow, playing with the remains of the bonfire,
and Asanaro took a last look at the dying flame, as if trying
to hold the image of it in his inner mind before entering his
tent. Once inside he settled his blankets and personal things.
Searching in his backpack he quickly found what he was looking for: a notebook that, not knowing why, he had brought
with him, and which would now serve as a log of his dreams.
He cleaned it and carefully placed it beside his pillow. After
slowly and ceremoniously removing his clothes, he did the necessary exercises before sleeping and, already lying down, he
blew out the last candle, made himself comfortable, and closed
his eyes. He worked with his imagination for a few moments,
before tiredness overwhelmed him and he fell asleep.

. . .

"How are you, Asanaro? Asanaro . . . can you hear me?" He didn't quite realize what was happening.

"Am I awake? But . . . when did I get up?" he wondered. "It's not cold, even though it should be . . ."

"Asanaro . . ." He was being called again. He turned his head and it was Alsam who was speaking to him, sitting next to the almost dead bonfire and over the strange figures he had been drawing in the dirt.

"But . . . Guide, what happened? I feel like I've missed something."

Alsam smiled, and there was a pause. Asanaro spoke again. "But . . . I'm in the Astral! I'm in the Astral! I'm sleeping and I know it!"

"Well, of course, Asanaro."

"I've really enjoyed this sensation before, but I've only felt it a few times. I feel free! But, Alsam, is this really you? Aren't I just projecting you, I mean, imagining you, or something like that?"

Alsam, or whoever he was, answered, "What difference does it make? Do you care?"

"But . . . is it you?" The Guide's figure started to vanish slowly, and the Apprentice said to himself, "Actually, it doesn't really matter. If I think, I waste my time . . ." And with that the Guide reappeared.

"Phew . . ." Asanaro exclaimed, relieved.

"Yes, Asanaro, doubt is just a waste of time. I've come to invite you on a short journey . . . but, now!"

"Let's go!" said Asanaro, and immediately they began to fly

fast, skimming the tops of the nearby hills, the mountains, and quickly they saw their camp below become smaller and smaller. Soon came the taller mountains with their majestic tops, so glittering with snow that they seemed alive. The sky was of the richest, deepest blue, lucid and warm like the ocean, neither too cold nor too hot. The beauty of the ground, the mountains, and the sky was so strong, so sensational, that it was overwhelming.

"Wheeeeeeee..." Asanaro yelled as he flew with Alsam. "This is amazing! I can feel the wind in my face and it doesn't bother me at all..." And in that moment a group of birds flew up next to him and looked at him, smiling.

"Wheeeeeeee..." Asanaro kept screaming. He looked to his side and Alsam was no longer there, and before he could think about it Asanaro was flying into a thick cloud, which only grew more and more dense. A few seconds later he was in a strange place.

"When did I arrive here?" was all he could say.

He found himself in the hallway of a very odd place, among huge mountains that at the same time seemed to form an edifice of solid rock. There were people everywhere, looking through windows and walking through strange tunnels made of metal or stone. All of a sudden one of them appeared close by, walking at his side. Asanaro turned to him.

"Alsam, is that you?" he asked, then observed the short man in greater detail; he was much older than his Guide, without being terribly old, and he wore strange, comfortable-looking clothes, somewhat like overalls, not too tight or too loose. Over these he wore a small and beautiful mantle. "It's not him..." thought Asanaro, and he kept wondering who he might be.

The man spoke quickly, and his voice sounded strange. "Go!

Go! Come on! Come on! Don't drool, already waits, already waits!" Asanaro, seeing the expression on this character's face, felt like an obstacle.

"What a welcome," said the young Apprentice to himself.

"What a welcome, what a welcome," imitated the man, "I'm telling you, don't drool, keep walking, heheheheh . . ."

All of a sudden a huge door opened in the side of the mountain, but it wasn't a mountain, only the high walls of an immense building. Many people passed very close to him but paid him no attention. The old man looked at him and Asanaro looked back; his face looked familiar, as if they had met somewhere before, but he couldn't remember where or when. As he was thinking, trying to remember that face, he looked to his side and took in his surroundings. He was inside a huge building with high walls and a floor that seemed to be made of rustic tiles yet was soft and comfortable as a carpet. People kept passing them as they crossed a long hallway. A thought came to Asanaro's mind.

"But . . . then, I'm conscious or . . . I'm projecting! Just like Alsam said. This is great . . . what an opportunity! This is great, great, great!"

As he thought this, the man quickly replied, "Mmmm . . . Yessssss, Good! Good! Good! Already walk, walk, good, and prepare because they has to see you."

"But, who wants to see me?" replied Asanaro.

"Heheheh," the man chuckled. "That'sssssss not important."

"But . . ."

"Heheheh . . . now quiet, quiet," answered the man. "We are already there."

They crossed beneath an arch formed by a pair of curved columns, high and narrow. When they turned there were various people seated at two semicircular tables and a tall, short-haired woman standing quietly between them.

Asanaro said, "I'm sorry, but is here where they wanted to speak to me?"

No one answered. The old man went to the table and exchanged some words . . . The woman was quiet, looking around as if she was speaking to someone. About fifty feet from the table there was a young girl hiding behind a column who would peek out to look at them, smile, then hide again behind the column. The Apprentice of Dreams was curious and thought about how strange things can happen in dreams . . . very strange things. The girl popped out from behind the column, looked at him, smiled, and hid again.

"Come on, is this the one?" He felt a new, solid voice in his ears, not knowing where it came from. "I think we are wasting our time . . . he doesn't have any capacity at all!"

Another voice, rougher, answered, "I agree. I don't know what he is doing here."

"This is a waste of time. He'd better leave," added a third.

With that, Asanaro realized that they were speaking about him, so he burst out. "This is too much! I come from Earth, where people have fun ruling and controlling others, full of bureaucracy, paperwork, rules, regulations . . . do people need certifications even here?" His voice was upset, though he didn't know why; he didn't even know why he was there, or what they wanted with him. He hadn't projected his mind to go to any special place, and he didn't even know where he was! He didn't even think he was capable of speaking in such a strong and direct way; he normally wasn't like that. There was a silence, something strange grew in the air, and the girl behind the column peeked out for a last glimpse at both the Apprentice and the lady in the middle of the room. She hid, and he couldn't see her anymore.

"Take him back!" said one of the elder voices sharply.

Asanaro thought, "This is where my journey ends, and I was starting to enjoy it . . ."

"Wait a minute," said the lady between the tables, gentle and confident. "I think he has possibilities."

Asanaro looked on her as his savior, though he had no idea what she was saving him from. The lady continued speaking, justifying him in a protective and understanding way.

"We should give him the vision, for he has some qualities, and these are the ones that must grow inside of him."

There was a silence in which no one spoke. She continued. "I know that there is a lot of ignorance and impatience in him, and perhaps he is too arrogant, but that is his own test, and I support his previously proposed labor."

Asanaro felt better with the woman's support, without knowing what for or why he was happy—he couldn't imagine what was being discussed or who these people were. He had no idea where he was, either, and everything still seemed like a very lucid dream to him, or what Alsam had referred to as a real Journey.

"That is fine . . . the opportunity remains open. Let him leave now," added one of the elder voices. The Apprentice looked at the lady thankfully, though he didn't know why he should be thankful.

He turned slightly and there was the strange man who had led him there, and he was smiling. Asanaro felt as if he could no longer stay there; everything became blurry and he felt a sensation of falling backward, falling . . . falling . . . Sleepy, he knew that he was about to wake up, and he was conscious. He tried to fight against it, but it was inevitable . . . it was his time, and he was awake.

Bit by bit the feeling of his body came back to him, soft and unstoppable. The weight of his physical state was complete, though even more than weight it was the feeling of physical density, first far off and then closer, more clear, with its senses whole and thick, nearly disturbing. Totally irreversible . . . he was awake, totally awake. Before opening his eyes or even moving he reviewed what he had lived, as he had already learned. He remembered everything, from the beginning—departing with Alsam, the cloud, the mysterious place, the mountain building, the strange, small man, the meeting, and the lady who had supported him. But, he wondered, what was the meaning of that discussion? Meanwhile, he began to feel the light through his eyelids and he began moving his legs and arms as he opened his eyes.

Dawn had come a couple of hours before; the sun shone through the top of his tent.

"What a journey!" thought Asanaro. "I'll go tell Alsam—he must be awake by now."

As he got up he felt extremely happy. Without a clue as to what it had all been about, or what a dream or Astral Journey really meant, Asanaro knew that something good had happened, as if he had passed a test, been approved for, well, something. He had nearly run out of the tent before he remembered the disciplines that Alsam had given him, so he checked himself and awoke quietly and ceremoniously. He arranged his clothes and things, made the Breathing Movements of the Dawn as he had learned, then wrote down in his log what had happened to him: It was his first page. After he finished he went out to look for his Guide, but he couldn't find him anywhere. He looked all around, under the trees and in the thickets, but Alsam was nowhere to be found. Asanaro looked toward the bushes along the river, coming closer to them, to the bank of the river, near the camp. Alsam was there, on the border of a gentle slope.

Alsam was practicing his Boabom exercises. His hands, making strange movements, were soft and strong, precise, quick, then slow and harmonious ... the Apprentice always enjoyed the shapes of the Art in the hands of an expert such as his Guide. He didn't want to interrupt, but he was so excited about his recent Journey.

"Welcome back, Asanaro. You've woken up earlier today." Alsam had not even turned in order to see him.

"Good ... morning ..." answered Asanaro, a little confused. "I'm sorry to interrupt you in your practices of the Art ... it's just that I had a special dream at dawn that I wanted to tell you about!"

Asanaro enthusiastically told his Guide the details of his previous night's adventure, and they spent some time discussing it.

Near the end of the conversation, Asanaro asked, "Alsam ... were you really there?"

"Well, well ... you haven't yet learned. Whether I was there or not doesn't really matter. Concentrate your mind on the pleasant sensations this encounter has left with you, and prepare, because what you've lived is a small preview, an announcement. Both your body and mind are slowly tuning to the universal frequencies you are trying to catch; what you lived means that if you continue with your practices, you'll have greater results soon. If that is the case, then you've received a special pass, so to speak, to a new state: the Bamso state. If you are well enough prepared for that moment, a big door to the Great Bamso Record can open to you ... but beforehand you will be tested ... remember! You will be tested! For now, you must continue your preparation in the three initial stages: art, mind, and body."

"Alsam, I'm intrigued again. What is the Bamso? And what is the Great Bamso Record?"

"Ahaaaaa! ... I'll explain it later, so leave it for now. You must be more prepared ... Let's have some breakfast, since it is already late. And speaking of preparation, I assume you've already reviewed the medium projected forms of the Art, for I think you haven't forgotten that today is your last Boabom lesson, and we have to finish your Major Movements program as well as the Non-action Tactics. Remember that soon you'll have a test to give ... don't forget that the first discipline toward achieving the control of dreams is the Osseous Art, in all of its forms."

Asanaro continued asking himself many questions, despite what Alsam had said. Among them, he wondered ... "Was Alsam really there, in that strange dream?"

IV.

Bamso

Another day had passed, and the new morning flew calmly by. The day was fresh and, even though summer was beginning, a light fog had settled in the mountains and hills, lending the whole scene an aura of quietness and introspection set in the cozy silence of the fields and the singing of the birds. After midday, when the fog had become thicker, Alsam told the Apprentice that he'd be out doing some work for a while. Asanaro offered to go to a place lower in the hills, a couple of hours' walk into the valleys from the Osi Mountains, to bring back some milk and flour for dinner. Asanaro knew that his Guide was very fond of natural foods, so he wanted to find some as a gift. He'd have plenty of time to go and return before sunset, and he could take advantage of the cool day.

The walk passed quickly as the student spared no time in

analyzing the many things on his mind and coming up with all of the questions he wanted to ask. After walking a while he surprised himself with a few Boabom movements done quickly, like a young, restless cat, as he imagined a scene or a specific practice of his Art, a defense, a step, before continuing quietly along his route.

After a few hours he arrived in the valley and quickly found the house that he was looking for, where a small family lived, raised cows and other animals, and kept a small vegetable garden. Getting the milk and flour was no problem; the only strange thing, Asanaro thought, was the shocked expression the peasants' faces had on seeing him, and that they didn't let him pay for any of it: They just gave him the food and some extra things in a hurry, as if wishing him quickly back from where he had come.

That return uphill was a little harder, but the fog continued to refresh the whole environment. The great Star-Sun still had a few moments before it started to set.

When the Apprentice reached the camp he left the things and looked for Alsam, who wasn't anywhere to be found. He heard someone not too far off, in a little clearing, so there he went. His Guide was there working. He had cleared the place and formed a large circle of stones. With dry sticks and branches he had made several figures and was placing them around the circle. Asanaro had never seen him do anything like that before, and he shivered.

Quietly he spoke. "Alsam, I am back with the food for dinner."

Alsam continued with his labor, creating a mysterious order among his work. The Apprentice stood silent; he was intrigued, and the figures that his Guide had made invariably caught his attention, like a spell. Alsam finished arranging some branches, made a strange gesture with his hands, and turned.

"I noticed that you brought a lot of food. Let's go and enjoy a big dinner."

As he returned to the camp the Apprentice was still spellbound and, though he did not know why, he didn't dare ask what Alsam had been doing with all of those branches and stones. But as he made the fire, without even noticing he forgot about the subject completely.

They were ready to share an excellent meal, with a big bottle of milk from the farm, warmed by and given the taste of a fire made of wood, not the cold heat of a "modern" stove. The taste of things touched by that rudimentary method . . . it was so different from the ways of the city. The value of simple, natural, and essential things was there in everything around them. There and then they didn't need any of the comforts of the city, only a good fire, a big cup of milk, and a thick bread, baked in the ashes, that needed nothing more than flour, salt, and water to taste good. And, of course, good conversation and a lesson, to feed the insatiable interior hunger.

While the fire danced, trapped in its stone circle, both teacher and student expanded on the subject and teachings of the Astral Journey, on the different practices and exercises that would help the Apprentice work better in what Alsam called the Multi-Dimensional Consciousness.

"Are you enjoying the fire and the dinner?" asked Alsam.

"Yes . . . this is really nice, the food, the nature surrounding us, even the fog, and especially your lessons," answered Asanaro.

"Haven't you wondered why it is so important for us to get away from the city?" asked the Guide.

"Well, I've thought that we always enjoy nature, and that it's the best place to learn ..."

"Yes, that's true ... but doesn't a particular reason come to your mind?"

"No ... I haven't really thought of a specific reason why."

"Do you enjoy the fire, the movement of the flames?"

"Yes, very much," the Apprentice answered. "I love it."

"Do you like the fresh bread and the milk?"

"Well, yes, of course, but where are you going with this?"

Alsam smiled, paused a moment, and then continued.

"Do you realize that you are getting ready for a higher dimension?"

"Well ... I don't know ..."

"You must prepare," added the Guide.

Asanaro paused a moment before asking, "But what do you mean by a higher dimension?"

"Pay attention now. What we usually call Astral, or what most of the people associate with dreams, is a state that possesses its own name and vibration. In order to live it more deeply you must evolve, and that must be done here, in this place. You shall give both your body and mind some finishing touches in order to be admitted into the Great Bamso Record, and you still have a long and hard trip ahead of you, where you will see things that few have seen, or, better said, that only a few have wanted to see, and for that you need a very special type of food."

Asanaro listened thoughtfully to Alsam, and when he finished, he said, "I've heard that word before! Please tell me, what is the Bamso?"

"In some way, I have already explained it to you," said Alsam. "There exists what everyone knows as dreams, but the truth is that it is a stage that every night opens a new dimension to the mind. You and every living being can project your mind into dreams, see beyond, travel, learn, feel; it's a wholly different dimension. When the projection is unconscious we call it dreaming; when we realize that we are dreaming we call it conscious or lucid dreaming; when we have a certain control in it, or when we are projected into something beyond the usual, it's an Astral Journey; but beyond that we can link to some higher stages, and those we call Bamso, the Art of Dreams.

"That's where the great trip begins, and you can be invited into the Great Record. Though you might not believe it, in that stage you can cross time and space, as both of them stop having real consistency. But remember, from dreams to the Bamso there is only one knitting."

The Apprentice always tried to understand what Alsam said to him, but sometimes it was quite difficult.

"If I have already achieved the first stages," he asked, "with your teachings and discipline, how can I get to the higher stages, like the one you were explaining to me?"

Alsam simply replied, "You need the best of foods."

"But Alsam, our food is completely normal."

The Guide took a breath before continuing.

"Let yourself be guided by your instincts and you'll understand. Each food from nature, the colors of its fields, the tones and contrasts from the mountains here, serves as a backdrop; the bushes, the trees with their quiet attitude, the birds and animals that surround us, the open sky. These are your best foods. Had you thought about this before?"

"Actually, I've never seen it that way . . ."

"Think," continued Alsam. "Each element I have named, even though there are many others, has its own state of vibration, which affects what it contains, what sees it, hears it, feels it, or smells it. In its own way, each individual element in nature, all of which are actually only one, affects you, affects your internal recording, your state and your energy and, therefore, it affects the possibility of your Astral Consciousness, your Astral Image. They are the keys to the Bamso, as they tune your antennae.

"Now look . . . why does a bird fly?"

Asanaro stared at him with a quizzical face and could only stammer, "Because . . . because he has wings . . . ?"

The Guide laughed hard. "Well, you are right, but if you continue that line of argument, you could also wonder why the bird has those wings, why it has a body, why it moves, why there is an Earth, why air and why space.

"So I could ask you again, why does the bird fly?"

"To be honest, I'm confused . . . I don't know." The Apprentice seemed troubled.

"Don't you know?" asked the teacher, his face intrigued. "Well . . ." He paused. "Neither do I!"

The Guide started chuckling, and as Asanaro joined in they both laughed in earnest. After they quieted down, Alsam continued.

"What I want to express with that example is that the bird starts flying because within her there is a series, even more, an infinite number of elements woven within, many or most of which go far beyond our understanding. These have allowed her formation as energy and body within a determined cycle, in a determined time on a determined planet, and within the sight of determined beings that with a certain understanding can watch her flight, value it, and create a concept of 'flight' along the lines of their culture . . . It is all part of what you may call Time-Fluid, the silhouette of time and its events."

Asanaro listened intently, trying to work all of the ideas through his mind.

"I'm sure you're wondering where I'm going with all of this," added the Guide. He continued, "You, too, want to begin flying, but your flight will be of a different nature. You want to jump from the common dimension of dreaming to the Astral, to go deep into the Bamso, and this flight requires that you realize several different elements before you can accomplish it completely and without difficulties. Not only that, since if you intend to reach the Great Bamso Record, you must be well prepared, you must gather in yourself elements that are at the same time both fine and strong."

"But why is everything that surrounds us so important?" asked Asanaro.

"Each element, each thing, is, unto itself, a constantly changing state of emanating energy, of vibration. This energy reaches you, becomes part of you through an amazing, almost magical internal process; it becomes one with you, with your sensations, your mind and thoughts. It vibrates within you, creating reactions or ripples that are linked to other, similar processes, other vibrations, in a chain that comes from infinite to infinite. The vibratory state of the deep Astral Journey is very refined, quite high . . . for now we can say that you will only reach it when you are riding the crest of the wave, but you won't be stable there until you're fully prepared, while around you remain some primitive energies of doubt, fear, and prejudice. These have been caused, in fact, by the same process we described above, though they come from the negative, the opposite of our search for the positive, for evolution.

"That is why, for people subject to the physical and magnetic alterations of a purely human environment, it is completely impossible to accomplish the simplest Astral Journey. It is not only impossible, but inconceivable; they cannot even imagine it, what it is, how it would feel, even that it could exist, and if you were to tell them about it, the whole subject would be so far off, so contrary to their traditional beliefs, that they would think that you had gone insane. That is why these teachings have been reserved for only a few people, and out of them, only a few have been able to fully achieve it. The Conscious World of Dreams has a big sign hanging above the door that reads FORBIDDEN, but no one sees that the door is actually wide open.

"Everyone brings their own tools along, but they don't know how to use them; when someone tries to show them they get scared and become aggressive, defensive, attacking that person and acting as fanatic guardians of their fear. For example, we see nature, energy, and the life in this place, whereas a real estate developer might see acres occupied by vacation resorts ready to be built, of cheap materials, and sold as quickly as possible. Think now of a 'civilized' hunter . . . how would he see these fields? He would come in his truck, bringing bright lights and his pride, and he would see a place for killing, where he could gain a feeling of power in front of a pure and defenseless animal . . . since he is weak and insecure, he would only see in this place a way to make up for his lack of strength, proving that he can be a cruel bully in the face of pure innocence. I say that everyone can, but who wants?"

The Apprentice, who had been listening attentively, asked, "I have a question . . . what do you mean by what you said before, Time-Fluid?"

"That is complicated," answered Alsam, "for it has many different aspects to it. I could say that the structure of things is in essence only one, just as the structure of time is only one, but a changing one. It is like a wave crossing water. To complete the work you have ahead of you, you'll have to learn to recognize the negative aspects of that Fluid, for you sail on it, too."

Asanaro wasn't sure if he had understood fully, so he asked further, "But then, what would be the most negative elements for someone who, as I have, has already decided to accomplish the deeper levels of conscious travel in dreams?"

"There are many *elements* that conspire against Astral Consciousness, but there is only one *reason*. The negative elements are numerous, though the principals are internal: self-values, self-respect, and self-esteem; and external: balance, energy, and vibration. These together create a group of attitudes that are unbalanced in each person, and this unbalance prevents them from enjoying one of the most wonderful senses that we've got . . . the Conscious World of Dreams.

"If you analyze a normal person, what do they concentrate their minds on? Three things are most important to them: the problems they have, the problems they have, and the problems they have!" They both laughed out loud. Asanaro enjoyed that Alsam always had a sense of humor, even while talking about the most complicated subjects.

"As you already know, there are basic elements that, by themselves, damage every attempt to come close to the Astral, without even mentioning the Bamso! You have what you feed your body and what feeds your mind. You know many examples of this already, since you have seen the madness that exists in your world, on all levels, even among those who consider themselves intelligent and intellectual; they often commit the worst and most terrible mistakes in the name of vanity, what other people might say, or trying to be accepted in the dirty media, ruled by the code of stupidity, of cultural appearances." Alsam paused a second before adding, even more seriously, "Are you ready to hear this? You might not like what I'm going to say."

"Please, Alsam," said Asanaro, "go ahead—I want to learn, so say what you must say."

Alsam continued. "I am going to give you many examples. Let's begin with the roughest, the most terrible and most common cases. Let's start with the example of a regular person, so watch what he feeds his body: recycled, trash food. And what does he feed his mind? Vanity, fear, classism, history, intolerance, and persecution. This is not his fault but his culture's, heritage from thousands of years of traditions imposed by power's vested interests, of religious-political control and its sole translation: materialism. This is inherited, transmitted, passed on, feeding the minds of all of those people. How can they even envision the Astral in its real state? They take their prejudices and stupidity to that level, too, and that is why they see nothing but what they call nightmares, nightmares, and more nightmares! In the best case they experience total darkness, a blank, the sensation that they haven't even had a dream.

"Take for example the drug addict, because he is the most pitiful. Not thousands but millions close the doors to the Astral because of drugs, drugs for all tastes, from the simple but no less harmful cigarette, derived from innocent and wise little plants, to hallucinogens and their terrible, elaborate chemistry. Can you imagine what damage it causes . . . ?"

"Yes," added Asanaro, "since living on Earth you always meet some examples. But it's almost impossible to talk to them about it, because they always take it quite hard . . ."

"It's normal, because their self-esteem is in play, which is one of the major elements I mentioned to you. In them, this self-esteem is completely wrecked, twisted, just as in one sick from too much materialism, ambition, and intolerance.

"Drugs damage the brain directly, and sometimes the damage that they cause is irreparable. It is as if you had an antenna all set up, pointing to the Universe, ready to receive the finest vibrations, to search the most remote and unknown corners of the stars, willing to hear the Great Message, the great truth that goes along with you, interlaced among the whole cosmos . . . that waits quietly, open to everyone. Then to that oh-so-delicate antenna, to that instrument of infinitely fine precision, they throw stones, metal, bricks, they cut its cables, throw acids on it that corrode its circuits, causing nothing more than an ugly, unstable, phantasmagorical image in the monitors . . . and after all of that the person foolishly asks himself why he feels so bad." Both Guide and Apprentice shook their heads. Alsam then continued with his explanation.

"It is really pitiful! Humorous, too, but so pitiful the way humans treat themselves. There's a lot more to this subject, especially related to the preparation to consciously travel in dreams. As I said before, there are many different kinds of drugs, and they are all harmful! Each one alters what they call the nervous system, which is a much more complex circuit than most people can imagine. The elements contained in drugs act like a poison that doesn't kill you immediately but has the terrible effect of mangling and twisting your antennae. It's like a spiritual death: It takes away every possibility of internal advance from you, not just in the Astral ... it turns terribly, terribly scary ..."

"But what do you mean?" asked Asanaro. "The person's dreams become totally unconscious, right?"

"No, Asanaro, it's much worse than that. If it were only unconsciousness, it wouldn't be so bad. It's actually something much more frightening ..."

"But, Guide, tell me! What does happen ...?"

"For someone who has been caught by this stupidity, or, better put, someone who has been caught as another tool of the great mafia behind drugs, the consequences for his Astral and Dimensional Sight are tremendous. As I said before, it's like tearing apart that delicate and fine system of antennae and monitors, and when I said 'phantasmagorical' I was speaking quite literally."

"Do they see ghosts in their dreams?"

"Worse, Asanaro. You will soon learn that there are Eight Superior Fields for the Magnetic Dimensional Sight; one of them can be 'tuned' directly, in flesh and bone, without needing to be projected into the Astral, or asleep in the case of a person who doesn't have control in that dimension. That is the first form of vision. The second form of vision is what you have learned through projection, the development of what we usually call the Astral or Conscious Dream. Both stages or types of vision are possessions of every living being, in differing levels. For common people, this first vision, in flesh and bone, is what they call premonitions and encounters with beings that they call abnormal, or out of this world. You will learn that it is only another cycle of life, which we can reach if we are prepared."

Asanaro spoke. "It's hard to understand these things quickly ... even though I'm sure what you're saying is true ... it's just, when I think about it a chill runs down my spine."

"Bit by bit you'll understand, and you will see that there is nothing negative or scary about it. For a normal being, fear is a very effective limitation that doesn't allow him to come close to those worlds or to those visions. At the same time, if that person has the slightest opportunity, that same fear will make him recoil before he even gets there, so that he doesn't crash, so to speak. In the case of a person affected by drugs, he is poisoned and his sensible channels have gone haywire. This brings the worst: Two great confused fields open in front of him, instead of two dimensions of magnetic vision. Those two negative magnetic fields are terrifying, unimaginably traumatizing.

"And as for dreams, what should normally be unconscious is altered by the conscious-unconscious sight. Drugs force that vision, and as they do they destroy all of the 'antennae,' doing so in such a way that each element that should be positive, pleasant, and wise turns negative, confused, and evil beneath all of the culturally prejudiced concepts the sick person possesses, since addiction to those poisons is a real disease. Imagine that person is projected in his dream, sees a beautiful mountain, which all of a sudden turns into an avalanche, into a dark, thick mud that covers him, trapping him. He becomes desperate but cannot escape. The mechanism of compensation that unconsciousness of dreams serves has been altered, and he simply can't escape, and though he runs away the avalanche becomes full of evil beings chasing him, all according to his imagination. They follow him, catch him, he escapes, shivering with fear, they catch him again, and his fear increases. He sees grotesque forms who laugh as they surround him, running everywhere, teasing him constantly. Each of these things exists, but the degree of evil is only within the distorted mind of the person who sees them."

"It sounds awful, but why don't they just change their Astral frequency? I mean, if the negative doesn't really exist," asked Asanaro in a troubled voice. "Or does it?"

"The truth is that in being it doesn't exist, but in reality it does."

"But what do you mean?" asked the concerned Apprentice.

"Well, it all depends on your point of view. Mind itself is incredibly creative, and in the state of dreaming it becomes even more so. If we see this creativity from the point of view of a delirious person, the body has encountered a severe difficulty, and this plunges him further into the field of nightmares. If someone is sick because of drugs, the same thing happens, but in a manner much more real and much more terrifying. His being, his fears, his own body and mind, accuse himself of the crime, the damage he is causing, pointing the finger of guilt inside. It's a warning that the abyss is drawing near.

"This state is so severe," continued Alsam, "that it also affects the primary vision, the vision when she is awake and lucid. His magnetic sight can be altered, and he'll see things from parallel dimensions but in a skewed, negative way, with the charge of terror that goes along with it. In contrast, if people who don't take drugs see something that they identify as from another world, then their self-limit of fear comes into play, as I said before. It's like an electrical fuse—it simply jumps, automatically, and the vision is transformed while the person is left in doubt, wondering if it was just his imagination. Of course, the culture of control that exists on Earth follows the policy of 'The less people know, the better.' This fear has been encouraged, so that this fuse jumps early, at nothing, and the people stay blind. This is why children are punished for having an imaginary friend, or when they demonstrate extraordinary capacities.

"For a drug addict, the norms are a bit different, even though the whole scenario is more or less the same. This fuse is altered and simply doesn't jump when they see something from 'beyond' . . . it gets stuck, and as with any electrical equipment, the wires start burning. The sick person sees beings who mock him, tease and provoke him. It can be entertaining at first, but it always turns frightening, as everything is malfunctioning. Whatever creatures he sees that trouble him, that laugh wickedly at him, he will see that way because he is not prepared and only sees what is negative or without form. If not for his blindness, for the fact that he is intoxicated and sick, he would realize that they are sending him a message, or, better put, a lesson to react to, to value himself, and to understand that he has only been led and tricked by a mob that uses him as a stooge, another poor, willing consumer who hand-delivers materialism to a small band of opportunists."

"That is awful Alsam . . . is there some kind of remedy?"

"It is hard, but there is. Just like fear, drugs are a disease that grows very deep roots. There are many primitive cultures, just as ignorant as the present one, that have encouraged the use of these poisons, specifically drugs and alcohol. They justify themselves by saying that these plants are beneficial, and foolish arguments like these have made many people fall. The tobacco plant, for example, is very useful, for example as a disinfectant for injuries, but that does not mean it is in any way beneficial to our health to smoke it and fill our lungs with that smoke, just as it wouldn't be beneficial to inject a liter of onion juice directly into your veins.

"If you think about it, you'll see that the Earth has many different elements, and these are our nourishment; we must get to know them, to use them in a positive way, not in a harmful way—that is insane! Many sorcerers and medicine men of many tribes forced themselves into trances in order to justify messages from 'the beyond,' so they could live off of the tribe. It looks as if the people of today understand this trick very well, since if you look closely, you'll see that the Earth is still the same, that those tribes who used drugs are still as ignorant as the others and as blind as their modern counterparts: priests and successful politicians."

"They're really causing themselves such great harm . . . they should just get rid of drugs, forbid all of those things forever . . . just wipe them off the map," said an upset Asanaro.

"Get rid of . . . ? Forbid . . . ?" Alsam scratched his ears and continued, "It seems I'm having trouble hearing . . . yes, I must be losing my hearing . . ."

"What? I meant to just get rid of them, so there aren't any more . . . drugs, I mean . . ." replied a doubtful Apprentice.

"Ha ha ha ha . . ." The Guide laughed hard, clutching his belly, playing with his gestures and words. When he finished laughing Alsam sighed before continuing.

"Don't get your hopes up, Apprentice. The negative elements within humans are not so easily erased, for they are part of the figure of human time, and in order to really overcome such decadent aspects, we must move into a more complex field, which, in part, you'll better understand when visiting the Great

Record. Also understand that in order to get there you must rid yourself of the prejudices of your Time-Fluid, just as you must rid yourself of the nearsightedness that it has caused. You shall stop seeing things only on the surface and begin to see their profundity ... which can lead you into fields that you may never have imagined."

"But what," Asanaro asked, "does this have to do with what we're talking about?"

"A lot, in fact. The previous discussion is a clear example of concepts that have been imposed upon you, which have a double standard, where good is a great evil disguised in a gold suit, and where evil is only a small player that's been involved to cover the great, real evil, which is dressed like a king and possesses only an insatiable ambition for power, for so much power, and for materialistic gain. You need profound sight within the mentality of the world of humans, for it is also a part of you, and that world is too tricky ... it changes its suit too often, and by continually shifting false appearances it is very, very slippery, very dangerous.

"If you'd like me to finish the previous example, I can ... but it will surprise you. You will see that one thing is tied to another, and though it may seem not to be related, it always is. I am afraid that I will have to use more Earthly and upsetting examples."

"Go ahead, of course! Since I am here to learn from every angle."

"I am saying this because when I must use your world as an example, I tend to be, well, unkind."

"Come on Alsam, continue. I think I am ready to listen, that I have an open mind ... at least I hope I do!" The Apprentice knew that when Alsam spoke directly, he was very direct.

. . .

The sunset was quite pleasant, and despite the light fog it wasn't too cold. In the distance they could hear the stream running calmly, carrying its cold water to the invisible wells of the valleys. A few bugs flew about the heads of the two men, who sat comfortably on the Earth that formed a natural mattress. They could just hear the birds returning to their nests. All was perfect for such a strong lesson, and Alsam, Guide of the Mind, continued.

"Pay attention, since I am about to make an inappropriate comparison. Do you see those trees? If you break off a branch, the tree continues living, right?" Asanaro nodded. "Well, now, if you look closer, do you see that greener part between the two thicker branches of that same tree? It's a parasite that has formed a cyst, living off of the tree. If you cut that branch there, you won't kill it, because it will just appear again, to continue sucking both life and energy from that noble tree that is, at the same time, living a struggle for its own existence. Only if you kill every last root of that parasite will you release the poor, innocent tree, and only thus will the parasite leave its existence as we know it. If we invert the example, the problem of drugs in your world, as well as the problem of fear, since they are tied together, are like the parasite in that tree. They are linked, do you understand?"

"I think so . . . but . . ." replied Asanaro.

"Listen. In that world of yours they have a terrible problem, if we listen to our example; it is the drugs that we are analyzing. But is that the real problem? 'NO!' more than a few people will shout, 'it's the drug dealers in the neighborhoods, and if we chase them out, we'll be rid of the plague! They're guilty of forcing drugs on us!' Let us take a poor country as an example, where from some corner appears Mr. Third World Politician, saying, 'Let's get rid of the drug dealers who stand on every corner,' while the ignorant masses repeat, 'What a brave man! So courageous!' Now think a minute more, consider this example and tell me, tell me who is the tree, and who is the parasite, and who are the branches where the parasite lives?"

"Well . . ." replied Asanaro, "the parasite is the drug dealer . . ."

"No, Asanaro! Think! Think!"

"I don't know . . ."

"Pay attention, now, think and don't think. Analyze the matter, as the worst evil is the one disguised as the good. I'll explain something to you: You have the people, the small-time drug pusher, the cops, the politicians . . . which of these do you think is the root?"

"I . . . I don't know anymore . . ."

"Well, in order for you to understand, I can explain it from various points of view. For one, I'll tell you that, superficially, the real parasite is Mr. Third World Politician, the modern feudal lord, the real root of the problem."

The Apprentice looked doubtful as Alsam continued.

"The small-time drug dealer is just another stooge, just like the people themselves, the masses who are ignorant, who have their uses and who are disposable, simple accessories in a billion-dollar industry. Mr. Third World Politician uses conveniences, they are his salary, and the rest is propaganda. I'll expand on this example, for Mr. Third World Politician is a good friend of Mr. Drug, the great provider, the kingpin. Not only this, Mr. Drug is also a large contributor to the advertising campaigns behind Mr. Third World Politician, which help him to pollute the minds of the people by buying the media. Understand, too, that people believe in the massive publicity that puts a nice face on power, that convinces. Many people could see but don't, they do nothing, for their minds are weakened from a lifetime of manipulation at the system's convenience, or from fear. Mr. Third World Politician, for his part, can't appear in front of the public as a friend of the kingpin Mr. Drug—this part of his life has to remain unknown—that public face—but when there's money for campaigns he takes it automatically, happily. They control 'public opinion,' too, through reporters, who serve as nothing more than another gear in the whole apparatus: useful, and disposable if they don't dance the right way. The truth is that it is just one long cycle of convenience that is never seen or heard. The modern feudal lord dresses himself up fancy, simply to hide the great evil that he carries inside, for his truth is only materialistic ambition for power and possession, and nothing will stand in his way. He would be called a social psychopath on Earth, where he only wants to appear in the social media, on the square box or in any other public forum, since that's part of what his consultants, or, better put, his sycophant retinue, call marketing. That is why he organizes campaigns against drugs with one hand while taking money from its trade in the other, taking all of the benefits from its distribution . . . after all, the rules of the 'market' are known to all of these people, and they know how well anything sells on the black market, and how much easier it is to inflate prices and influence the whole business when it is underneath the law, because what is forbidden attracts and can then be manipulated by only a very small few.

"Now think about this," continued Alsam. "Mr. Third World Politician calls the cops on a 'poor guy' who pretends to be a mafia type, thinking how cool he is, and has no idea what he's getting himself into. Well, they catch this guy and send him to jail, while Mr. Politician calls his second tool, the journalists, who believe themselves to be the conscience of the public, which means that they are the ones who carry out the orders to influence the minds of the masses. The small-time trafficker has been caught, convicted, and abandoned in a jail. The people are satisfied, but what they don't know is that the people at customs, sitting at the border of power, let through a few tons of the same poison without anyone noticing or, better put, without any of the regular people noticing.

"Or take the rich country for another example, sitting across the divide and conquer, I mean border, from our poor country of the previous example. The First World Politician is now swearing to the people of his country that he will stamp out drugs, that he needs to stop them at the source, of course the poor country. The politicians of both countries then go on television together, saying that they'll get rid of Mr. Drug, though neither of them has any intention of doing so at all. But now the rich country is giving money to Mr. Third World Politician, and his country owes even more to the rich one; Mr. Third World Politician becomes like the small-time pusher, taking money from everywhere he can, but afraid because he knows that whenever the rich country wants, it can replace him for another who will do the same job. So when that does happen and Mr. Third World Politician gets kicked out, everybody in both rich and poor countries cheers on the advance of 'democracy' as the new Mr. Third World Politician finishes his lunch with Mr. Drug before going to accept his new position of 'power.'

"These examples shows us the dirty side of human ambition, and I am being very, very . . . simple. Politics forbids drugs, thus lining the pockets of the clever ones even more. By forbidding drugs, only a few gain the power to manipulate what they cynically call law, or the instruction manual for ambition and materialism. They can easily condemn any fool who dares publicly compete with them and get away without a problem; at the same time they can use this condemnation as advertising in the public conscience whenever they need, by chastising whomever they please.

"Think, Asanaro . . . think, and not only about this example. Think about wars, about arms trafficking, business interests . . . it would be terrible to keep on digging!"

"This is a very ugly subject, Alsam . . . I had never seen it in that way before, nor had I thought that everyone was so manipulated." Asanaro's voice rose as he spoke. "People should do something about it!"

"No, Asanaro . . . nothing must be done about it."

"But why! If that whole controlling mafia is the parasite in your example, the one killing the tree . . . now I see it, so clearly, and I feel duped . . . We need to cut the parasite out, root and all, and save the tree!"

"It's not that simple, Apprentice. Tell me, if you're so sure now, what exactly is the root of the parasite?"

"It's the political mafia, of course," replied Asanaro, now a bit mutinous and revolutionary, "with all of their awful associates."

"No, no ... it isn't that easy ..." answered the Guide with a calm smile.

"Now I don't understand ... You lecture me about Third World politicians I could care less about, you show me that they're the ones who truly manipulate the system and the people's will, and now you tell me that it's not quite that way, that it's not so simple!" Asanaro paused and lowered his voice. "I'm sorry, Alsam ... I just got caught up in your explanation."

"If you want to avoid tricking yourself in this square-dimension, you must pay more attention. Once you begin to see things more completely, you'll be able to see with more clarity into your world, the Astral World, and yourself, and you'll understand the examples. You'll understand that they are only examples.

"From a certain point of view, what you called the political mafia isn't the root of the problem; there remains one more powerful than it."

"More powerful, Alsam?" asked Asanaro, at the same time wondering what exactly square-dimension meant.

"Yes, much more powerful. There is a power involved on all levels, and it has gone beyond even politics' own tactics, experience, and terrible cleverness. If you wish to advance, you must take care with it, learn to recognize when you are facing its tactics and plots. If you want to come closer to the Great Record, you must have a very lucid and strong mind. If you see with clarity and an open mind on Earth, you will see with clarity and an open mind in dreams, and not only their shadows ... not only their shadows.

"Everything you've seen on Earth," he added, "is tricks and

false appearances, and you carry them with you whether you want to or not. All of the examples I've gone through, all of that conflict is inside your mind, too: politics, laws, journalists, and so on. Now it is your responsibility to recognize that mistake, and not to let it control and confuse your vision and superior projection, for this is a field so delicate that any doubt, any confusion, can change utterly everything designated to be shown to you. And that would become one more illusion."

"You mentioned something about a higher power. What is it?" asked Asanaro, now wondering what Alsam had meant by "everything designated to be shown to you."

"Don't worry . . . you will see, with your own mind's eye, and you are preparing for that, in order to have the correct vision of things, and thus to have the correct vision of the Great World of Dreams, and through that to get to yourself. This is the real Art of the Deep: the Art of the Bamso."

V.

From the Osseous to the Subtle

That night's conversation with Alsam had been long and hard, and many questions remained in Asanaro's mind. As he thought about each aspect of their discussion, about everything they had analyzed, he realized that he had never been so bothered before by Alsam's use of politics and religion as examples. After all, he had his own ideas about them, but what should he do with them? How should he bring what he was learning into focus? Asanaro spent the night mulling over these questions, but he finally decided it much better to listen and learn, because, after all, he was there because he wanted to be.

Days passed and Asanaro, despite his disciplined dedication to his practices, hadn't uncovered any new surprises in his dreams. He felt, however, that something would come, even if he didn't know when; though the vision of many things was changed in him, he knew he still had a long way to walk.

Usually Alsam would isolate himself in the mornings, making those strange drawings in the field nearby, while in the afternoons they would gather to continue the teachings, scrutinizing examples of daily life, of the "outside world," as that singular teacher liked to say. They spent the lessons developing the values and the vision necessary to realize the great adventure destined for the novice in the superior dimension. The Guide explained the complexities and subtleties of that voyage on the line between fantasy and reality, as well as the proper respect for correct training of the mind. He taught how to rid oneself of prejudices, fears, and ignorance, and how these stages have limited the psychical capacity of people throughout the various eons of existence; he taught how to act upon oneself and how to protect the imagination so it would not be interrupted by negativity.

Every meal was a special moment to patiently stoke the fire that cut like a clear energy into the luminosity of the mountains. They cooked together and Alsam laughed while boiling the vegetables, cutting them in unusual ways. "Laughter is important for food," said the Guide. "If you cook laughing the food gets in a good mood, too, and after you smile while eating it, and it puts your energy at its top!" They both laughed a lot, and in that way they spent the night, the afternoons, and the few days between the lessons and the teachings.

On the afternoon of their eighth day together in those mountains, Guide and Apprentice were preparing for a different class.

"The week has really flown by, Alsam. I've really enjoyed this place and your teachings."

"Good! As you already know, it's time for you to continue in the Osseous Art, Boabom. We have adapted the body to these mountains, and it will do you good to keep on advancing in the movements and techniques for controlling and improving the body."

"Of course—I haven't been able to stop thinking about it! I've been waiting all morning for my physical class with all of its different forms."

"Let's wait until the sun begins to set; then we'll start your lesson. Soon you will have your examination for the Major Step in Boabom, and that will require a lot of concentration and fluency in the movements. Besides, it's best for you to be in optimal physical condition for what we'll call your Astral invitation."

"But, Guide, actually . . . what does Boabom have to do with projection of the mind in Astral states? Since those aren't physical?"

"What you name as physical is directly linked with the subtle. In fact, if it weren't for this part of our sciences, Boabom, the one everyone sees as simple physical exercises, or perhaps as a strange dance—at points delicate, at others warlike—without it you could never have accomplished what you have achieved in the Astral. If you wish to continue advancing in that field, you need to keep advancing in your Body and physical Mind."

"But how are Boabom, the Mind, and Astral Projection related?"

"Well, you've already learned the importance of a healthy body, free of toxins, as we spoke about the other night. Aside from the toxins that people choose to consume, there are more subtle 'toxins' that you can't avoid simply by running away from smoke and pollutants. Your own body and mind generate them, simply by being alive."

"What? Those toxins are inside me?"

"Pay attention. Our Art is a science for self-healing and equilibrium of the three fundamental energies: the solid energy, or
physical; the mental energy, or cerebral-nervous; and the fluid
(or magnetic) energy, pranic or auric. Observe these physical
Arts, Boabom and Seamm-Jasani, that you have studied all these
years, the effects that they produce—and for right now we can
refer to their forms as if they were fused into only one, though
we could study them individually, as if they were different organs
within a single body. The Boabom Arts are a complex pattern
of movements covering various aspects, from simple relaxation
or stretching of the muscles to breathing, to movements that
take life, passing through great works of motion, which, as you
know, make you sweat in a unique way. They are also linked
with concentration, with the isolation of the mind, with the
possibility of polishing every muscle, like the strings of a fine
musical instrument, stretching them and making them sing. You
know well that every movement in special states gathers the
gentle and, at the same time, what we could call the Noble Art
of Defense, meaning the path of projection of fast and precise
movements, combining speed, technique, and mental projection
into one motion.

"All this," continued the Guide, "which you know already,
would sound very complicated, very foreign to someone who
hasn't lived and experienced it. In your case you will understand
it better. A moment ago I mentioned three basic energies: the
physical, mental, and magnetic energies. Each energy produces
its own benefit as well as its own toxin, if you want to call it
that; we could just as easily say that each has both high and low
cycles. These low cycles form a sort of delay or harm to us,

which is normally produced the evolutionary labors of daily life. Now our physical studies make the higher cycles predominate, and we can quickly get rid of these lower cycles in order to avoid this delay, or self-harm. However, you must also consider that these three fundamental energies work together, chained or interlaced as one whole, one more stitch.

"The body is easily damaged by drugs, alcohol, tobacco, or other toxic chemical elements, like smog in the cities. It is also damaged by exaggerated or unbalanced food, the excess of meat or fat, although a person's needs depend upon the zone of the planet where they live, as well as their particular metabolism." Alsam stopped, as if waiting for Asanaro's comment, which in fact came quite quickly.

"I understand what you say, since I've met people who drink, smoke, or eat in an unbalanced or excessive way, and I've seen that damage them in a more or less visible way. But I've also found many people who take to excess who are generally quite kind, understanding, and open-minded, and many people who consider themselves 'pure' who are in fact terrible, irritating, and extremely prejudiced. Sorry, I'm not trying to interrupt or contradict, but it seems that intoxicating your body isn't always a sign of, well, being 'less evolved,' to put it one way."

Alsam smiled. "Don't rush off to the end of the story, Apprentice of Life! Observe what I intend to explain. There are three fundamental energies, each chained to the other, each affecting its partners, and within each of us they have different roots, which results in the differing degrees of evolution you can see in every living being, its gentleness or its ignorance. Not intoxicating the body with the various poisons that can be produced on Earth, such as drugs or alcohol, is no guarantee of internal evolution, yet it can help in having a healthier body, with better qualities for higher works. But if that health and care are the result of restrictive rules, of fear of an authority corrupted by its own rules, or to political-religious fanaticism, then the result in your mind might not be so good.

"The sum of all this is simply drawn: Impositions on your body, without a pure example for the mind or a warm transmission of magnetism, is ultimately useless.

"Haven't you," he added, "seen enough repressed and traumatized people in your world? Haven't you seen the damage that the political-religious world has caused, organized through fear into contradictory commandments, punishment, sin, the promise of terrible hells and reincarnations, cruel karmas—in sum, persecution if you don't obey the interests of an authority that always breaks those very rules that they hold up as holy and unbreakable to everyone beneath them?"

"Once again, Alsam, you are right..."

There was a silence between them, while the melody of the birds and the gentle breeze blowing through the leaves of the trees created a perfect setting for discussion and meditation. Calmly, the Guide continued.

"The mind is easily intoxicated, but by much more subtle elements. On one hand, it is linked strongly to your body, forming a single tool; thus, whatever you do to your body, you do also to your mind. But the mind is not only affected by the food of the body, for it has its own nourishment and digestive organs apart from what it receives from the blood (with its own positive and negative charges). These organs are directly related to the world, offer their information and feed the mind, but they can intoxicate her as well, encourage her into generating negative states, which send orders opposed to the material body, making it susceptible to disease, exaggerating its illnesses, or even producing diseases that it never should have suffered from in the first place. This is the way in which the mind's toxins function, and from which the mind needs to balance and detoxify: the Art of Centering the Internal World.

"Think of a construction worker," he continued, "who eats well, in a more or less balanced way, who doesn't drink or smoke, but who in his work is surrounded by machines that produce a terrible cacophony of shrieking and of cracking rock and steel. His ears suffer, of course, but even worse, this situation can affect his mind, which will consume information that is too toxic. The worker will return home in a bad mood, irritated or overtired, needing to balance that abuse to which he must subject his will, needing silence . . .

"For the last, the third stage, or fluid energy, has also its own cycle, related to both body and mind, with its own organs of magnetic nourishment and its own forms of emanation. And just the same, when taking in, it can become intoxicated by the wrong energies, which it needs then to release.

"These food elements, as well as the toxins, are more subtle, strangers to a common mentality, but not because they do not exist. Because the external world doesn't understand this, it has devoted itself to materialism, luxury, appearance . . . they look for their 'magnetic food' in a completely twisted way. They become intoxicated, poisoned, and convalescent without even noticing; they live a superficial life. It can be a life rich in vanity, but it is empty on the inside . . . its laughter is false, every cackle sounds hollow, only like a cry for help that becomes more urgent as the diseases become more severe."

Asanaro listened carefully, and without meaning to, developed a sad, melancholy expression. His Guide interrupted, "Don't you see?! You are already being influenced by the magnetism of thoughts about the world . . ."

"I felt sorry about what you were saying . . ."

"You should laugh instead of feeling sorry for someone who isn't asking you to."

"I don't understand."

"People do not need sorrow, or understanding, or a campaign for help. Alms are cynical. What they need is to wake up, to become free from their own ignorance . . . they need to understand that it was never necessary to take the long road, that the answer has always been close."

Alsam stood up, and with that gesture apparently intended to end the lesson. Quickly, and before the Apprentice could speak, he added, "Well, Asanaro, later on we'll have time again to expand this discussion; there is time for the world, but not for you! Now, let's go back to the beginning, or have you forgotten already your class in Boabom, the Osseous Art?"

"I'm ready! Whenever you say!"

"Good. The sun is in the right place, and it will be good for you to free your physical, mental, and magnetic state; it will help you prepare for the correct Astral Vision."

The setting sun was beautiful: The light that remained was perfect, yet the distressing heat was gone, so the exercises and subjects Alsam would teach would not be exhausting. They went to a nearby place that every morning Alsam had been preparing patiently for this occasion. The small field had been enclosed by a rudimentary circle of stones, and Alsam had made strange markings around it. There was a primary figure that called the student's attention, and he wondered where it was pointing. Each figure or diagram was made of little branches, tied with dried grass and held with small sticks from that same place, the lichen and bark still on them. The space had its own strange character, and the Apprentice felt a certain respect and a singular calmness. Now the field had its unique life, its own heartbeat, and one could almost hear it breathe.

Before entering the circle, Alsam said, "Go and put on your clothes for the higher stage, and come back for the class."

The Apprentice went quickly and silently. He returned almost instantly, tightening the traditional suit of his Art and School as he ran. The Guide, who was now inside the circle, allowed him to pass.

Facing each other, they began with a very particular greeting, like a short, elegant invitation to a mythical dance. Alsam then made a similar gesture to each figure, with special emphasis to the one in the middle. They then sat down, closed their eyes, and started breathing in a distinctive way, making an indescribable sound, a vibration that slowly invaded the silence of the place. The sky, the fresh air, and the sounds they made formed a unique, harmonious composition, part of the same painting, of a parallel world, a balance. After a few moments they both stood, again making those same gestures they had begun with. Alsam began what seemed like a sacred chant, counting in different tones, and the Apprentice followed with strange movements, fast at first, then gentle, then alternating. His hands made circles in the air, up, down, to his sides, spirals and twisting. Sometimes he would stop with his Guide to breathe deeply before continuing. With each projection he would exhale with different sounds, like a cat, a hummingbird, or an old lion roaring as he wandered his territory. They were strange sounds that could calm or could quickly alert.

The class continued, and, like any other of Alsam's lessons, it was a true piece of Art, profound and entertaining at the same time, mysterious and clear. With certain movements that Asanaro already knew by heart, his Teacher would interrupt to add a complication, a detail, a new form of execution that would have made its weft even more complex and indecipherable to a watcher who had not been well guided in those teachings.

They devoted part of the class to fast movements of the arms. Alsam closed his eyes, and by simply hearing how each technique cut the air he knew if it was well formed. He would only say, "Mind, tendon, muscle, air...ear, mind...are but one...listen to your body..." The next portion of the class was focused on steps, movements, and positions of the feet and legs that resembled no dance from this Earth, at some times gentle, even caressing, at others lightning quick, striking the ground, which thundered back, voiceless. The skilled student would move backward and forward, forward and back, twisting and stretching lithely, like an agile macaque yet with the strength and purpose of a jaguar.

There had been more than two hours of intense physical work, and still the student and teacher continued. In the final part of the class they worked on projections of the legs: high, middle, and low, then twisting and taking strange leaps. Then followed something like a review of the exercises, in which all of the techniques were joined in fast and slow patterns that were fierce yet beautiful to behold. The student was covered in sweat, his heartbeat visible in the veins protruding from his bright red arms and face; a soft steam rising off his body made him seem halfway outside of this world. In sparkles between the movements he wondered: This Art that Alsam taught him, where did it come from? Why did he feel as if he were reviving something strange, of another world? Or was it a dance formed like a spell to call upon dimensions and forces unknown?

When they came to the end of the class the student looked as if he had gone swimming in his clothes; he was drenched with sweat. The next step now was the rest that awaited him as both Apprentice and Guide sat down, the one following the other in their mystical greetings before resting, silent for a few moments, mentally digesting and savoring all that the class had developed. In Asanaro's mind stood an image of the circle of figures and, although he could not translate them, he felt an awareness of their meaning.

The night was clear and calm. After bathing in the pure, clear water of the river, the student put on clean clothes and went quickly to his bed. He could barely even practice his exercises for the Astral before he completely surrendered to the superior dimension.

VI.

Beyond Dreams

For the Apprentice, the lessons continued. In the midst of the plain marked by the stones, he was alone; his practice was perfect and light, and he felt neither sweat nor the physical weight of his movements and coordinations. He was more flexible than usual, could turn farther, jump higher, and as he did he formed, without thinking, movements that he had never been shown . . . it was all familiar yet not normal.

A voice interrupted. "Energy good . . . for only an Apprentice . . . hehehe . . ."

Asanaro stopped and turned around. On a flat stone just next to Alsam's drawings, someone sat, watching him. He looked at the man for a minute before he remembered: It was the small man who had been with him in his dream of the mountain-city. Asanaro twisted through the air as in his practices of the Art and, without any effort, stood next to the man.

The visitor spoke again. "Heheheh ... restless ... expected already ..."

The Apprentice intended to say something, but the man added, "Blink, now. Blink."

Without thinking why, Asanaro closed his eyes tight, then opened them again. They were together on a large rock at the edge of a tall cliff, Asanaro standing there and the man sitting on the other side, dangling his legs and looking down at the valleys several miles below.

"But ... ? what are we doing here? You again!?" asked Asanaro, confused.

"Shhh ... quiet ... concentrate on the now, remember ... the now ..."

Asanaro noticed that the little man spoke strangely; however, he smiled and understood what was meant. Rapidly everything became clear, more full of light.

"Yes, now ... prepare and you me follow."

The unusual man suddenly jumped off the cliff with no fear and began to fly, and, without even thinking, Asanaro followed.

From such heights the beauty of the mountains was beyond description. The snow was whiter, the sky bluer than ever. Everything shone gently, with a light that did not bother Asanaro's eyes. He was overcome with happiness at visiting this dimension of dreams. What freedom he felt! What a sensation of cleanness, of liberation! The visitor looked over at his guest and knew that this part of the journey would soon come to an end; it seemed that he had just blinked and he was in a large room, comfortable yet without an end.

The short man was there, too. "Moment this is for you to

value what you learn before ... and come you with me in a short trip-time, remember, it is only a blink ... want to?"

"Of course," answered Asanaro, although he did not fully understand the man. "Where are we going ...? And by the way," asked the smiling Apprentice, "who are you?"

"Hehehe ... am I ..." And he added, in a deep, booming voice, "Ooooomboni ..."

Asanaro felt that he already knew that name or, better put, that sound. He asked again, "Omboni? But who are you? And where did you say we were going?"

The strange little man replied, "I being like a worldarian ... hehehe ... now, remember lessons and know we going ..."

Asanaro wondered a moment before asking, "Are we going to the Bamso?" as he thought that a worldarian might be like a world librarian.

"Hohoho ... that being how you call it now ... want to come or do not want to come? Or, better said: when-where going? And ask, how-squareculture will you understand?"

"I am confused ... I mean ... I understand ... I understand ... I understand ..." Asanaro repeated to himself, recalling that his dimensional state was unstable, as Alsam had taught in his lessons, and that he should accept whatever came.

The short man added, "Aha! ... first travel State-Fluid-Space-Time. Wake up from being awake! Hehehe ..."

"Okay! Now it makes sense ... well, at least I think," answered the Apprentice, remembering his Guide's warning that at any moment there could be surprises. "But ..." he added, "I can't help it! Why do you say 'how-squareculture'?"

"Mmmmm ... feel Apprentice, feel ... already know you ...

your journeys in this field having been basic . . . now will you
see . . . beyond, stages complex, telling truth simple and chained
they are. Your how–squareculture, as resident of your Earth
changing your images momentarily, avoid that, awake from being
awake! Your primary journeys may not have had a big conflict,
there are no forces at fight in your human memory, no–conflict.
This trip different, bigger, already has it being explained to you.
You know."

By now Asanaro had begun to relax and his vision had
become clear; he felt confident, willing to face whatever would
come his way. The great adventure awaited him!

"I seeing you remembering," said Omboni, "must remember you the right lessons, remember what is needed, not what
weighs. Knowing being perfect, not-knowing, too. Beings like
you are copycats . . . hehehe yes, much copycats, assume what
seen and what not seen, because you being just what you being.
You have done incorrect and you have not been you, you have
done correct and you have not been you. Your line, your squareculture affects. Prepare, you will see beyond your world, the
un-shown.

"Listen, now I have a silly task, you learn fast and we leave
Earth. Now I carry you to experience your advance; unready
would suffer great crash, will see a raw truth, as jumping from a
cliff in a solid body . . . hehehe . . . hurts. If you have much 'I am . . .
I know,' if persists this and remains big, if it like this, it will change,
misunderstand you will what you see automatically, because it
will not allow you to find the raw reality, I say, you faint before
falling to the bottom and crash . . . hehehe. If your pure-me is prepared, you will see it and normal it seeming, and already known,
and if that being the case we could continue, traveling through

what you call Bamso . . . hehehe. What a name! And recall . . . here no-time, no-space, no-impossibles, only limits you acquire from your worldly contact. Wish you me to continue?"

"Of course, Omboni! This is becoming more interesting, and it's for this that I've been preparing . . ."

"Good . . . mmmmmhhhh . . . good, this imaginary room is only stop to jump in time-space and temporal-river . . . we will travel different places, different ages, it does not matter when in squareculture human years. This your first lesson, for that you have been authorized. You will see examples of man-development . . . when be-are in the ages of the most dense or most interesting temporal-river, I will make you remember, for you to pay more attention. Much better this than what call in your world the time machine. All this being necessary, for you must see for yourself."

Immediately the room became strange, as if its walls were melting. Everything changed suddenly, but gently, and without even noticing Asanaro was among the trees.

A pleasing sound was in the air, a harmonious chant whose words he couldn't decipher. All was peaceful and inexpressibly warm. He did not even bother to ask why he was there; it did not matter. The place was beautiful. The trees were greener and emanated a heat that he could delicately touch. He flew weightless between them, branches brushing his face, and even though he was aware that his state was not as solid as it was on Earth, he could feel that close contact. "I should pass through them, or they through me," he thought, "because I'm not using the body that Earth has given me . . ." Yet he could still feel them touching him, caressing the surface of his skin.

In front of him he saw dozens of birds darting happily through those same trees. They sang in concert with the ambient chant of the trees, and through this unison created a subtle melody, magnificent and simple, and Asanaro felt a deep emotion, felt joy, nostalgia, and liberation, all united with a feeling of detachment unique to being asleep and outside of your body. One of the birds flew in circles around him, as if inviting him to play. Asanaro smiled at the bird, brushing and gently grabbing at it. The little bird continued its flight, closer now, then farther, seeming to smile back as it joined its friends flying close by, playing. The Apprentice could not explain his feelings of happiness and nostalgia, and wondered at their intensity as the bird returned and without words said, "Remember me?" As these words registered in Asanaro's mind, he looked at the bird, and both his happiness and melancholy became clear. When seeing them so free, so happy, so innocent . . . Was it only in this state, so far from the influence of the world, that he would be able to see things like this? In that moment the Apprentice remembered his past, when, nearly a child in his idiot culture, stupid with youth, he had been so cruel to animals, like this little bird . . . In a certain way he did not want to remember, yet he did, the fact was there. He looked back at the little animal, not knowing what to say. It was not even necessary to say he was sorry; that little bird was not there to judge his past stupidity but to teach him. The prey he had chased as a certain and relentless hunter now gave him his best lesson.

Asanaro now understood that melancholic happiness, and he felt that he was setting himself free. Even though he considered himself to have moved beyond those past episodes, in that instant he understood them completely. All life on Earth is precious; every life in existence is unique and irreplaceable, deserving of our deepest respect and admiration, even though it may look small to our eyes, large as they are in ignorance. Within the smallest plant or tiniest being, there is a universe.

In that moment he could not help feeling deeply touched, as he had not been since he was a child.

The little birds flew happily, continuing their subtle and beautiful song, and Asanaro floated, sunk deep in his thoughts as he flew among the green, profligate leaves of the trees.

Omboni appeared, unnoticed, next to Asanaro.

"This necessary for your advance. You must release the mistaken in life to evolve and correct. Now can we continue our trip beyond, in the weight of the world."

Asanaro smiled, relieved and fortified.

The strange being of dreams continued, "Many things will you see related to many mistakes you have made, seen, and lived on Earth. Prepared must you be."

The Apprentice nodded.

Everything transformed then, again, softly, as if coming in a wave from the background. Now they flew over vast prairies as the sea, forming a semicircle on the horizon, simultaneously approached and receded from them as they flew toward it yet rose higher and higher.

"Where are we going?" asked Asanaro.

"Do not worry!" answered Omboni, loudly now, as they were moving through what seemed to be strong winds or turbulence. "We being come into a temporal-river, meaning to

you something like a current! Hehehe...That current being
the one conjugating your apparent world! The one you living in
the lower state! When you living flesh and bones!"

They were moving farther and farther from the Earth. Their
flight took them though the last tiny wisps of clouds and beyond.
They could see the roundness of the Earth and how it shone, and
in front the Star-Sun, fountain of Earthly life in the dimension
he had known so far, which he was now leaving behind, shone
brightly but without accosting the eyes. They came rapidly to
the moon and Asanaro felt pure awe, amazement, thinking only
of enjoying that instant, of enjoying consciousness, immensity,
and the great freedom offered by the Astral's superior state: the
Bamso. They were beyond the Moon now, which fled quickly
behind them. Everything suddenly was dark, and the Apprentice
heard the voice of his Guide for that dimension.

"Now we going to where-when, as already explained."

"What is where-when?" asked the Apprentice.

"Mmmmmhhhh...listen well. Where-when being a magnetic recording emanated to what we could say the Universe.
Remember, the Great Galaxy is a Great Record of the Everything! Being a Grand Universary!"

Asanaro was puzzled and curious at this explanation, perhaps
also because he was beginning to better understand Omboni,
who seemed to link words and sentences more clearly. The singular being continued.

"Hehehe...yes, yes...you understand me well...it is
normal...will sharpen the frequency...The more understand
you my frequency, my words melding better with the ideas and
concepts in your mind.

"The Big Record is infinite light," he added. "For you to

place it into what you knowing, it being like a light-ray from an extinct planet. You seeing light from the Earth's angle, but the planet no longer existing. Now what we will do, as already explained, is to project us. You say: the Bamso, the Great Record. We project us with the speed of thought, similar to throwing ourselves fast from Earth to a far corner of the Galaxy, seeming less time than a flesh and bones heartbeat; in this way we will capture the thin light-ray from your original planet in the past. The velocity of that light-ray being physical, and less than one of thought, so it being reachable. We can arrive in the age we want, without limits, aside from your how-squareculture state, as I have said before, If ready . . . this is your time!"

"But, Omboni, tell me where we're going!"

"Ahaaaa . . . surprise! But remember, it is not a determined place but a subtle recording of what happened in your square-dimension . . . demension . . . dimension! Dimension!"

Suddenly the loud rushing sound of the strong wind, current, or whatever it was that had been following them for a while vanished, and there was silence. The immense darkness that surrounded them began to form into shapes and it became apparent that they were approaching a planet. It resembled Earth, but in what age Asanaro couldn't say.

His Guide in that strange

adventure said, "As practice, I taking you to points of temporal influence on Earth! Those being very dark moments, so ... hold on tight! You will see the weight of shadows! Maybe you will see what you did not want to see, but what being necessary for you to learn!"

TIME OF GROWTH

I.

The Weight of Shadows

The planet started to grow larger. Asanaro had the sensation of being part of a mirage as all of a sudden they were inside an old building, desolate yet ornate. It was cold, but he was not disturbed. They walked together through a dark hallway, full of odd adornments and furniture of an old epoch. There were many surprises, and Asanaro was attentive to everything. He remembered some strange conscious dreams where everything seemed very, very real, and he tried to compare them to this experience. This time, though, he was amazed: He could feel every detail of this place as if he were really there. There was the peculiar smell of a dank, closed place. The sensation of walking, too, was real, and the hallways seemed new, though their shapes belonged to centuries long passed. He was so impressed that he could not speak.

Omboni spoke. "Do not worry ... we are already being in a

wave of the temporal-river. What you see, feel, smell, hear, and taste no longer exists for the solid dimension of the Earth-planet; we could say, in words for your mind, that this is its past holographic projection. Nothing here can affect, touch, or harm us. If you not being prepared, you could not consciously being here. You would be afraid, or simply transform this scene into another strange dream . . . or an awful nightmare. All depending on the mind. But well, now you pay attention! What you will see is, in straight Earth words, a small history lesson. It being the true story of your world, and will explain a lot of what you are and in what you believe, and why you believing it . . ."

"It's disturbing to be here, Omboni, but to tell you the truth, I don't feel very interested in learning about the history of the Earth. I could have gone to a library to find out about it in a very Earthling way, and nothing more."

"Mmm . . . Apprentice . . . if so simple, you would not being here. What you see here, now, is necessary for your vision of the reality of the world from which you come; you having no vision of it, not knowing who you are. I see in your mind, the history of *you* has been fixed for the convenience of those who want to shape other beings. You will see that in your world many think what only a few decide they should think. You will see the weight of shadows, which covers those from your time. Because of this they do not travel here. Now, live what you must live, accept, and your line through space will open greater fields."

"But is this really necessary?" replied Asanaro. "This place isn't very pleasant."

"Yessss . . . being necessary. I was telling you that we are in a wave of the temporal-river. What is happening here affects much of the future and evolution of human beings. You, whether you like it or not, being involved, and being affected by this fluid, with its errors and duplicities. This must be clear in you, for you to someday discover who you really are ... but the *real* you, not the one fashioned by another squareculture in the immense temporal-river ... not ... you-them."

"Now you've made me curious ..." responded the Apprentice.

As he spoke he saw a man approaching, dressed in clothes that fit that place. Asanaro tried to slow down so as not to collide with the man, who walked directly between Asanaro and Omboni, without hesitation, his side and arm passing straight through the Apprentice.

"Wow, I thought we'd run into each other, and I really felt him moving through me ... what a strange sensation!"

"Concentrate," replied Omboni, "not being so impressed by those sensations, for if they are too strong you will quickly go back to your body on Earth, having wasted this opportunity."

"Yes, yes ... I understand that. This is only a projection of a past time, and has no consistency ... I have no reason to be impressed."

"It being that way," answered the Guide of that strange journey, "nothing from here can affect you, and neither can we in turn affect or change anything that is happening here, for it has already happened! We are observing a Galactic Record, lost in the expanses of space, and all that construction being-was, and all those we will see were. Even though you tried to have telepathic contact with them, like you could on Earth during your travels in the Astral of the flat-time dimension, here it is impossible. Remember that this being another vibratory time, beyond what you name as dreams, being like a ghost, but very precise in facts—it being the facts!"

They advanced down the hallway, coming to what appeared to be a meeting hall, not too large but luxuriously adorned, typical of that ancient place. They could see a group of people talking, discussing something. Four of them sat at an elaborate table, while another who wore fancy clothes stood and spoke in a tone different from all the others. Of medium height, he had a hard face set with small, intriguing eyes, above lips gesturing strangely, curved to one side and showing a certain nervousness.

From the entrance of the room both visitors from the Astral World watched the scene. "What language are they speaking?" asked the Apprentice. "I won't understand anything they're saying."

"Come on, remember, remember . . . in this state it does not matter what language they speak, or the one I do . . . (if only you knew the way I speak . . .). Simply use the telepathic frequency in which these facts are recorded and you will understand perfectly, without even needing to know the language that they are speaking. Concentrate . . . this I have already explained."

Asanaro relaxed, and just as if he had changed the tuner on a radio, he understood perfectly everything that those people were saying.

"It's incredible how easy it is. Languages . . . they don't really exist!"

"Of course they don't, for they are only codes of sounds recorded in the brain, attempting to interpret your thoughts or intentions, but never accurately. Now, since you have entered the field, the frequency of their thoughts, you can understand directly what they are saying, and you will even notice how among themselves they lie, mislead, and trick without any problem, without even blinking. It is basically natural for them, hehehe . . . But remember, you can listen only but cannot intervene in any way."

Together they came closer, and with Asanaro's growing confidence they walked around and sat down at the table unmolested. No one in that room could possibly know that they were there, for even though everything seemed very real, it was only a projection of what had occurred centuries ago, a scene stolen from time.

"Please, my Caesar," one of the oldest seated men addressed the standing one, "we all know that public relations in politics has been handled, mainly and fundamentally, by the priests. If they have worked well for the Empire for such a long time, why must we change things now, for you and your domains?"

The standing man frowned, serious, as another of the seated men spoke.

"Many of our subjects have their beliefs already, my Lord. Most of them follow Mithra or the old gods, and some even follow Zoroaster, not to neglect Serapis. They won't be happy with your plans. Anyway, the Caesar's religion has never been involved with those people. This hasn't changed for centuries, so why do it now, my Lord?"

The room became silent. The visitors of time could read the men's thoughts, which were not pleasant but shadowy and unimaginative. Each one of them was doing the math, weighing benefits against costs, trying to protect himself from the betrayals of the others. Fear and cunning pervaded the room.

"Omboni, these people want to kill each other, yet they argue as if they had a great fidelity; here you can only feel economic interest, ambition for power, and a terrible sensation of . . . fear, yes, so much fear."

"You are beginning to see the reality of the history of your world ... hehehe ... but raw, just as it is. Aren't you curious to find out just where-when we are?"

"Of course!" the Apprentice answered quickly.

"Mmmmm ... Well, in time Earth we are more or less in the Maus, eons after the Era of Water ... hehehe ..."

"What?"

"Let me translate to your mind, mmmm ... We are-being four centuries after that in west-cultural-Earth call ... mmm ... Christian era. During this journey you will see it isn't exactly what they call it ... hehehe ..."

The Apprentice was intrigued by the strange little man's explanation.

Omboni continued, "You see if you want to see, for your people like naming the river and the water. Yet the river does not stop, nor does it dye or change itself from one minute to another to create a new river. Your people calling this 'Christian Era,' but this not being a new era, being the continuing of the idea-village of what was known as Rome and other villages, and even before and before in that time-shore. Actually, this place where we are now being a palace in the western part of that city, and the one you see standing, we could say that he is the first in beginning that 'new era,' which is nothing new. He being another one in the river, but he *thinks* he being an important Boss from the squareculture, which he *thinks* he will create, and which he *thinks* will prevail in that side of the world for the next many hundreds of twists around the sun. If your prejudices are still strong in you, you will know it immediately, for what you will hear and what is happening here being very strong, very direct. No one who has lived later on in the temporal-river would be willing to understand impartially, even to hear what happened here. It would be a terribly strong blow that none would accept; they would react skeptically and angrily, as these facts would touch the sensitive, internal channels that have been formed by the squareculture of the time-river in which they have lived, that which is directly connected with their preformed I and to their supposed knowledge of what life should be, of what is and what is not. The one who does not want to see cannot continue this journey; the Astral World only speaks what is."

"Okay Omboni," answered the Apprentice, "I feel all right, and I want to see things as they have happened. I want to see and listen for myself, without the predetermined stories from my world. This is not pleasant for me, but if it is necessary, I want to live it, to understand it now, directly. I don't consider myself delayed or narrow-minded."

"Hehehe … well, let's continue. Pay attention, for the thief with the title … oops! … for you to understand, I mean, this man that you see standing there, who the others calling Caesar, is worried; he is afraid of losing power over what he has already stolen: land, gold, and everything with weight, that he cannot carry without a body. He fears for his own life in its wrapping, and as you have already sensed, he is paranoid, images of death floating around his mind. He fears that everyone is plotting against him, and he does not know how to control the situation. Can you feel it?"

"Of course … it is so tense here!"

At that instant, the man standing, who was already very upset, raised his voice and spoke roughly.

"What Empire are you talking to me about? What beliefs are you talking to me about? This is not the Empire, this is

not Rome, for we own only the backyards and not the palaces!
I want everything, not just crumbs!"

All the others lowered their heads and listened quietly as he
went on.

"The Empire and its beliefs are undone here, in Rome and
in the East. People believe not in the old religions, but out of
fear of our sword, and that sword is growing weaker. Our armies
are not those of our glorious times, understand! People do not
believe, and if they do not respect us, they do not fear us. It will
be our ruin, sooner or later. We will not win the war against
Magnentius in Rome and less against the Empire from the East.
I want it all . . ." (The Apprentice was able to hear him say, inside
his mind, "Only there will I be safe, for I do not want to wake
up with a sword in my back . . . I will not lose . . . I will not
lose . . .")

They all remained quiet, and the cruel and despotic gaze of
the man became clouded.

"Are you all conspiring against me?!!!" he shouted.

After a terrible silence one of them, fearfully but with
thoughts of hatred, fear, and envy, spoke.

"But, my Lord, what benefit do you see in supporting that
new religion through all of your vast domains? Things might
not be very good, but they work, and they have worked . . . And
in what way will it influence our campaigns?"

Another man, the older one, added, "Lord, we have supported you through all of your battles, and things have worked
out, just as they did for our ancestors. The rabble from north
to south, from east to west within this Empire, have only been
able to understand two things: First, the sword, and later the Pax
Romana, our peace from commerce, our taxes. Our order, or

death. My Lord, that absurd religion you speak about is directed by a mediocre group of fanatics; it is a low-category sect. The Empire has known hundreds of religions formed by better people and based on more logical arguments."

A third man, dressed in some kind of military uniform, now intervened. His voice was rough. "Sir, with all the respect you deserve, I would like to speak."

"Go ahead! Speak! Speak!" replied the Caesar in an equally rough tone.

"I have always been a faithful soldier to my Lord, you know me well. But I must say that this sect, the Christians, is a group of degenerate fanatics. I have had problems with many of them in the areas under my protection and they have infiltrated part of the Army, but anyway they are and remain a minority even if we have never been able to fully control them. They riot constantly! You are well aware of the hate they have even for themselves, not to mention against other sects within the Empire. The Mithraists have always been more trustworthy. Christians have scandalized many Roman families, converting and perverting the minds of their sons and daughters, making them believe in Gods foreign to our traditions, breaking up families; many, many people I know personally have had problems with them. You, my Lord, are a soldier, and because of your form you know of what you speak, but you must have an iron fist if you get involved with that . . . rabble!"

All went mute. The Emperor paced restlessly around the table, nearly touching the visitors of time as they watched and listened to that lost scene, reflected in the secret and mysterious corners of time and space.

The Emperor finally spoke. "Sirs, I have fought hundreds of

battles and wars, and I have achieved my place in this Empire; I've earned it bit by bit. I know well that each war is won with two battles: one by the sword, the other in the world of the divine."

Many frowned, surprised. The Caesar looked at them and quickly continued, laughing hard and proud at the expressions of his councilors and allies.

"Hahahaha ... ! Look at your faces! I haven't changed what I believe. I have never been a stupid superstitious fanatic; if I were, I wouldn't be Caesar! I am not interested in gods, and for that reason I am a God! That is more than enough for me. But it seems that your vision blurs and you understand neither my purpose nor the never-ending change that I want my future Empire to live. Listen quietly, and you will discover that I am the real God Rome has always wanted.

"The lands of the Empire are vast; they contain the four corners of the world. They include hundreds of cities and towns, along with their old religions, cults, beliefs, and superstitions. They also contain villages of different races, customs, and traditions, and we have always kept them, with one form to unite them: by the sword! And then, afterward, negotiations. But superstitions move masses, stir them up and direct them ... the decisive factor in their minds! You are well aware that our army is not the same as it once was, and that negotiations do not always succeed; it is because of their beliefs that more than one town has rebelled against the Empire. And our Army," as he cast a sidelong glance at the general who had spoken earlier, "is always more faithful to its pay than to myself.

"The Empire," he continued, "has too many enemies, not just our servants but what they believe in. The agreements we make with the provinces are not always sufficient and stable enough to keep power and influence. I need a new army, with only one servile town; I need a faithful ally under my complete control; I need an army for the minds, guardian of the minds of all those who live in our lands and the Empire's, from here to the East. I need to kill the old system and be reborn with a new and better one, one that can finally fulfill our need for absolute control ... yes, control! More control! Control that the whole of the Empire has never seen before. Control is everything ... everything ..."

There was a profound silence, and all in the room looked at one another, pretending not to, and sensed that their Caesar was stubbornly decided. They all had a sickly feeling.

After a pause, the Caesar continued his frenetic speech. "If you have the peoples' stomachs, you have half of their bodies; if you have their minds, you have the whole of them! My people! My new Empire will need a Great Guardian inside the mind of each of its inhabitants: slaves, peasants, merchants, the wealthy ... even aristocrats! Now they are all my enemies; any of them can conspire against me. For this reason I need an army to control them, yet if I control their minds, they will be faithful allies, their own guardians and keepers, their own judges, their own unmerciful executioners. I need to educate all of them again from nothing, it is the salvation of our Empire, the perpetuity of the Empire ..." ("It is my salvation," thought the Caesar, heard only by the two visitors.)

Tired yet enthusiastic from his own ideas, he sat and spoke more quietly.

"The near future is essential for my plans, and I need your help. I must become closer with the sect of the Christians; they, with their unceasing chatter of tameness and obedience before their god, will be my best allies in gaining absolute control. That tameness and obedience will now belong to me . . . I want their leaders to trust you and your emissaries; I want them to believe in that trust and know my honest interest in them. I need their names, to know their most important people, their beliefs, their superstitions. They will be my allies, my best allies, and will lend me a new and improved image . . . I will be . . . their Father . . . yes, their Father . . . Today, their Caesar! Tomorrow, their Emperor! Their Supreme Pontiff! Their God!"

Several of those there thought that he had really gone mad with power, like so many other Caesars in the history of that Empire.

The eldest man there thought, "This vulgar son of that prostitute, horrible barmaid, and lover of that cretin, his father . . . he is really insane. That mediocre cult has always been a problem, a low-class plague, and this idiot is planning to use them . . . he might even get it into his head to walk around naked, like the Adamite Christians used to do . . . it would do him good! But on the other hand, I'm not sure, for either he is an ignorant and arrogant imbecile, or he has a brilliant plan to ensure that nothing happens to him, as usual. All the Caesars have been the same: They just want to become God before learning how to rule. And I am tired of being only close to these usurper thieves."

The visitors of time and the Astral listened curiously to what those men thought, as well as what they said. They looked at each other and smiled with pity.

"This, you see, occurring many times in history . . . ambition for materialism and power being a normal path in your world . . . mmmm . . . bad, very bad. Much cynicism, lies, deception, that are later admired."

"This is incredible, unthinkable," answered Asanaro.

"Better to say it being normal. What you seeing now being the standard and typical development of beings like you, only that these being a group of thieves with a great ghost of power. For normal beings, being impossible to even think that this might have happened . . . they respect thieves with power. They can less believe that it happens in their own space-time! On the contrary, if people knew of this, they would not believe it at all, they would be the first to defend those who have deceived them for centuries, for thousands of years. That is why I have brought you here, for you to clear your own vision and, at the same time, to understand that in many beings beliefs are too deep-rooted. They cannot visit this place, being forbidden to them."

"But why? If they really want it, there would come a time for them when they could travel, be approved, just as I have been, and could visit this place and see the truth of their world and its past for themselves."

"If it being so easy, many would know this truth already. Be patient, for you still have certain things to see, and you will really understand why few can visit this Universal Record. We have many things to see . . . past, and later, future! Hehehe . . ."

"That sounds great, Omboni. Can't we just skip all this stupidity and go straight to the future?"

"Patience, Asanaro, patience. This being necessary, take it as an exercise in comprehension, as well as an exercise in tolerating images that can collide with the time-river to which you inevitably belong, that you are living in your four-dimensional world. If you were not prepared, all of this confronting you, and this journey you are taking would lower its frequency to semiunconscious, from which it would become contradictory unconsciousness, meaning a nightmare. That is why it is forbidden. What you see becomes a shock if you being not prepared, and if your primitive beliefs being very deep-rooted in you, they create a short circuit with the real part of the vision. You want the future . . . first accept the raw past . . . or else you see the unreal future. See the real past . . . see the real future . . . and see Univeeeeeeeerseeeeee . . . Hehehe."

The Astral Apprentice was absorbed in the words of his Astral Guide, while the scene he had been watching was frozen in time, a parenthesis in which each character ceased speaking, ceased transmitting thoughts, and ceased moving, as if all were halted by a spell in a blurry and obscure image. Omboni continued with a curious but typical expression of his, frowning and lifting his ears.

"Hehehe . . . Asanaro. Now we must continue our Astral time-space tour. If you've noticed, the scene we were watching has paused . . ."

The Apprentice looked around, amazed.

"Wow! I hadn't noticed. While we were speaking, everything stopped. What is going on?"

"Do not worry . . . hehehe . . . Remember that all of this is an image recorded in a projection of light, interstellar and infinite. Even though you might not understand it, we are traveling in space. We are going away from the Earth of your time, approximately seventeen hundred sun turns, assimilated to light . . . hehehe . . . meaning, I translate to your mind: seventeen hundred light-years. Then we go back and forth, for example, as if we were searching along a tape. If we come closer in thought to Earth, we advance in human history, which, at the same time, has infinite channels. We have followed this channel of events, for they are important if we wish to clarify your doubts about beliefs and superstitions that govern the beings of a great part of what you would call contemporary Earth."

"But I still don't understand . . . why has everything stopped?"

"Mmmm . . . simple, Asanaro, for as we began talking and analyzing the matter more deeply, directing magnetic waves to form our conversation, we instinctively halted our journey. Even though it may sound strange, we are resting in a specific wave, many light-centuries away from Earth. In order to follow the scene we must move closer to the Earth—that's it. If we moved too fast, we would jump to another scene. Or we could jump to another place or wave and our apparent location on that planet would change, regardless of the time, or even the planet!"

"But," asked the Apprentice, "if a traveler in space, made of flesh and bone, flew away from the Earth, would she be able to see the past?"

"Hehehehe . . . It is not so simple, for she would find two difficulties. First, she must travel at the speed of thoughts, where the speed of light means nothing. And second, she would need an incredibly precise device, a transceiver the likes of which you have never seen before, with which to connect to the right frequency, which is almost impossible for a mind four."

"But we are doing it," replied the Apprentice.

"Hehehe . . . Of course, but we are not using any metal spacecraft or any body linked to any world. We use mind as a conduit, or radio, to travel in the superior dimension of conscious dreams, and at the same time, we need a little push."

"And what is that push?"

"Mmmmm . . . you will remember." The Apprentice was thoughtful as Omboni continued.

"But for now we must not waste this journey, for I have many things yet to show you." On saying this he looked at the scene, which immediately resumed its course, as if the whole of the travelers' conversation had never taken place.

The Caesar continued, "I have already told you many times, sirs, that I will not be weak as my predecessors were, and I will not die by any imbecilic traitor. On the contrary, all those who in the future rise up against me . . ."

"Will rise against God," the old man added apathetically, after carefully following the Caesar's every word to that sinister council.

"Yes . . . yes . . ." replied the Emperor, with a tone and look of suspicion at such a quick and uninspired conclusion from one of his most venerable councilors.

"Allow me, my Lord," continued the old man, in an attempt to undo the doubt of infidelity broadcast by the Caesar, "I believe I understand now, and I think that you are right."

While inside that old man's mind, the travelers heard his thoughts: "This idiot is only going to suffer the same end as all of the others before who have believed themselves gods. When the sword comes, gods die like dogs."

Asanaro thought, "If they would die like dogs, they would die nobly, with a clean mind, and fearless . . ."

To which Omboni sent a positive answer, "Mmm . . . we already know, Apprentice. Continue listening, for this will become interesting."

The old man spoke on. "Yes, what you say is true, my Lord. The people need to believe in something; unfortunately, our gods are a little . . . exsanguinous!" The council laughed cynically. "But how will we get those ignorant fools of the Christian sects to help us? How will they aid us in better controlling Rome? I know some of them, and they are terribly divided—I cannot see how they will be more efficient under our service. To which of their many groups will you make address? To which of their many heads? And how are you going to convince them? Or, more to the point, how much will that convincing take from our coffers? After all, I do not believe them so confident, for they were public enemies of the Empire until not so long ago."

At this another councilor, short, with beady eyes, curly hair, and thin lips amounting to a very nasty look, who had been silent up to this point, spoke. "My Lord, you are well aware that I have always been in charge of your public image, and that I am your best servant, for you also know well that your image is a great weapon." He spoke submissively. "In that labor, you are certainly a genius. With only a small part of our treasures we can buy many wills. You know how magnificently I fulfill my role, that I can control all of the news, which with gossip and rumor has become a great influence within the Empire. If we organize well, I am sure we can take hold of one of these sects and make it our servant, with you considered their Royal Savior, their Protector and Father, as you wish. They will feel so honored at your interest in them that they will easily and quickly betray themselves so that they may continue to count on your favors, and they will become the greatest communicators of your message. After all, the days when all of them were undesired fugitives are not so far behind us, fugitives as so many have been, and still are, within the Empire, and I am sure that they have no desire to return to that!"

At the end of this speech the general, who was still confused by all that was being said, cried out, "My Lord Constantine, our Army is faithfully yours until death! Why shall we mix with those people?"

The Caesar looked at him with such contempt that the general could say nothing more and simply kept silent. Constantine sat down and spoke again, tired and with spite.

"Fear and greed are the greatest unifier for these people ... For all the rest, propaganda. As for the Army, no one really believes anymore. I want an Army willing to do anything," and as the others considered what he said, he thought to himself, "and the best soldiers are the idiots, not those who believe they can think, and so ask for a general's salary, like this buffoon. The future incentive of them all will be their superstitions, as it has been before, but with a new face, the face of my making. The people will give all they have, the mothers will gladly send their sons to my wars, my wars that will now be sainted, holy, and if they die there they will be blessed, all by the new God, of whom I will be the representative, the Supreme Pontiff, the only interpreter, I, Constantine, the New Emperor, will rule as no one has before, with a control beyond what those here can even imagine!"

He went from thought to words and spoke categorically. "Let's not talk about it anymore! Enough words—for now I want results, and fast. First, I want your messengers to accomplish what I have commanded throughout all of our provinces, and I wish to have, as soon as possible, the list of all of those with power among the Christians: I want to know in which areas and zones they have the greatest possibilities, I want to know who their direct enemies are, and, most important, I want to have the strong ones in my presence. I also wish to know their contacts in Rome and in the Eastern Empire."

The oldest man interrupted. "My Lord, I can introduce you to several of them. Among my contacts there are several agents who work for me and belong to that sect. But I must respectfully insist, my Lord, that there are others as much and even more popular than that one, and I can also put you in touch with them."

"I have already answered you, no!" replied the Caesar sharply. "I want the Christians at my feet! Those fanatics once burned down Rome, and now I will burn the whole world with that fanaticism. They might believe that a pact with the Empire is possible, but those ignorant fools have no idea who they're fooling with. My Empire will survive and will be perpetuated through eternity, disguised in their arrogant belief. Everyone will think that they adore their prophets and their God, but they will be adoring me: I will be their leader, I will mold them to my taste, in the way of the Empire, of the old gods, of us. Their famous fable of . . . what's his name?" he asked, eager to continue with his plan.

"Jesus! Jesus!" shouted the old man, wishing to put an end to all of it.

"Yes . . . that . . . Jesus! The fable of Jesus will serve us perfectly . . . we will take all of its benefits in accordance with our inventiveness. Was he not a miraculous magician? Now he will make miracles for me, he will build and strengthen my Army . . . I will take the whole Empire . . ." and, to himself, he thought, "I will be their God . . . I am a God!"

The old man continued thinking, "This maniacal imbecile is truly insane. How does he think he can convert those fanatics into collaborators in his war against Rome? I have got to see this . . ."

"I have been analyzing this for a long time," continued the Caesar.

And in the mind of the old man, "Don't I know where he gets his ideas from? From that bartender, his mommy, and her cult of despicable ideologues . . . why didn't he call them here, instead of me!"

The Caesar's exclamations continued. "My plan will consume all of the Christian sect's beliefs. If it is successful to my expectations, I will give it a category, a social level, and an image, and I will turn it into the religion of our New Empire. A religion that will be dressed in our imperial dress, a religion that will carry our forms, even our hairstyles, a religion that will acquire the form of our temples, our grandiosity, my calendar, and my majesty. My creation will control the whole world for millennia!"

The scene stopped, and a thin fog appeared. Omboni spoke to his Apprentice, commenting on what had just happened. "Mmm . . . well, Asanaro, you having seen enough, do you think?"

"Yes, enough. I can imagine how this whole thing ends. It's incredible, and if I hadn't been ready, I would hardly have believed all of this. But, I mean, is this truly where the whole Christian religion was born? From here, in this form, is this how it was conceived?"

"Hehehe . . . no, Asanaro. Still missing is a big part of our trip. This will clarify, with time, many doubts. Also you must realize that one thing leads to another, and then, the time-river is infinite. You belong to it in its whole, we belong to its Universe, and all the actions of the human beings, as you, have been influenced by others, forming a chain that is impossible to completely walk. What you have seen now being only a small part of that chain. I have shown it to you because it being symbolic for how humans act concerning power, control, and, more than that, materialism, so much materialism. The wrong human desires are infinite in the past."

The Apprentice was trying to understand what Omboni was saying, but his mind was still thinking, flying around his previous question, so he asked again, "Then, Christianity was born with Jesus? Isn't that true?"

"Mmm . . . no, Asanaro, it wasn't born with him. You will see for yourself that the Being you mention never spoke about any new belief-mind; those who came later made their own conclusions, combinations, and conveniences, as you seeing now. This subject requires further analysis, but for now I would like us to continue with our path, and continue in this period of the time-river, which includes not so many years."

"This is getting interesting! Let's move forward, as soon as you say!"

Images and sounds faded away.

II.

Gold, Rumors . . .
Bread and Circuses

All was a blur. That strange sound, like wind, returned, and as the Apprentice blinked both travelers found themselves in the corner of a great room that, little by little, was becoming clearer. As Asanaro slowly fixed his vision on this new place, trying to tune in to the scene, he could hear Omboni's commentary.

"Hehehe . . . We have made a small space-time jump in our journey. We have advanced a few sun-turns, close to that last place, close to that time. We are following the path of that . . . mmm . . . big thief! Or Caesar, for they are the same. Watch what will happen here, for this is not written in most of the books in which beings like you record what has happened. You will understand why . . ."

"Where are we, Omboni?" asked the Apprentice.

"Your mind knows this place as Nicea . . . Now watch."

The room they had materialized in was growing ever clearer, all of its details and forms sharp, precise, and very real. It was much larger than the last room, grander, with high ceilings and well decorated; there were statues everywhere and the walls were elaborately frescoed. The room was lit by many candles burning in elaborate candelabras, despite the fact that daylight filtered gently in, trespassing the openings of the windows. Both candles and daylight showed that the room was full of luxuriously dressed people whose garments broadcast their taste for gold. There was a general noise; the people spoke and argued among themselves, apparently waiting for someone as they formed small groups. Meanwhile several other people who seemed to be servants brought small, exquisite bits of food, which the others received in a careless, even contemptuous fashion.

In that place, lost in the memories of both time and space, a grand reunion was taking place, which the two travelers of mind watched from the heights of that luxurious palace. As they stood in one of the cornices beneath the roof, both prepared themselves as two anonymous and ghostly spectators; or, rather, the great event that was about to take place was ghostly, and they the most solid and tangible things in that moment and time, lost in the depths of the records of the Universe and its strange dimensions. Attentively they observed what went on and what was said.

From what they could tell, those moments preceded a great council or formal gathering. It was clear that the people there had come from the far reaches of that epoch's Empire; their dress was ornamented and bejeweled, each in its own way showing the ambition of its wearer. Many of the people conversed in harsh tones, while others argued about strange concepts, beliefs,

and ideas, taking the posture of great intellectuals and philosophers. Others spoke of their wealth, of the sums they had
gained, boasting before others who were not so fortunate.

Another group spoke discreetly about the benefits of coming closer to the Emperor. One of them, the eldest, was thin and
serious, with a presumptuous look; he spoke with the four other
men as if he was with old friends.

"Since the Emperor began supporting our cause, we have
made our followers even more faithful, though in this vast
Empire there are still many who do not believe. I think that
Constantine will soon have to take more drastic measures. Ours
is the true belief, and those who don't believe and don't pay the
tithe, well . . . they will have to pay the consequences!"

Another, portly and shorter than the first, intervened in a
vexed and fearful tone. "I wouldn't dare say another thing to
the Emperor . . . he has his ways . . . it's very possible that it will
be worse for us to speak too directly. I've known many who
thought themselves close to him only to fall from his favor, or
who have had their heads fall from their shoulders on the same
account . . . anyway, we're fine as we are now. He keeps us as
princes; what more do we want? He hasn't even respected the
necks of his own family . . . I don't want any trouble."

"In our province," a third began to speak, "since we have
counted on the support of the Emperor everything has gone
along perfectly, and for me, too! I do not need to add anything
about greater benefits or doctrines; who cares about doctrines,
anyway? No one eats from a doctrine, and for one point more
or one point less, well, I don't think God cares. In my province
we can count on all the Imperial support we need. What else do
we need? Isn't that enough of a signal from God?"

"Brothers!" The most presumptuous of those strange men suddenly spoke again. "We are the Empire, and we must know how to impose our will and speak our minds to the Emperor. I have several contacts who can assure me a personal meeting with him, and I know that His Excellency would approve of my suggestions. Think about it. There are churches that he has favored too much, and we cannot be left behind, for after all we are protecting the interests of the Empire before the ignorant rabble. Remember that his victory at Milvian Bridge was made possible with our aid; our people fought there, to the death, all for the Glory of God... He owes us many things..." And, he thought to himself, "And not only to our greedy and selfish brother, that despicable Bishop Ossius of Cordova."

A fourth introduced himself into the conversation, attempting to calm the others. "My brothers, I will be happy if the Emperor places the Army directly and definitively under our control and helps us to eradicate once and for all the old religions, the pagans and, along with them all of those dissidents who are damaging our belief. Besides, all of those audacious philosophers who call themselves thinkers, mathematicians, and whatnot, they are all a plague on the Empire and should be killed... to the arena with the lot of them! As long as those people with their strange ideas exist, we will not be safe. Have you never thought that our Emperor might not live forever? You know well that there are many plots against him. What if one of those succeeds, and we find ourselves with another Diocletian in control, dictating this and that against us, to favor another religion? What if they take from us our well-deserved benefits? There are still many who could usurp our position, which would spell our doom. We must act now to make this

last forever, for we have engaged and identified with factions
for too long."

The eldest interceded quickly. "But brother ... brothers ...
We are the Empire! There is no turning back, neither for us nor
for the Emperor. He knows it, and he needs the support and
belief of the ignorant masses, the belief of the people! Who have
been his best agents all of these years? We have. And who
have been his best soldiers? Again, we have. Who are his best guar-
antors before the people? Who can certify the sanctity of the
Empire but ourselves? Who are his best propagandists? Aren't
we? And who are the ones who expose the people and are his
best informers? We are.

"Now, without our support," he added in a lowered voice, "he
is only Emperor, Saint, or Vicar of the Dead Christ, as so many
others have been who haven't lasted so long in the throne." He
sighed. "My brothers, understand once and for all. We are the
Empire! And the Empire will live forever in its new form. There
is no turning back, not for us, not for the Emperor, and not for
those under our command."

All stood thoughtful and perspicacious, analyzing the situation for themselves. One, whose silence through the whole
conversation had called Asanaro's attention, thought without
speaking.

"I truly do not know what to think, or what's best for me ...
and I don't know where this stupid, arrogant old man finds his
arguments and justifications, as if Christian superstitions meant
anything to us. We all know that the Emperor and his court
rule everything, with an iron fist, and that we are his servants
whether we like it or not. But it is better that way. If the Empire
needs a religion to survive forever, so be it, for after all I'm an

honorable aristocrat, much more noble than these peasants here. My ancestors must be turning over in their tombs, knowing that I've had to become a Christian to keep my influence and to save myself. Irony of ironies . . . life is one big irony."

All of a sudden they heard several loud knocks, perhaps made by heels on the floor, announcing something. Several people entered in a line, looking like an honor guard or something like that. The Emperor followed immediately behind, the very same person Asanaro had seen moments ago, in another time and place. He looked much older now, more tired and worn. His robes were extravagant, white embroidered in gold and encrusted with precious stones. He wore a strange, conical hat that drew everyone's attention, for it was tall, pointed, and, denser in jewels than even his robes and shone from afar. His guards wore a stolid, vacant expression, taking after their master. Behind them walked a full retinue, dressed in luxurious clothes that marked them as members of ecclesiastical ranks.

The Emperor's entrance was accompanied by a general silence. All in the room turned to face the Emperor and his retinue; Asanaro could see, in their appearance as well as in their emanation, apprehension, even rancor in some of them. In others he could see a servile admiration, but all of them shared one common emotion: fear . . . so much fear.

As they contemplated this scene, the passengers of time analyzed it.

"Asanaro, mmmmh . . . would you like to go nearer? Being good for you to analyze these things up close. Just follow me."

"Whatever you say," answered the Apprentice.

They crossed together from one point to another in that grand hall, from the front cornices to the lower floor, on the opposite corner, where the master of that sinister reunion sat. Gently flying, they gained a strange panoramic view of the whole scene, invisible ghosts of time that they were. Once they had reached the floor they came closer to the large chair on which the Emperor was sitting. His expression was serious, his gaze hard and decisive, and his thoughts were no more pleasant than his expression.

"Watch all of these people," Omboni said suddenly, "for from combined facts they have created a wave in the time-river; they are the result, and at the same time they being in one of the impulses that will increase that wave. Yet not even they can measure the results, even though they believe themselves in control of the whole situation. As a matter of fact, many of the people here will lose the 'Boss's' favor; some it will cost their wealth, and others it will mean their lives! For them, it being collateral damage. Watch carefully, come to your own conclusions, and take this as an example of the destiny of Earth. This being nothing extraordinary, for from time to time darkness gathers."

While the Astral Guide was speaking, Asanaro felt unnerved by the look of that Emperor, Holy Man, Boss, or whatever he was. It was the worn-out and careless look of his teeth that called Asanaro's attention, as did a scar above his eyebrow, perhaps a reminder of an accident or battle, but his teeth, they were the worst part of it. Asanaro tuned the Emperor then, whose thoughts were no different from his look.

". . . These despicable people are always the same . . . they only want gold, and more gold . . . while they play and pretend with me about doctrines and beliefs . . . to me! Speaking of doctrines . . . of Gospels . . . as if I believed or even cared one bit for them! They may think me an idiot, or that I run my domains because I believe in some god . . . Here, I am the God, I am his word and doctrine . . . for I am God . . . I am the Emperor, Caesar, the Father . . . I do and undo here, I am unique, and my religion, which I have made in my own image, is, and will remain, unique . . ."

He then cast a contemptuous look to his side, addressing a man who seemed by his clothes to be of some importance; he came forward, and the council began. After not too long a debate began, on subjects that were unclear and made little sense. Some there only listened, while others intervened excitedly, followed by a general murmur from the others.

"I really don't understand why they're arguing," Asanaro said to Omboni, "because what they say doesn't coincide at all with what they're thinking. It makes understanding all of this very complicated."

"Hehehe . . . Yes . . . this being something that not even they can understand well, their thoughts troubled, on one side, by appearances, of not looking bad before the Emperor, and, on the other hand, for justifying that they have some dominion in the realm of religion, even if they might not believe in it . . . hehehe . . . Observe and focus your thoughts in stages, for you being able to clarify this a bit, but most important being that you see it as an example, not being very productive for us to keep digging in here, for you will find the same garbage, always . . ."

One of the men was speaking intensely, in a slimy and cynical manner.

"Your Holiness, Magnificent Vicar, my Lord Constantine, you know of the support of my Church and faithful toward you; well you know it is unconditional. Also, for the good of our faith, and for the sake of the Empire of God, I absolutely support the motion and concept of Jesus-Christ, of God-Jesus;

he must be consubstantial to God, he must possess the same category. This is the best and strongest method to maintain his divinity and the unity of the true belief against those of our enemies.
Besides," he added in a low tone, "the people like that," then
continued in a stronger voice, "how could they ever adore with
the same strength someone who is not at the same time their
God? I must add, my Lord, that nowadays there are many false
prophets ... false Gospels ... and, excuse my supposition, but
tomorrow any one of them will want to compare himself to our
Prince of Heavens, our Lord Jesus. The situation for the future
must be clear: He is also God, and being God, who would even
think to compete with him, to touch his name?" He continued,
in his own thoughts, "Therefore, no one will dare to touch us ...
if He is divine, then so are we ... Our power will be absolute
before the superstition and ignorance of the masses ..."

The murmuring rose to take over the room, and the man
continued on with his analysis, which became long and tedious
in the extreme.

Meanwhile, the Caesar thought, "These despicable fools
are really boring me, for I already know what they are here
for—they only want more support from my coffers ... and I
will give it ... for it is always convenient to keep them happy,
it is the best way to maintain the stability of my dominions:
one God, one State, one Church, and all will faithfully obey ...
So many disquisitions try my patience! I have already decided
everything ... but then, appearances must be maintained, and
so long as those idiotic and ordinary followers of Arrian don't
appear, all will go smoothly. My Empire does not need scandals,
for people are always susceptible, and everything has been perfect so far ..."

The man who was holding forth with his theory on Jesus was claiming justification in several sacred texts that they possessed in their monasteries, relics that would help them legitimize this and that. His speech jumped from one point to another, and Asanaro found it difficult to follow.

"Mmmm..." Omboni interrupted the thoughts of the Apprentice once again, "calm, Asanaro, there being not much to understand."

"These people are so strange ... what are they getting at with all of this?" asked the Apprentice, still watching the gathering.

"Well ... you having seen enough to understand a little more. What you have seen here happened more or less three hundred sun turns after the life of Jesus, the one they talk so much about. You might think that he and his life had something to do with this whole reunion of opportunists. Now, we'll follow our journey and you'll see that he has absolutely nothing to do with these people. That first. Second, I must explain that this man, Constantine, who you see here, was just another of the Caesars who ruled this part of your Earth, and just as you observed before, he having been planning this moment already, a long time ago. All these years he has been executing a campaign, with the help of his closest advisers, to gain control and to create a new mask before those who fear him, and those he uses for his advantage. He took the mask that seemed most appropriate, most popular, or simply the one that being easiest to control. He needed servile allies, adapted to his Empire, and here you seeing how the different lines in space-time have converged to form a complete system in the great time-river, which is the destiny of people such as you. Consequences of what was lived here have damaged many people, more than you can imagine. The next thousand years, many centuries more, even, being affected by an expansion from this moment. An era very, very . . . daaark."

"Omboni, if this had been stopped, would that whole Dark Age have never happened?"

"Mmm . . . not so easy, Asanaro, for this that you seeing here is only one link in a biiiig chaaaaiiin . . . If this had not happened . . . it would not affect the great current. The weight of past facts being so heavy, that what being coming would have happened in one way or another. The time-river having its own inner strength and inertia."

"But if this Caesar had not existed, maybe this could have been stopped," replied the Apprentice.

"Mmm . . . no, again I tell you, it being not so simple. Things happening obey temporal-fluids, which have their roots in deeper and more complex factors than you are prepared to imagine. Do not blame . . . there is only a torrent . . ."

"What if those churches had not existed, then the Caesar wouldn't have had anything to support him," insisted Asanaro, stubbornly wishing to change the events.

"Hehehe . . . you are trying to change something that has no solution through 'events' or 'not-events.' You still have long to walk, to understand these time-rivers among human beings, and on Earth in general. If that sect, or whatever it is, had not existed, I can assure you that nothing would be very different. Recall what you have heard, that in those years there being many other sects that would have served the Caesar's purposes in the same way, such as the Mithraists you having heard about in our last scene; they possessed the same arguments as the Christians. If not being one, being the other, and nothing more. Those same beings naming themselves 'noble citizens of the Empire,' who you see here, now, created once the old religion and now the new one, are the same in one case or another, only with a different title. Small changes in their speech, and I can assure you even that is almost nothing. Being the same, and with the same Caesar. You learning . . ."

"Omboni, it's hard for me to understand all of this. I try to follow their explanations, but I only get confused. Are you trying to make me understand that all of this was inevitable, one way or another?"

The council continued, though more and more slowly as the scene lost its sharp detail, became blurry, ghostly. The Guide of that strange adventure continued calmly instructing the Apprentice.

"Mmm . . . you having much to learn, much to live in the superior world of dreams, and much to value in the world of your four dimensions, trying to explain too much and judging, too close to condemning . . . that being a word of your thought, here useless . . . useless to you. Be patient and you will be understanding better with time in your state of Earthly existence. All this being necessary to clarify who you being . . . Now, observe and complete your experience of these facts."

The scene in front of them dissolved as if by magic, and before the Apprentice could notice that a change was happening, all was transformed and they stood in the highest galleries of a great Roman circus.

The new place-time was full of people. The sky was clear and Asanaro could see everything, down to the finest detail. The building itself was enormous, and although its shape and design immediately called to mind past epochs of history, the building was well maintained, felt solid and kept up. There were certain details that showed its age and use, marks and scars in the walls and galleries.

People were laughing and shouting, and the whole scene gave the impression of one giant party. To the amazed Apprentice, traveler of the Great Record, the manner and attitude of those people reminded him instantly of things he had seen in his own time, in a "modern" stadium where people looked on while a confrontation took place. The Apprentice thought, "The passion of the people doesn't really change . . ."

"Hehehe . . . that being true, Asanaro," Omboni immediately answered Asanaro's thoughts. "The beings from this place sound familiar, and that being normal, they navigate in the same river."

"Yes, and it's strange," answered the Apprentice, "as the attitude of these people is the same that I have seen so many times on Earth, how they get together and transform themselves, watching a game of something, or when they crowd around someone who's just had an accident, not intending to help, only to satisfy their morbid curiosity in the face of someone else's suffering."

Omboni nodded in agreement and began walking among the people in the galleries. The Apprentice followed him, nearly hypnotized by the people he saw, their expressions, their faces . . . he couldn't stop staring at them. What most called his attention was how they held expressions while emanating energies as contradictory as hatred and pity or fury and terror. Suddenly a man jumped up, screaming hard enough to distort his face; clearly he had been drinking heavily and his face was tough, its poor shave matching perfectly with the intensity of his anger. Asanaro was disconcerted by the proximity and reality of it all, but he managed to remain calm, remembering and reminding himself that it was only a projection, and the crowd was neither more real nor more solid than he.

From a corner Omboni called the attention of the Apprentice, away from staring agape at the raucous scene in the stands. With a beckoning gesture that was at the same time a special emanation from the Astral Being, Asanaro turned toward the center of the arena, which he hadn't yet noticed. His face, or really his energy, became so contracted before that vision that he seemed about to lose consciousness of that Astral Journey, but he took strength from deep inside his projected mind in order to remain lucid, immutable, and strong. He only thought, "Nothing can touch me . . . nothing from here can touch me . . ."

What was happening in the arena was as painful to watch as it was cruel. Blood stained the ground in different spots as a great lion tore into pieces something that had been a human being, while several still-living victims tried to run away or defend themselves pitifully from the other felines. All were quickly overtaken and tossed to the floor like limp puppets. One of them, with one leg left and parts of his body severely torn, escaped from the implacable claws of the animal, which made no effort to follow him. The man fell over and began to drag himself when, suddenly, the lion sprinted and jumped on the man again, easily finishing his task. Meanwhile, the people screamed deafeningly, muting the cries of the victims.

"Calm, calm . . . mmm . . . truth never being cruel. Have not you prepared for it? Calm, Apprentice . . . center your mind, for you being here to learn from these examples, and our work still being long ... neither I finding this pleasant, do you not think I know better than you that your world being from a very primitive state, both yesterday and yours ..."

As he listened, Asanaro reacted and began to regain, slowly but securely, the scene that he was living. He thought, "This is only a record of what happened and I am a projection of my own mind. My form is insubstantial, timeless ... and I want to go further."

The scene returned, solid as it was before, and immediately the Apprentice addressed the Astral Being.

"Is it really necessary for us to see this?"

"Mmm ..." Omboni immediately answered, "yes it is. From the moment you took the road of knowing the Astral World, you deciding to know it all, the good and the bad, the gentle and the rough, what pleases you and what you find unpleasant; you must walk through it all to finally discover what you are really looking for. What you seeing here today forming part of your time-river, that being undeniable. Crimes that you see here today will repeat again, will continue repeating through an extended period of the fate of your four current dimensions: Earth. You see past, I seeing present."

A memory and a thought crossed Asanaro's mind, and immediately Omboni answered, "I know what you remembering has helped you getting upset before this scene. It is true, even in your era, which calls itself so advanced, public cruelty being celebrated and rewarded ..."

"Yes ... I recall the cruelty of bullfights," the Apprentice added sadly. "How can anyone have so much hate for a poor, defenseless animal, already wounded? Here, today, they celebrate these lions killing those poor men, but these animals are pure in their actions compared to the cruelty of the audience and their captors, who use them in this bloody spectacle.

"I was thinking..." he continued, "why are human beings so cruel, so inconsiderate, so blind before their own crimes, and why do they justify them so cynically? Their cause may be political, religious, or whatever, it doesn't matter, but they always have the stupidest justifications for their cruelty. What is worse, even, is how they feel satisfied and victorious after the abuse. They seem to feel mighty, knowing that there is someone who is weaker."

"Mmm ... already understanding, Asanaro. Must value much of yourself before what you are seeing. Beings, called humans," Omboni added quietly, "monkeys transitioning through doubt inevitably belong to their own time-river, and since they being so weak they cannot escape its influence. The I-pure in themselves, as it has been in you, knows what is right but is tiny, tiiiny, and weeeak ... The I-external, that is, the idiot controlled by the time-river, conforms to a whole system of influences, interests, of filthying the mind of beings over beings. That I-external is the one who takes any argument, no matter how stupid it being; it is the one who accepts going to a bullfight, even out of curiosity ..."

Asanaro's energy became opaque, for he knew what Omboni meant, and remembered perfectly how once he had been invited, and went, to one of those cruel spectacles, for which Alsam had deservedly reproached him.

"Heheh ... now you understanding why this scene has been so disturbing, to the point where it almost sending you back to your body. If being so, that crash with your carnal wrapping being so sudden you would have forgotten all of these lessons, at least in the conscious ... hehehe ..."

"I am sorry Omboni, I must be honest," Asanaro answered sadly. "But I thought I had already overcome that foolishness. With the lesson that Alsam taught me I felt I had learned more than enough, but I can see that it still affects me."

"Of course, Astral Apprentice, here nothing you having seen and lived in your bodily state being easily undone. The recordings are deep, and all of the errors and states in which you have allowed yourself to be negatively influenced by the warped time-river, those being here proven inevitable. That is why it being necessary for you to experience all of these scenes; you will see yourself, your world, your river and time-fluid, which also being yourself. I ask you . . . what kind of being will you end up being? Hehehe . . ."

A little bit lost in the explanation, Asanaro asked, "What exactly do you mean?"

"Mmm . . . all in the moment . . . Patience, Apprentice of Dreams, relax now and concentrate mind on our adventure. You have much yet to learn from it!"

The scene returned to life, and the noise continued throughout the entire circus: the screams that had been muted as the Cosmic Visitors spoke returned instantaneously. People bet on who would die sooner or would last the longest, screaming encouragement at the lions and their victims. It was all insane, though nothing too strange when compared to the scope of normal human behavior.

Already grown more accustomed to that reality, the adventurers of the Astral continued their conversation.

"But tell me, Omboni, what era are we in?" The Apprentice's voice was already more calm.

"Hehehe . . . well, discover for yourself. Come, follow me!"

They both began to fly, nearing the center of the circus while avoiding the arena itself, for Asanaro wanted to avoid that direct vision. From where they now were they could clearly see in the center of the building a great balcony overlooking the arena, emphasizing the presence of some important person.

Immediately Asanaro recognized Constantine. His expression was contemptuous as always, but now he looked especially ferocious. He was easy to spot from afar, with his long white robes, exquisitely embroidered with gold and jewels. The man looked more worn out than ever, and his look showed that so many cruelties and machinations had not been in vain.

"It's the same Emperor!"

"Mmm ... yesss ... same character we having watched before, being very shocking to you! We simply followed his track, so you could complete your vision of him, for he influenced in some way the apparent fate of a great part of your world."

The Apprentice was confused. "But, well, what is he doing here? I am trying to be logical with the dates, and if this man took Christianity for his Empire and government, this scene, which is after that happened ... it shouldn't exist, for supposedly after that there were no more Christians thrown to the lions ..."

"Hehehe ... Wanting to solve the enigma? Follow me," cried Omboni, "and forget your logic and memories, here not serving you, being only distractions. Go and listen for yourself, not to the tales that other beings have told you."

The travelers came to the Emperor's balcony, which was crowded with guardians and other Lords of the Empire, all laughing and enjoying the horrors in the arena below. The Emperor, however, kept his usual cold, rancorously cruel expression. His forehead was now marked by years of anger, his mouth seemed frozen in that same expression of twisted spite that characterized him, and now the side of his neck showed the scars of some peculiar skin disease. He emanated a strange sensation of pride, but nervous, though he knew himself to be master of the whole world. Pretending to participate in the laughter of his comrades, he forced a laugh and spoke with disdain.

"To the people, Bread and Circuses!" He thought to himself, "And to those surrounding me . . . gold . . . and rumors."

All on the balcony forced their laughter as loud as they could.

"Mmm . . ." the Astral Being spoke to the Apprentice, "now tune into the thoughts of this man, and you will see that they have not changed."

A few seconds passed, and Asanaro understood the whole situation.

"But . . . how!" He was upset. "He, on the advice of his closest bishops, has given the order to prosecute and execute the men who are being sacrificed in the arenas of this circus . . . Why? . . . Why?"

He answered himself, "They were enemies of the new religion of the Empire . . . But how! I don't understand . . . he is supposed to be a Christian . . . and he is killing those who do not think as he does, just as his ancestors, the Caesars, killed the old Christians . . ."

"Mmm . . . yessss . . . Christians died in old times, but these being others. Now they govern in the name of them, and anyway judge and determine who lives and who dies." Omboni continued after a pause, "Apprentice of Dreams, learn: Power is always power. And as it is said by the beings of your dimension,

I can see it in your mind: Power corrupts, and absolute power corrupts absolutely.

"The new Being-Religion of the Being-Empire not being any new religion, as you can see for yourself. Simply, the Empire took the idealism that sounded better to them, or was more popular in a given moment. Took it for himself, built it at his own caprice, with his own rules, though now trying to pretend good through public relations and propaganda. Persecution always being persecution, abuse always being abuse, power always being power, since the oldest rivers and flows of time. Nothing new in this Being-Emperor who wants to dress up as a god, saint, or savior. Be it in the name of Ra, Zeus, Caesar, or God . . . ignorance and error are the same."

There was a pause; everything spun inside the thoughts of the Apprentice.

Inevitably he asked again. "But Christianity . . . it must have somehow changed the world . . . or the people, right? Maybe not so perfectly, but . . . it must have accomplished something? Didn't it?" he added, doubtful of what he said, doubtful of everything.

"Mmm . . . Apprentice of Dreams, Walker of the Great Record, open your mind, free yourself, and you will see reality. Ideas, religions do not change human beings and their conditions. No, it is they who create those things, at their own measure, their own stature, weight, time, and necessity. And much, muuuuch more . . ."

"But tell me more!" insisted Asanaro, anxious.

"Mmm . . . as a matter of fact, what you say, what your mind calls religion not existing, only another being-invention. Religion having never existed . . . neeeever . . ."

. . .

The Apprentice was perplexed, deeply insecure, and though he had already advanced so much, perhaps his evolution was still too undeveloped, and what he had seen perhaps too strong, too much for a novice and one journey. His Astral-head seemed about to explode, and everything around him became blurry, less and less precise, as he lost the cruel scene before him, feeling and hearing instead that indeterminate wind, though now it seemed far more eerie.

In a second, or after a long time, Asanaro awoke.

He opened his eyes brusquely and sat up in his bed. He glanced abruptly around, trying to clear his vision, but he could not manage it as quickly as he wanted. He remembered what he had lived, and the dialogue of a few moments before, or who knows when and where it had happened.

"Where am I?" he asked himself. "What time is it? Where am I?" He repeated his words in a stupor.

He was slowly recovering his sight and could finally focus his vision on what surrounded him. There was someone there, though he didn't know who it was until he focused his eyes a bit more and saw clearly.

"It's . . . you . . ." He spoke weakly. "But I'm awake . . . you shouldn't be here!"

"Hehehe . . . sure that you being awake?" replied Omboni, answering the question with another one. "Relax, do not think too much, just relax."

"But, but . . . I'm confused," the Apprentice said.

The Astral Being answered, "Mmm . . . calm down, you have

awoken, but not to your four Earthly dimensions. This is a stage for care, to which I projected you so that your waking on Earth not being too harsh, nothing more. Also, in this way you can make a choice about the path you have taken."

The Apprentice answered, "All right, Omboni, I want to understand . . . I understand slowly." He paused, then continued, "We had a long travel in space and time, and we were analyzing what we had seen. Why are we here now? Did I do something wrong?"

"Hehehe . . . no, nothing, Asanaro. Only that you seeing things that for your Earthly teaching being too strong and too contrary to what is known by beings such as you."

The Apprentice answered in a compliant tone. "But I had already prepared for this. After all, many of these things I have already spoken about with Alsam, and we have analyzed them together; he is very direct in saying what he thinks. I don't know why this journey has affected me so much."

That whole place seemed incredibly clear, too clear to be properly defined, and the Apprentice felt as if he were lying in bed.

"Hehehe . . . well, you not being so well prepared. You are prepared for hearing, but not in the deep facts of yourself. One thing being hearing, taking that as a conversation or a curiosity. Living it, seeing things directly, that being another thing entirely . . . Hehehe . . ."

"Yes . . . Alsam would say, 'It's one thing to sing, and it's another to get on stage, with a guitar' . . ." the Apprentice added as he remembered, laughing at himself and his inexperience. Trying to relax, he added, "Or he'd probably say, 'It's one thing to cover one's eyes, and another to be blind!'"

"Hehehe ... Good! I see you are more relaxed," Omboni responded, "being normal that subjects which you have spoken about in the past, to open your vision to the things of the world, being very different when you are traveling in Universal Record and seeing for yourself the fact that you have truly been conforming to your current in the time-river. These visions being too strong, stronger even than if you seeing them in their real time, in the ages when they actually happened. What you are living in this adventure, you have caught from many directions, like a kind of telepathy, an emanation of the energy of others, and many details that are beyond normal states.

"Mmm ... if you being from that era, as you are from yours, meaning if you being in an equal dimension to the people you have witnessed, you not seeing mistakes in the same way ... for you would being soaked in the same river, in the waves of your moment. That clouds the vision, and being why there are few visionaries in your world.

"What you seeing with me," continued Omboni, "touched the depths of yourself, to your roots, your deepest feelings. For this, few being prepared to know the truth, and many fewer being prepared to live the truth. You have sensed this example for yourself."

The Apprentice rested, analyzing what he was hearing. He tried to focus on the surroundings, but everything remained undefined, with a green tone, like fresh wood. As he tried to discern the background he noticed that there was someone behind Omboni. He tried to look at the figure, who kept hiding and appearing again, and it seemed to him that it was a young girl.

"Where are we?" he asked. "And who is ... she ... ?"

"Hehehe . . . this being a state for resting, a state I could not explain with a where or a when. It simply helps, as a station for recuperation and definition," answered Omboni, saying nothing about the Apprentice's last question.

"What? Of . . . definition?" asked Asanaro as he tried to get a good look at the strange visitor. She seemed familiar, but perhaps, he thought, he was only confused and dazed from everything he had experienced.

"Mmm . . . yeees, I spoke that way so you can understand that in this stage you must come to a decision."

"Yes . . . yes . . ." Asanaro replied distractedly, paused, and continued more attentively. "Tell me, please, explain to me, what kind of decision?"

"Hehehe . . . it being simple," answered Omboni. "There being two choices for you now, based on your having suffered several alterations in the face of what you have seen, and the harsh reality you have discovered. In this moment, you can quietly return to your body and rest with several hours of unconscious dreaming, recover your energy, and calm yourself completely. The other alternative being for us to continue, to complete at least our first stage of this journey through the Great Record, what your mind calls Bamso, being a stage still difficult, but necessary for you to see."

"No problem," replied the enthusiastic Apprentice, "I want to continue without doubts, no matter what I have to see. I am willing and I take full responsibility for myself. Let's get going!"

"Hehehe . . . Okay, liking your enthusiasm. If choosing to go back to your Earth-dimension now, you would have lost the consciousness of all you have seen and advanced."

The Apprentice was surprised and a little upset. "But why didn't you say that before? If I had chosen to go back, I would have lost everything . . ."

"Hehehe . . . your decisions must being without interests, natural, must be born from you, not conveniences."

"It's all right, I understand. I only want to continue this journey with you."

III.

The Agony of Lights

Asanaro lost his perception of the Astral Being and again felt the initial sensations of movement and sound that came every time they jumped within the Great Universal Record. After a few seconds, if those impressions could be measured in time, the Apprentice began to notice clouds, and then the majesty of great plains, deserts, and mountains. They flew high above those landscapes, at an indefinable speed, and the sensation of freedom Asanaro felt was splendid; the vista before him was beautiful and clear. He could feel the wind, but it did not disturb him, and looking down he saw the desert below change slowly, first with occasional bushes and then with more dense, Mediterranean forests that calmed him, reminding him of the other Astral Travels he had taken. He was overwhelmed by the beauty below, and Omboni, who was flying alongside him, smiling, began to speak.

"Hehehe ... I can tell that you are enjoying these scenes ..."

"This is amazing!" answered the Apprentice.

"I should tell you that what you seeing is a part of the Record not in real time, for I simply wanted to bring you indirectly to the scene we are going to visit, through a parallel channel. Being better this way, for you will follow this more calmly, since what we are about to see follows the same line of the time-river that so shocked you the last time. This entrance serving as a break for you, and also I can explain better the circumstances of what we are about to see."

"This is wonderful ..." replied Asanaro, "I don't care what time or place it is or isn't!"

"Hehehe ... Enjoy!!!"

They were cheerfully flying quite high, just below the clouds, though when passing a mountain they would fly higher, to avoid it and to get a better view. After a while, the Astral Being continued.

"Mmm ... Our latest jump having taken us about one hundred Sun turns beyond the previous scene ... unpleasant. Now, we are more or less close to that last place-time we visited. The wave of the events produced by the Constantine-being, and the willing-beings close to him, has already had many effects. By passing his plan on to the other Caesar-beings who followed him, continuing and increasing the idea while increasing the power, control, and absolute influence of the Empire-being over its useful-servant-beings. It being necessary neither for you to revisit again and again the scenes of crime and murder organized and committed by these so-called holy-beings, nor to visit each of the persecutions they enacted against other beliefs that they considered enemies of the new Empire, already become a religion. What you seeing now, in one certain form, represents this whole wave in the time-river, a wave of decadence from wisdom, an age that turned your world away from any search for knowledge, calling it a strange word that your brain knows: sin. Knowledge became an offense against the power established by the Emperor-being, disguised now as his new Spiritual Government. These sequences being typical in your human-being world, since the beginning."

Asanaro responded with only one question, "Omboni, why do you call everything 'being'?"

"Ohhh ... hehehe ... hahaha ... I taking that word from your mind, to adapt to an idea that your mind does not have. Lord, empire, caesars, governments, religions, servants ... they do not exist for me, for they are just beings. Hehehe ..."

"But you are always speaking of human-beings ..."

"Hehehe ... you will see ... you will seeeeeeee ..."

The sea appeared quickly below them, and the water sparkled with its normal splendor, which can only be truly appreciated in the superior state of dreams. The waves were crisp as the two travelers flew high above, gazing down upon the beaches of white sand. They could see one or two boats far off, floating like weak nutshells in the majesty of blue. The Apprentice, as always, was intensely enjoying all of it.

"Haaa!" Omboni called. "Prepare! We are approaching our new objective."

Asanaro understood, though he continued to enjoy the beautiful sights. He noticed another ship with its sails unfurled. Closer now, he could almost see the men on the deck, almost understand the orders that the boatswain screamed as loud as he could. The ship looked new, though its design was from an

ancient epoch, its sails quite rough yet effective. The Astral Travelers descended lower and lower, and the Apprentice was now
able to distinguish clearly the crew on the deck; they were wearing clothes that looked strange yet comfortable. They were restless, anxious to arrive at their port, which seemingly must have
been close by. Asanaro turned, and he saw clearly a great city of
ancient times. Its buildings and monuments were beautiful and
shone in the sun, and the Traveler of the Great Record knew that
they hadn't advanced too far in time and were still wandering in
past centuries.

The city grew bigger and bigger as they approached.
Asanaro could now distinguish the silhouette of a great building,
ensconced in an island at the entrance of the bays that formed
the port. The closer they came, the more ships they saw coming and going from the place; there was a lot of activity on
the coast, reminding Asanaro of the activity of a modern port,
though scaled to that era. The Apprentice could barely contain
his curiosity, and despite his intention to just let go, he couldn't
help but interrogate Omboni.

"Where are we? This is a huge city, but it seems that we
haven't advanced so far in time, right?"

"Hehehe . . . patience, patience, Apprentice . . ." replied the
enigmatic Astral Being. "Enjoy the view!"

They continued flying together, over the city now. The
streets were alive with people, the buildings were numerous and
well kept. They were still within sight of the port and could
turn to watch its activity, the loading and unloading of the ships,
the many carts pulled by animals that brought or carried away
the goods. In front of them they saw people eating in the streets,
in front of small shops that made delicious-looking dishes out

of who knows what. Their vision was wide from those heights: the rooftops, the buildings, the carts, carriages, and animals, the shops and the people everywhere all spread out below. Omboni began descending slowly, and as the Apprentice followed, they came closer to a building that was different from the rest. It seemed to be some kind of public building, elegant and majestic, with an eclectic mix of Roman, Greek, and Egyptian styles. It had beautifully carved columns, and once the travelers touched the ground they could appreciate the exquisite craftsmanship of the floor itself, covered as it was in mosaics that seemed to represent several gods from old times. They began walking toward the open entryway. As they approached, two people, in the dress typical of those times, left the building and walked directly through the travelers, for, after all, they were only two ghosts wandering through the projection of a scene that, at the same time, was only a mirage lost in the infinite dimensions of space.

They continued walking into the building, and Asanaro instinctively kept silent, not wanting to ask any questions; he felt that place needed such silence.

"Mmm . . ." Omboni said after a few moments, "I see you being very silent, expectant . . . you wanting to ask any questions?"

"It's strange," answered the Apprentice. "This place looks and feels like a library to me . . . it's silly, to be honest."

"Hehehe . . . no, Asanaro, you being right, we being actually in a library . . . your instincts being correct."

"I'm assuming that we need to be quiet, then."

"Hehehe . . . not worrying about speaking. Remember that this being only a projection recorded in the Bamso, and that even if we tried to be heard, being impossible. This and they belong to a different time-space, and this being the remains of what has actually happened on your planet many centuries ago. We being just visitors, projections only, although not stopping being real, as much as you are in the four dimensions of your Earth when you use your wrapping."

The Apprentice continued his instinctive silence. The place called his attention, and he felt a certain admiration, combined with curiosity. They advanced together until they reached a new central hall, surrounded by hundreds of shelves made of beautiful carved wood, each shelf separate, divided, containing not hundreds but thousands of papyrus scrolls. In other shelves there were things that looked like paper stretched between wooden boards. The Apprentice was absorbed in observing all of the details of the library.

The Astral Being spoke again to Asanaro. "Mmm . . . I see that you now being very interested. You look calm, curious, and fascinated."

"Yes, Omboni. Coming here has been a real break from all of those other places we've visited. The vibe is different here, as I would say if I were awake and inside my body."

"Mmm . . . and what else can you feel?" asked Omboni.

"Well . . . there is a certain tranquillity here that I like a lot. I feel the energy of a desire to learn . . . but . . ." The Apprentice paused in doubt before continuing. "But . . . there's also melancholy in this place . . . yes, a certain sadness."

"Being right," answered Omboni, "you have perceived well the sensations of this place. However, you just beginning this new path, and you will see that bit by bit you will be deciphering each of your sensations, and you will discover why I have brought you here. You will see that this being a very important and significant episode in the fate of your world, despite being forgotten by it."

In that moment, three people entered the room, speaking to each other in a strange language, though the travelers spontaneously deciphered it telepathically. The people passed by the travelers, carrying on their conversation about writings and papyri. The Apprentice was now able to appreciate the place in greater detail: The walls were covered in mosaics, as were the floors, and there were many statues taller than an average person. These monuments seemed to represent various Greek and Egyptian gods, and perhaps some from other places that were unknown to him. Far off he noticed several people working at some tables and, curious, he moved closer to them. They were writing, transcribing manuscripts, and each put special care into what he did, making very little sound. Reading their thoughts, Asanaro understood that they were completely absorbed in their tasks, that there was no thought disturbing them other than to be as loyal as possible to the original texts that each of them was copying. Their pens were made of strange feathers, and the paper they used was thick and yellowish.

"Hehehe . . . I see this place calls your attention."

"Yes, Omboni, I like it here. I don't mean to complain, but finally you've brought me to a more pleasant place in the time-river than the ones we've visited before."

The Guide smiled and answered, "I had warned you that the experience of our first journeys would impress you a little, since you must seeing for yourself how the time-river in which you live on Earth has been formed, and I know it not being very pleasant . . . Plus, I did not bring you . . . you always being coming . . ."

"But . . . well, it's all right, Omboni. Please don't tell me that something terrible is going to happen, that there's some genocide or something like that planned, because I'm satisfied with what we've seen already."

"Mmm . . . well, Asanaro, enjoy the positive now and later we will learn what we must learn. Follow me."

The Being of Time began walking again, toward another room adjacent to the one they were visiting. When they entered they saw a lonely man sitting at a desk covered with enormous open manuscripts; he was absorbed in his study, intently reading one of them and making notes on small pieces of paper. Both travelers came nearer until they stood right next to him.

The Apprentice looked over the man's shoulder and asked, "What is he doing? I'm trying to catch his frequency and I see a machine, the design of a machine. This man is thinking of how he could build this machine, which seems like a sort of steam engine . . . What a mess! But tell me, Omboni, where and when are we?"

"Hehehe ... I am amazed, Asanaro, that you still have not guessed. But I have made you think about it, so now I will tell you. As I explained before, this is a great library, but now being in decline. This city being known in your mind, and from those times, as Alexandria, and therefore this being the Great Library of Alexandria, or what being left of it ... in the place your mind calls Egypt."

"Well, that's why! I've always wanted to see this place! From what I know this library gathered manuscripts, books, and compilations from many eras and many writers, scientists, and philosophers. It's amazing! But, Omboni, please explain something to me: How is it that this man, in this time and place, is designing or trying to understand and build a steam engine based on the manuscripts he has there in front of him? Steam engines weren't invented for more than a thousand years."

"Mmm ... interesting ... interesting," replied Omboni to the astonished Astral Apprentice. "If you wanting to know the truth, go see it for yourself, not from what being written in comic ... I mean history books ... hehehe."

"Do you mean to tell me that in this time there were already steam engines and things like that? Because that's what I see."

"You are right, Asanaro. What you seeing, really being-was. Here, around twelve hundred sun-turns before the memory of human-beings recalls the creation of steam machines, here in this instant out of the time-river, they were beginning being designed and ready to be tested and put to work."

"But why isn't that written in human history? Why wasn't it known?"

"Mmm ... well, Apprentice of the Astral, you already saying human history, the same as politics-being or Religion-being. For those in your planet, everything being an arrangement according to the consequences and circumstances of the moment."

"But Omboni, what happened then? Where did all of these projects go?"

"Asanaro, what you will seeing later will explain the why. I am afraid that being the sad part of this visit, but being necessary for you to know, and you will understand many things that will help you appreciate the behavior of your contemporaries and what their reality being."

After a pause, the Astral Being continued his explanation. "Mmm ... you can say that this being the last remains of public wisdom in this era, on this side of the world, that you seeing here. Here, in this library, there being gathered thousands of writings from every corner of your planet ... hehehe ... mmm ... they wanting to imitate the Great Record ..." Omboni's tone then became more serious. "Here being formed a 'soup' of learning, to call it so that your mind can understand. This soup being strong food for an epoch with a weak stomach. Those who being restless, who do not let themselves be carried by temporal-rivers, could come here and use that knowledge in a positive way, but they being dying lights in a river growing turbid. That being the case of this old man who being by our side. I will tell you a little bit about him. His mother being from a place your mind calls Syria, his father being from Greece: They naming him Horace. He has traveled all his life, first inside Greece then reaching the being-city Rome. His great goal in life being what humans call Physics, Geometry, and the mechanics of things and their practical applications. He has studied these subjects his whole life, being, as some might say, crazy or eccentric in his time to the rest of beings. In your world always calling 'crazy' the ones who move forward in the time-rivers."

The Apprentice was absorbed in Omboni's explanation and, curiously, at the same time he could tune the old man perfectly as he studied at that table, gathering sparks and flashes of the old man's life as the Astral Being explained it.

"Mmm..." Omboni continued, "well, when this old man lived in that village Rome, after many years of searching, he found another curious character, restless as he, who showed him the basics of what he had investigated and concluded, and spoke directly about this library: the Great Library of Alexandria, and especially about another character such as himself, Heron, who wrote many centuries ago about different types of machines that could work independently; through this, the interest of coming here being born inside him. Being the line of those who creeeeate."

After a moment Omboni continued. "The ideas of he and his workmate called the attention of the hierarchs, or the recently formed church-being of the city, now already owner of the Empire, or the Empire owner of it, or whichever way, it is all the same ... and that is when his problems began, because he had the foolish idea of talking about his project: creating a machine that would replace slaves and galleys, claiming that his ideas were based on the ideas of old Greek and Egyptian scientists, all considered contrary to the thought of the new religion-being. Worst of all, he declared himself not a 'devout believer' but a 'truth-seeker'... Imagine what happened!"

"I can see something," Asanaro answered, sadly, "and it's not pleasant. It seems that this 'institutionalized ignorance,' as Alsam says, always wins."

"Mmm . . . yesss, you speak well . . . but conclude too fast. Not being pleasant to see that, as you say, 'institutionalized ignorance,' how it chases those who trying to think for themselves. Remember well, and make Alsam remember: This will always happen . . . but only from that vision does ignorance win. I clarify your words, even though this may confuse you more, being the institution the one that institutionalizes ignorance, by its own measure and interests . . . only depending on minds, not believers. But, before going deeper into this, let us follow the lonely thinker you see here.

"Unfortunately, he and his partner, after many years of work, not wanting to terminate their experiments and their relations with other thinkers who also not participating in the new religion of the Empire. They were taken, and as is usual in your world, accused of something such as breaking the divine law, or whatever it was not really mattering, it being all the same. What being real, his partner was killed in prison, and Horace escaped after a few years, thanks to riots as well as a few payments his friends had made in his favor. Of course he having to run immediately away from that village Rome. Now you seeing him here, trying to remain unnoticed and complete his project from plans made by other ancient thinkers and scientists who have had the same questions as he, who have tried to create their own line of time."

Horace, meanwhile, patiently attended to his studies. He looked at the old hand-drawn plans, examining them carefully, with an almost sacred respect. Soon he was absorbed in his thoughts, trying to draw some conclusions on the idea of his strange machine, thinking of the quality of the metals that he should use, how to increase their strength and make them function better. He frowned, closing his eyes and seeming on the verge of sleep.

"Hehehe..." Omboni spoke suddenly. "Watch Asanaro, watch and you will learn."

"What is it? What should I watch? I can only see the old man sleeping..."

"Pay attention, and learn. Do not see things with the vision of your world. Is it not enough what you have lived and learned already? Watch carefully, calibrate yourself and use the sensitivity that this state gives you, and you seeing something common in the great thinkers and searchers of the Earth..."

The Apprentice tried to focus as carefully as he could on the shape of the old man who, with his hands on his stomach and comfortable in his chair, had nodded off and fallen asleep. Bit by bit the Apprentice saw the energy of the old man's body duplicating itself, forming a second body as solid as the original, as if a double of itself was forming and rising, while hundreds of little threads united the new to the physical body. Strangely, those threads looked thicker in certain places than in others. That man, or the figure that was separating from the original, stood up and began to walk around the room thoughtfully, as if he were still analyzing the same problem that had put him to sleep.

"But how is this possible?!" Asanaro asked Omboni. "We can even see his projections inside the Astral?"

"Hehehe ... well, yesss ... this place or state being the reflection of a projection of hundreds of years ago, in the past of your world, yet at the same time containing even the tiniest detail of what happened, within the four dimensions of the Earth and within the superior dimensions of the Astral. Each detail being

there, recorded forever, only in the finest frequencies, being why
I had to help you to see a little bit beyond, or better said, I had
to help you tune a little more precisely within this projection,
which is outside your time and space."

Horace's projection then turned to the plans, remaining
connected to his body projected in the Astral. The Apprentice
watched, curious, for the old man thought himself still awake
and did not notice his other body sleeping at the table as he
stood there, studying the plans. He then continued pacing, meditating over the problems that he had in his mind, and Asanaro
felt a little strange, believing that this man, because he was also in
the Astral, could see them both, but Omboni quieted that fear.

"Hehehe ... you being quiet, for he cannot see us, from a
certain view being impossible. It is true he being in the dimension of dreams, but what you seeing here being only an energetic material projected here a long time ago, as I have explained
before. What you seeing here, now, being only a more delicate
tuning of something that already happened. But for now keep
watching, and we will follow the path of this character. It will
be interesting for you."

The whole scene transformed itself, and suddenly they were
in a strange place, with no relation to the one before: It was a
room without walls, full of singular machines. The Apprentice
was amazed, for it seemed they had jumped time and place in
a blink. And there was Horace, pacing as before, now inside of
this new space. Asanaro turned his head and Omboni was still
standing next to him, just as before, as if only the backdrop of
the scene had changed.

The old man began speaking to himself as he paced, his voice
growing louder and louder, though there was no one to hear.

"I must go deeper . . . I know I can make it work by itself, like the wind leads the galley, yes! Like the wind leads the galley . . . she moves by herself. Why can't one do the same on land? There must be some form, the way the water moves the wheel. I know there is a way, I know it . . . and as soon as I discover it I will go and tell Hypatia, yes, for she must be the first to know . . ." In this way he continued.

"Hehehe," Omboni intervened. "Surprised, Apprentice of Dreams?"

"Yes, I am surprised," answered Asanaro. "How did we get here? And Horace followed us also in this projection!"

"Well . . . being honest, we have not 'come' here. Better said, we being 'tuned'; you have noticed that the person we watched still being with us. I know this will sound strange, but the truth being that we have followed him, for one way of saying it. We have tuned in to the projection of this being. Him, his material body, being where we were, and the one you seeing now, whose path we are following, being only his Astral Projection . . . the fine-tuning of the facts that you were watching before. Now, the old scientist has vibrated in such a way with his studies that he projected himself to a new state inside his mind projection, to which he being semi-unconscious."

"And this new place, what is it, Omboni?"

"Hehehe . . . a bit difficult to explain that to you . . . but I will give you an example. Remember when you went to visit the mountain-city, that was what you called it, the place in which you seeing me for the first time?"

"Yes, I remember it perfectly. I was surprised, very nicely, of course!"

"Well, your own vibrational energy, which is what shakes

and fascinates you, which calls your attention and dedication, both conscious and unconscious, being the engine that made you come to that place, which in truth being a state more than a place. This state has meant you being authorized to see new states, especially the Bamso, or Great Universal Record, that being the frequency where we are accomplishing your research now. But, I ask you, what began this adventure?"

While the travelers spoke, the old man studied, engaging himself with several small machines that stood in that place, or perhaps more accurately, formed there, for they were like three-dimensional sketches that constantly changed their shape. They would appear instantaneously and would change from their rigid forms to something malleable in the hands of the man as he experimented with them, transforming them into various shapes, happy and curious as a child.

Omboni's last question rang in the mind of the Apprentice . . . what had brought him there? The Apprentice answered to himself, "I assume . . . that it was . . . your help!"

"Hehehe . . . no, Apprentice, that help is first earned, and you earned it by vibrating, simply viiiibraating. . . . Each being its own sparkle . . . and when it being prepared its moment comes. At the same time each being has, whenever it wants to, the opportunity to evolve. Just like this old man, whoever really wants can visit the infinite records that exist throughout the Cosmos. Each record can give that being a key, an answer that can be realized in any world. How do you think great musicians create their music . . . or artists create their work . . . ?"

The Apprentice looked perplexed.

The Astral Being answered, "Vibrating and Dreaming, Asanaro! Viiiibraating and dreeeeaaaming . . . !"

After a pause, Omboni continued.

"This person we have been watching is a being misunderstood by his time, but, being honest, it makes no difference when he was born: He was born with that special sparkle, making him different in any time-river. He might be influenced by it in many aspects, but his essence being too strong; he can't help dreaming, as they would say in your world. We could say that he has the great energy of imagination in his favor, and that energy being what brought him here. He now has dreams, and while dreaming he enters a new state, according to his restlessness. He can now create freely. Tell me, Asanaro, do iron and wood attract in your world?"

"No, not really . . ."

"Hehehe . . . well, that being how imagination and Astral Worlds work. If the person is positive, a dreamer, and has a strong, constant, and pure imagination, being transported to one of the countless states of the Astral or of the Superior State: the Bamso. Each stage is full of curiosities, full of secrets, for each is like a library, to put it in a way that you understand, or like chambers where you can connect to a specific frequency that at the same time connects to your vibrational state and speeds your knowledge, clears your thoughts, and gives you keys, impulses that do not exist on Earth, and they being the most interesting! In some of our later trips remind me to visit the Astral World of the true musicians, of those who vibrate . . . ! Being true food to Astral ears! Mmmm . . ." he added, "for now, pay attention and observe our example."

Omboni called the attention of the Apprentice to the old man, who stood close by, entertained with different and curious toys. Bit by bit one of them grew larger and began to take on the shape of an old steam engine, with strong parts made of iron and wooden beams. Horace didn't look so old anymore, but younger and more dynamic, enthusiastically engaged in fixing and modifying the machine: He was fascinated. All of a sudden it started moving, working, and Horace observed its every detail, going over every inch of every piece, and as he did the machine worked better, or changed its shape unusually, shrinking or stretching as if it were made of some special rubber that was adaptable to his thoughts. After a few moments the machine had transformed completely; it was smaller and more symmetrical, producing a soft vibration that lifted it from the floor, where it floated gently in the air.

The Apprentice was captivated by what he saw, and asked, "But Omboni, what is happening now? It looks as if he's making a machine that can even fly! There are some things I don't understand. For instance, the Astral does not need machines, so why is he building them here, in this state? And how can he be projecting or thinking of a flying machine, when in his space-time there was nothing like it?"

"Hehehe . . ." The Astral Being smiled and answered quietly. "You still having a lot to learn. Not good assuming . . . Think, Asanaro . . . the unconscious state of dreams not being classified with being or not-being . . . it simply happens. The mind projecting, vibrating, connects to channels that maybe do not exist for you, or seeming strange, and that being why they not being, but not meaning that is all. Mind that thinks in being or not-being halts vision . . . halts advance.

"Our Horace," he continued, "being in a state in which he not being completely conscious, therefore he drags into this state many of his dimensional rules, but also, and thanks to it, being in a more free frequency such as this, he can investigate all kinds of theories without prejudices. In more simple words, nobody here tells him 'This is impossible! You are crazy! You are a fool!' Hehehe . . . Thanks to this our Horace will liberate his investigation from rules and dictates. His curiosity is free, and he can experiment with different machines that he can rediscover each time he projects himself. As well, he has another factor in his favor, and this is that much of the knowledge he has acquired is manifested more clearly in this state . . . it becomes better organized. On the other hand, and most important, even though it might sound crazy to anyone from your world, Horace's imagination and vibration form an antenna, and help him to obtain several keys or messages that exist in the infinite states of knowledge in the Universe. As a matter of fact, and thanks to those keys, he can leap past several years of investigation and make great discoveries for his era, such as creating a steam engine over a thousand years before, according to you, it was to be invented."

"This is fascinating . . ." added the Apprentice, watching that scientist playing with the strange machine that was now moving up and down in the air, like some toy from the future. "Why didn't I ever hear that this machine was built, or that there were even these kinds of investigations in this man's era?"

"Mmm . . . being easy and unfortunate the answer," replied Omboni. "Simply that no one ever knew of this, since it was never made solid. This man, his ideas, all of the material he had gathered during his life to build this project, all was simply erased from your being–history. For you to understand we must continue . . . For now, watch."

With a blink, both visitors of the Bamso came back to the

hall of the Great Library of Alexandria. There sat Horace, sleeping quietly above his precious plans, dreaming, imagining, creating in his mind and in the superior dimension what in practice could have meant centuries of advance for humankind.

Asanaro looked compassionately at the old man, thinking about what Omboni had just said, that in fact all they had just seen would remain as dreams for that studious man.

Omboni interrupted these thoughts of the Apprentice. "Mmm . . . not being sad. I know that what I will show you will disappoint you, but that not meaning that this searcher, like so many others, has failed. On the contrary, they have won for themselves, and it is your humankind-being that has lost, if we must speak of losses."

They continued walking slowly, heading away from Horace, who continued sleeping quietly, a soft smile on his lips.

The travelers now explored the building, and the Apprentice couldn't help but be amazed by the whole place, despite its age, for there was dedication and care visible in each and every detail of the building.

"Omboni," Asanaro asked the Astral Guide, "I have a question, something that's still in my mind after your explanation from before."

"Yesss . . . I know," answered Omboni. "Tell me."

"Why, a few moments ago, did you say that Horace could 're'-discover certain machines?"

The Astral Being smiled and answered quietly, "Hehehe . . . you being a good Apprentice . . . but for now, I will leave that question for you. Later you will know why."

They continued walking down those hallways of the past.

"Where are we going?" asked the Apprentice.

"Mmm ... very close ... we are going to that room," answered Omboni, pointing out the entrance to a room opposite where they were coming from. "That room being a few feet and three months from here ..."

"What?" asked the Apprentice, intrigued.

"What I mean is that you thinking we are going merely from one room to another, but we are not only moving a few feet in what your mind measures, but also some months inside the same channel ... inside this same place. You won't notice any change, just follow."

They entered the room, which was smaller than the last and had many holes in its walls, as if those walls themselves were built to house special documents. Most of the holes were full, and there was a great desk covered with writings and parchment scrolls. There sitting in front of the desk were two men dressed in long gowns, discussing something and often referring to the several open documents that lay in front of them.

Both travelers came and stood closer in order to see what was happening. They could feel some tension between the two men, who would argue, then read again the manuscripts in front of them. The younger of the two, who seemed a little younger than thirty years old, spoke again to the elder.

"Celio, tell me what you think. Should we take these writings to Rome or Constantinople? There are many people who need to know what is written here."

"Please," answered the elder, a man with gray hair, "maybe you are no longer sane. Don't you think that the authorities from the Empire will find out where these writings came from? Are you planning to risk your own neck for these documents, which might not be as authentic as you believe them to be?

I want to continue living, and I will not risk myself. Mangazar, you must be more careful and more reasonable."

"But this is too important. Besides, you know they're authentic, and you know how hard it's been to get them. The original scrolls, the ones I have here, are written in Pali, an old Eastern language, and the rest are translated into Hebrew. These documents are unique; the family that brought them comes from too serious and ancient a tradition for it to be otherwise. So come and see what I've found . . ."

The young man rose enthusiastically and took two scrolls from a saddlebag. He handed them quickly to the older man, adding, "What you see here certifies what is written on these parchments. You know it . . . this is no heresy, it's the truth. It also speaks about the Saint of Issa. Both these and the originals speak about his pilgrimage through the East in his youth, about his life as a fugitive, and especially about James, who was his disciple and rightful successor; this scroll tells things that everyone deserves to know. Can you imagine the commotion in Rome and Constantinople once they know about these writings, translated right here in Alexandria, in the very same place where the Gospels were translated before they cut them and extrapolated them at their own convenience?"

The older man, Celio, stood thoughtful and silent. The Travelers of Time spoke to each other.

"What is going on here, Omboni?" Asanaro asked his Astral Guide. "I can sense some strange and contradictory things, some tension over this subject they're discussing."

"Mmm . . . yes, Asanaro, what you discovering, what is beginning here, being another episode in the conflict between the desire for knowing the truth, being able to understand it, and the prejudices and conveniences of the time-river that assault the thinkers."

Meanwhile, the two men continued poring over the manuscripts in front of them. The Astral Being continued speaking to the Apprentice.

"Search within the minds of each one of these men, and you will discover the bottom of this whole thing."

Asanaro concentrated on them for a few moments, then spoke.

"The youngest seems very interested in these writings; it seems that he is some kind of archaeologist or linguist of his time. The writings concern the Saint of Iza . . . Issa . . . but why does another name come to my mind . . . ? Jesus . . . of Nazareth? I don't know . . . all of this is confusing!"

"Hehehe . . . you being correct. The Saint Issa being Jesus of Nazareth, the prophet, for your mind. His history causing so much commotion between these two people."

"But," the Apprentice said, "I've never heard that name refer to Jesus. Why are they calling him that?"

"What has happened, Asanaro, it that you having perceived one of the names by which Jesus was known in the Eastern part of your world. That form being never popular inside the Imperial Religion–being, and less so in this era, in which the new politics of the Caesar-being, Emperor, or whatever you wish to call him, being strong. One of the great state politics or . . . justification of abuse . . . hehehe . . . being to make what you call public image very stable. Thus in this stage of things in your world the new being-religion that has been established must be invulnerable to any drastic change, and, even more, to any change that means questioning the truth of the story that they have spread based on their interests, never on the truth. The time-river of humans being created like that.

"The writings that this young man has found," continued Omboni, "meaning to discover many contradictions and legends that the new religion-being inserted in the true facts. The Empire did not need radical changes; it required orderly and obedient subject-beings, not thinking. Simply arranges a belief to its own form, and the form that fits the people, not demanding from them anything out of the ordinary for the time-stage that they are living.

"You already heard the Caesar say, 'Bread and Circuses!' Now, after many sun turns being the same expression, perhaps a little more complex: bread and circuses for the minds of those not wanting to see beyond. That being what your mind identifies as dogmatism and sectarianism, their biggest distributor being religion: belief creator."

Asanaro listened closely to the words of the Astral Being, trying to grasp and understand everything this time, but it was impossible. Then he relaxed, analyzing patiently, for he knew that just as he had learned through so many lessons, understanding comes with time and experience. Meanwhile, he again asked a question of Omboni.

"But why can't I feel anything positive from the older man here? There is something strange . . ."

"Mmm . . . you must being more sensitive if wanting to see clearly the panorama of what will happen from here on, but what I will explain to you will help to develop your sensitivity in the Projected Bamso or Record of the Future. What you perceiving from the older man being energies of greed and contradiction: On one hand he feels admiration for the knowledge being presented to him, but on the other hand he is scared, and that fear is convenient, for he knows it being dangerous to confront the Empire's Religion, especially with this city's Bishop. But ... at the same time, he feels greed, and a temporal-branch has formed in him."

The amazed Apprentice asked, "But what is a temporal-branch?"

"In practice you will understand the idea better, but I can tell you that there being many stages of himself that have created a conflict within him, therefore he will have to make decisions that will affect his future. Not even himself knowing the consequences that these will bring to him, or the consequences they will bring to other people, and how they may interact with the results of his own decisions. These determinations, in this instant, in him, are inevitable. There is a plot that not even his partner senses."

The two men continued speaking, analyzing the manuscripts over and over, comparing them with others they had taken from within the library, conscientious in their study. Then, all of a sudden, the younger man spoke.

"We must take these writings to a clerk we trust, so he can copy them as soon as possible, and bring the translations and clarifications necessary. These writings are too important to have only one copy."

"No!" Celio answered quickly. "That would be too dangerous. The fewer people who know about these writings the better, and they will remain unnoticed here amid the papyri. No one ever searches through this section, and the Bishop's men even less often. Better to leave them here, where no one will know of them, and we can decide what we must do."

"I'd like to copy them and bring them quickly to Rome," added Mangazar, preoccupied, "for I know many people there who I know agree with our thinking, and who will support us. It is imperative for people to know the truth about the Saint of Issa, for they have been telling fables of him for four hundred years. I think the truth must be spoken, not hidden, prearranged, or forbidden."

"Please . . . don't rush," replied Celio in a conciliatory tone. "It's better for us to act with caution; an accusation of heresy would be very serious for both of us, as it could quickly be considered treason to the interests of the Empire. Many bishops would gleefully send us to visit with the executioner. Remember the persecution of Theophilus, right here in Alexandria! Keep quiet, and the safest place is here. The library is too extensive to be searched; it is like hiding a grain of sand on a beach. Here not even Hypatia will know that these documents exist."

"We should tell her!" the young man spoke, amazed, and then continued in a softer tone, "she is so special . . . She will understand, and I'm certain she will advise us well."

The older man put on a skeptical expression, and Asanaro sensed within him an energy of contradiction and deceit. He spoke sharply.

"No, boy. Do not be influenced by your admiration for her. She cannot confront the Bishop, or the Religion of the Empire. If you really care for her, keep quiet and do not let her find out about these manuscripts; that way she will remain more insulated from the Church, which, by the way, has a big appetite for her. Better to save her from more troubles. Listen to me; I am an expert in these things . . . better to stay quiet."

The young man was thoughtful and, after a moment, nodded

his head. The two of them soon continued studying the documents laid out over the table.

The Astral Adventurers stood by, discussing what was happening as they observed the scene like two invisible ghosts.

"I have a question . . ."

"Yes, I know. Tell me," answered Omboni.

"That energy," replied the Apprentice, "that the younger man demonstrated when he was talking about that other person, what was it? Hy . . . Hypatia, that energy called my attention. I noticed something different in his emanation."

"Ahhh . . . hehehe . . . that which you having seen in him being a very normal energy in your world. In that man there is a mix of admiration toward . . . well, I'll make it clear, toward her. Hypatia is a beautiful her and he being touched by her form and character."

"And what is her relation to the documents they are studying, or to this library?" asked the Apprentice, curious as always.

Omboni paused before continuing his explanation.

"Mmm . . . you having to complete your path in order to be able to understand what happening here, and the ultimate direction of this whole chapter of the time-river. But I will tell you something: Hypatia being an exceptional woman for her dimension, also being the type who jumps out of her time and space; you can say that she being the great axis of this place. She having protected many thinkers, philosophers, and scientists in this period, like Horace, whom you've already met. She also being a great researcher, and her passion being this library."

"I would like to meet her. Can we locate her within this time-fluid?" Asanaro was becoming more and more curious.

"Hehehe . . . it will be so, Apprentice. You are already ahead in this fluid. She being the objective of our next visit in our next adventure, and with her we will slowly begin closing this stage that being so necessary to show you. Come, and follow me . . ."

They left that place quietly, leaving Mangazar and Celio behind, still investigating, reading over and over the different manuscripts.

HYPATIA

The Astral Travelers crossed the threshold of the doorway, and as if they had jumped in an elongation of rational space and time, they found themselves in a totally new room.

This room was more comfortable and carefully adorned. The walls were decorated with beautiful figures of flora and fauna, portraits of crocodiles, cats, cows, and other animals interwoven with mosaics of onions, lotuses, and other vegetables, all surely sacred in that time. A few statues and living plants complemented the whole room very nicely. At the left of the room there was a large shelf, full of writings and scrolls.

Asanaro spoke: "This place is very comforting, really very pleasant. It's been a while since we visited such a pleasant place!"

Omboni smiled as he replied. "Hehehe . . . yes, being true, and you will like it even more . . . hehehe . . ." And he smiled again.

Someone was just then entering the room. It was a woman, and she came slowly into the Apprentice's vision as he began to see her in more detail. She was beautiful—she wore a loose, comfortable gown of fine linen and peculiar sandals that fit her perfectly. Her beauty was exceptional, not the sort of beauty imposed by a cultural fashion, the Apprentice thought, but the sort of beauty that carries its own lineage, regardless of time. He was very impressed. She walked elegantly to stand in front of the table.

The Apprentice, after gazing at her for a good while, could no longer hold his curiosity and asked, to confirm what he was already thinking, "Tell me Omboni, this is Hypatia, isn't it?"

"You do not need to ask me what you already knowing, Asanaro. You have felt in the correct way."

"I can sense from her energy that she is an extraordinary woman, as extraordinary as she is beautiful."

"Hehehe . . . yes, being Hypatia, as I have said to you before, being from the beings that jump beyond their era, and because they doing so, they bring more than one trouble to themselves. Because of her, this place survives in some way."

The enchanting woman quietly sat down at her desk. She opened some manuscripts, taking exquisite care with them, very gently extending the little scroll she had opened and, with an energy of total immersion in her studies, began reading it. Her fingers were long and she was a bit taller than average, and despite the fact that she was likely in her forties, she emanated a young woman's energy of restlessness and curiosity. She had a face that, without being perfect, was incredibly attractive: Her nose was slightly elongated and she had well-defined lips that perfectly matched her black, almond-shaped eyes and her olive complexion. She wore her dark brown hair tied behind her head, and a few locks fell gracefully on her shoulders.

The Apprentice of Time watched and admired her, captivated. The graceful shape of both her neck and chin drew his attention, and he recalled the energy Mangazar had emanated a few moments ago in another room of the library, and Asanaro felt a little sympathy for the other man's transmission.

"Hehehe . . . Asanaro . . . Asanaro . . ." The voice of Omboni came sidelong to his mind. "Do not let yourself get too involved . . . remember that she, and what you have seen in Mangazar, like all else you have seen here, being only a ghost, and you must not see it as yours, or as inside of yourself. Only learn from what you see."

Coming back to his own reality, the Apprentice spoke doubtfully. "It's just that . . . I don't know, but it's . . . looking at her is just relaxing. Her room, the way in which she reads, her attitude, her elegance and beauty, are not common or usual. It was starting to feel like a dream . . ."

"Mmm . . . I can tell you, though," answered the Astral Being, "that this, in the wrong meaning of the word, being a dream! Not the common dream, being Conscious Dreaming, and more than that, dreaming directed into projection toward the Great Record, where being now. If you want to continue being like this, do not lose your concentration or sensation of reality."

After a pause, while the Apprentice tried not to lose the vision of Hypatia, Omboni continued speaking.

"Asanaro, if you become too emotional with any of these scenes, you will cause the current of consciousness to be interrupted, producing an interference within the stability of your current projection. If reaching the point of bifurcation, your mind will act falsely, and what you clearly seeing now, with all of its details, will become just another dream, with all the normal blur of unconsciousness."

"Excuse me, Omboni," replied the Apprentice, "I just got a little carried away."

"Save excuses for your dimension, not being necessary in this state. Now you must focus, keep your form stable, far from too many emotions, which inevitably end up contradictory. What you seeing here see just as it is, with all of its rawness, for that will serve you. If you involve your emotions, your mind will alter the vision of these facts within this delicate Astral tuning, as if your mind took information that, being too strong to process, you automatically transform."

"I understand. Alsam spoke to me about this, and warned me about what could happen. He also spoke to me about the transformation state, where the dream becomes only what you desire it to be, taking you to a different channel and away from facing the raw reality of a determined state."

"Hehehe ... being so," answered the Astral Guide. "Mind, being a complete universe, Apprentice of the Bamso, which can mold everything in relation to itself, can transform reality. This being positive! But when living in your world, one needing to know how to control it. Now relax, and continue with our visit here, and pay attention to what is about to happen."

In that instant a knock came at the door. Hypatia carefully left her papers at the desk, gracefully stood, and walked toward the door. When she opened it a short, well-built man entered, his face rather flushed.

"Come in, Akena, what brings you here?" Hypatia asked kindly, addressing the visitor, who seemed worried and was breathing hurriedly.

"My lady, my beloved lady, I am very worried, and I need

to talk to you ..." The man spoke sadly. "If I am not disturbing you."

"Please tell me, for it is always pleasant to speak with you," replied Hypatia, leading him into the room to a comfortable seat. Once seated the man continued panting, still upset but trying to breathe normally.

"But, please tell me," she added, "what has happened to you? What has agitated you so much?"

"My lady, my lady ..." Akena began speaking, carefully addressing Hypatia. "I fear for your integrity. I've heard awful things in the markets ... I am worried for you ... this is terrible ... terrible ..."

"But, well ..." answered Hypatia evenly, trying to calm her guest, "do not exaggerate. I know that many people do not like me ... but I am used to it! Many times in my life I've been slandered. How serious can it be?"

The man was rubbing his hands together nervously, still upset. He took a deep breath and began to speak more normally.

"I am very worried, my lady, for you know how much I appreciate you. I have served you and your desire to save what is left of this library for my whole life ... I respect you as much as I respect this place, and I couldn't bear anything happening to you or our little ones, you know I call them that, our books, our babies. I was in the market this morning, buying some things, you know how I always visit the same vendors, for they already know me and trust old man Akena. Well, one of them, who also sells on a daily basis to the Bishop's servants, told me what he heard, that someone is plotting against you, my lady. He told me that there are rumors everywhere, that the Church is very upset with you, they consider you a bad influence, a heretic, and many other terrible things ... I am very worried, I'm afraid this could end very badly."

Hypatia thought for a few moments, and answered quietly and kindly.

"Akena, I know how much you appreciate me and this place, which we have both been taking care of, making it grow again. I also feel the same way as you for our library, for our little babies, and if you look at the situation through your feelings, you are most likely exaggerating what you've heard. I think you should not worry so much."

"Please, my lady ... my lady, you must be careful, somehow. If something happens to you, who would take care of your work? Who would take care of me? You are too important to let anything happen to you ..." Akena had calmed down, but his eyes were sparkling and sad, as if he sensed something inevitable.

"Akena, please, you are worrying me now. This whole situation is not so serious as you say, for I've never broken the law or done anything that I must regret. Why should I fear? Tell me, what should I worry about? Besides, what you are saying is nothing new to me, for the Bishop and I have known each other a long time, and you know well how we've never seen eye to eye. He knows perfectly my position on the old sciences, and I know his as well."

"Yes, I know my lady ..." answered Akena, disheartened.

"Akena, gladden your spirit, nothing will happen to me. The Bishop will never accomplish his objectives, and he will never have what he wants. This place is beyond his influence and control. He only wants to scare us, so that he can control this final bastion of knowledge. That is all."

"Yes, my lady ... but he is powerful, and if he asks again

to speak with you, please accept. Remember the destruction
Theophilus wrought, and he is the uncle of our current Bishop.
Please, if he asks you . . . please speak with him."

"No, Akena! I won't do it. I have no intention of speaking
with that man. He just wants to seize the manuscripts that we
have managed to keep, the oldest and most important of all.
Can you imagine what he would do with them? He has made
offers to me, and I have sent them all back to him. He cannot
make himself the God of Knowledge, for Knowledge belongs
to us all, each one of us owns it. No one can come here and
tell us what we must do, or how we must think. This Bishop
cannot forbid people the desire to learn and know . . . that is
what this is all about, my esteemed and faithful Akena. Nobody
can prevent us from investigating the reality and the beauty of
things, nor the wisdom of nature. That desire to grow and learn
does not belong to a religion, to any religion! The same way it
does not belong to a man, to any man, not even to the Emperor,
the Empire, or its Church. Knowledge, Akena, investigation and
nature . . . they belong to us all, and that is why I will never
cease my work . . .

"The paper on which the Bishop and his circle write," continued the impassioned Hypatia, "or the clothes in which they
dress themselves, were not created by a Christian or by anyone
with a determined belief; all of them were created by human
beings, by curious, creative, and free-minded people. Yes, Akena!
Free! That is what I am, for I think for myself, I am aware that
I do not know everything, and that is why I want to continue
being free, to continue learning! It is better for the Bishop to
save his threats, I pay them no mind . . . his Empire has no territory inside of my head, my heart, or inside our Library; here

only curiosity prevails; freedom and respect for the mind of each. This is something that is beyond the reach and understanding of Mr. Bishop. No matter how much he might threaten me or how many rumors he spreads, I will never leave this place, I will never stop teaching or learning, just as I can't stop being a woman! Even if that bothers him!"

There was a pause. Akena did not share Hypatia's passion; he was dispirited, and along his face a small tear fell.

"My lady . . ." He spoke in a very low voice. "My beloved lady . . . I was afraid you would say that . . . I was afraid. An old and simple man like me should take that risk, not you. You have so much to give to humankind."

Hypatia answered him gently. "Akena, calm down, nothing will happen to me. Gladden your spirit!" As she spoke she touched his shoulder affectionately, trying to assure him, to bring him out of his deep sorrow.

From a corner of the room the Travelers in Time followed the scene. Asanaro was extremely attentive, and with every passing minute his admiration for Hypatia increased, for her most striking qualities were her form of expression, her kindness, and her strength and courage.

"Mmm . . ." Omboni said, "she being one of the great women of the last time-river of your world. I think you have understood what is happening here."

"Yes, I understand," said Asanaro, "but not completely. What is that Bishop's obsession with troubling Hypatia? Isn't all the power he already has enough?"

"No . . . not being enough for him. This library being run directly by Hypatia, she being its central axis, as you may have noticed. And thanks to her enthusiasm, her vision and hunger for knowledge, she has made this place flourish again, but too much, out of synch with this so perturbed stage, in which the Empire being in a difficult stage of instability. The Empire-being, as always, being only a treasure that each great thief wants for himself, that the main thief not wanting to have taken away from him."

"But Omboni," asked the Apprentice, "what harm are this place and Hypatia causing the Empire, its Church, and all those people who consider themselves so powerful? Compared with them, these parchments and these people who care for them are so small . . ."

"Mmm . . . that being the way it should be . . . apparently, but I have already explained . . . this journey being for you to look beyond things, prepare for the real, superior teachings, which surpass all of these events, as well as those from your own time-river.

"Here you will see for yourself," continued Omboni, "how strong people can being when possessing ideals. The Empire-being does not feel hurt or upset by this place as a place, itself; instead hurt by what this place represents. Think that what your mind calls Christianity was used, infiltrated, and transformed to every whim of the Emperor, to perpetuate his power and the form of his power through idealism. Being so, one controlling people with their thoughts, not from outside. Understand this idea?"

"I am trying," answered the Apprentice.

"Mmm . . . I know. With time, you will better understand everything that you have lived here and everything I have shown you. Well, to speed your teachings I will explain as we walk . . ."

In that moment Hypatia was still speaking to Akena, now

about less serious matters, trying to quiet his fears. Unfortunately, the beautiful image of that woman and the man with her was slowly pulled away from Asanaro as the scene transformed.

In the closing and opening of an eye, both Travelers of Time found themselves walking outside of the library, through the beautiful city of Alexandria, still in that remote epoch. There were many people and many shops selling strange wares. The smells were particular, new to Asanaro, constantly changing as Guide and Apprentice walked through the city.

Smiling, the Apprentice interrupted their stroll.

"This is really tourism in time! Everything looks so alive, so natural, as if it were real ..."

"Hehehe ... well, being! The magnetic wave that we are walking through in order to see these things, being as real as the facts themselves, only seen from an eye that being incomprehensible to you. But, well, relax now, for a little while."

"You were analyzing everything that is happening here ... I'd like to hear more of it."

"Well, Apprentice, I will develop the idea a little. All of the people you seeing here being potential enemies of Empire-being—that is how it sees them. But at the same time, through idealism, the powers of the Empire discovered that those same people could being their best allies. In normal ways, they having to threaten these people to control them, to use the materialism they demand, which means, making the people their servants, as they liking to say. The sword works, but it takes too much energy. In some era, this power discovered that ideas moving the masses better than the sword, thus coming to the conclusion that if they controlled an idea, making it prevalent, they would have total power. The commencement of these facts, for the time-river that we are analyzing here, being illustrated by our last visit, to that character you liking so much . . . hehehe . . ."

"Yes, of course I remember," answered the Apprentice, "how could I forget him! He had that face . . . ambitious, zealous, perfect to play an Emperor."

"Hehehe . . . yes," added the Astral Being, "indeed, this parenthesis in the development of the time-river symbolizes the typical problem from your world . . . materialism! And to achieve it . . . power! Both holding haaaands . . . Analyze what you seeing, deeper and deeper, and you will discover how astute and vicious being human-beings when it comes to gaining this state of power-materialism: He quickly transforms into a cruel entity, for which conscience being only a word for common people, not for the so-called elite who assume control."

The street was crowded. There were many merchants, and people speaking different languages, and to Asanaro it looked like any other open-air market, just without the gasoline-powered vehicles and electric cables draped along high posts.

"Hehehe . . . see these people. They trade, speak, they relate to each other and exist, or better said existed, does not matter, for our example they being seen as normal people. What would happen if one day they said they not needing the Empire-being, or whatever it is?"

The Apprentice was perplexed. "I don't know."

Omboni smiled and continued speaking. "Well, the question I asking to you being the greatest worry of those who having the power: They too ask this question of themselves. What if the people simply came to the conclusion that they do not need them?

"Then, the Emperor-being, fearing the end of his power, and more than just the Emperor but all the clans that ruling with him, concluded that the best way in which to perpetuate themselves and their power being to take an idealism and shape it to their conveniences. Now here we are, within the development of that plan, its perfection, and trapped in the middle being poor Hypatia and her lonely, defenseless parchments. The final plan, which you will see, being repeated over and over again in your time-river, being the 'wiping the slate clean.'"

The Apprentice, confused, stopped and asked, "What do you mean by wiping the slate clean?"

With a wave of his hand Omboni called the Apprentice to him, and they sat on the corner of a small fountain, as if they were both as solid as that place, not ghosts from another dimension. The feeling of rest at sitting was as real as it was on Earth. Calmly, the Astral Being continued.

"Mmm ... well, Asanaro, seeing that you awaken whenever I take a phrase from your memory to explain a situation. Well, it being very simple. The Empire-being has dressed itself as a Church, with all the ostentation, belief, et cetera, but if I take another sentence from your mind, I saying to you that you can't make a silk purse out of a sow's ear. This meaning that, no matter how many times the Empire-being changing its clothes to gain respect, that is to say, fear, from the people, there remain too many people who do not swallow this story. There always being groups of people the Empire calls heretics, dangerous intellectuals, or whatever; this group never being so easy to fool, for they having access to information showing that the power is still naked underneath its new garb. Thus the power wanting to keep that information hidden. For this stage of the time-river that information being represented by the remains of the Library of Alexandria, and therefore those who care for it being dangerous."

"But how can that place be dangerous? What harm can it possibly cause the Empire or its beliefs?"

"Mmm . . . being simple, Apprentice of Time, being simple. The Empire-being, by creating the Church, created a whole fable, a superstition adequate to the mediocre mentality of the human beings and serving the Empire's own interests. Those who visiting the library being mostly those who know what the Empire has created, and that it being only that: a creation. Even more, many of them possessing documents to prove, as we said before, that it being only new clothes, the same body and the same mind. These documents and books being the memory of your world: If they exist no more, your world no longer has a memory, and any legend of history or religion being told the same, for no one being able to contradict it, less even after whole new generations being formed within the invention. Imagine what will happen when the time-river advances in darkness, without memory, with no light."

The Apprentice was very serious now, and worried.

"This stage of our journey won't end well, will it?" he asked.

"Mmm . . . we must continue forward, Asanaro. Whatever it being, you must see it for yourself."

"But if it's like you say, it would never have been possible for Earth to evolve . . . or change . . . I don't know . . ." the Apprentice trailed off in doubt.

"Well, from a certain point of view, thinking you that the Earth has changed so much? We can analyze it . . .

"From another perspective, the lines of time, or the chains of it, having so many infinite factors that form them, that the Empire-being could never control all of them, even though that being its strongest desire. I will name you two factors that make results different from how the power wants them to. On one side, in your world there being many isolated villages that have had their own, parallel development, and for those who being pilgrims, for those who being curious, this fact gives them subconscious keys that showing them that not everything being necessarily how they learning it in childhood or in its original place ... and this creating a new question, a restlessness for searching. The person can start to question, asking, 'So this means that not everyone has to follow the rules I was taught? Meaning that others who do not follow these rules can also exist and live without problems ... or with fewer problems? Then ... then ...' Understand me?"

The Apprentice looked at Omboni.

"Well, yes ... I understand ... that's what happened to me, from a certain point of view. When I was a child and people spoke to me about Christianity or Catholicism, I always wondered just that, what if someone was born in a far away place, where no Christian could go, and what if that person was born, lived, and died without ever having heard of a God, or for that matter a Buddha, or heaven and hell? What would happen to that person? Where would he or she go when they died? No one ever gave me a reasonable answer to that question ... with time, and after traveling to many different places I realized that there is no good answer to that question. Now I realize that religion is only a passing fashion, if you look at it from the immensity of time."

"Hehehe . . . I see you starting to understand, Asanaro, and you will see that there being much yet to learn."

"Tell me one thing, Omboni. If this fact that each village on Earth has its own ideas, without the need to believe in the ideas formed by another, if this is one factor that makes one think, then what is the other one that you mentioned?"

"Hehehe . . . you tell me, Apprentice. Don't you see?" Omboni's voice was intriguing. After a pause the Apprentice answered.

"I . . . I don't know. What is it?"

"Ahaaa . . . very simple, Asanaro. Where being you now?"

"Here, sitting by your side . . . well, speaking . . ."

"Hehehe . . . you seeing starts, I seeing the circle. Where being you now, Asanaro?"

"I . . . I don't understand you . . ." replied the Apprentice, but after a few silent seconds, he spoke again, enthusiastically. "Well, in the Great Bamso, of course! In the Astral! Hahaha . . ."

"Well," Omboni smiled, "there being the answer! This place, or better put, this state, BEING FREE! Understand? Here the Empire-being can never reach, nor any other of its like, whatever you name it. Here neither prejudices nor religions with their threats can reach. Here you can see that which has been forbidden, whatever dimensional-temporal-fluid you coming from, it making no difference. Here nothing being forbidden, nothing being hidden . . . or ugly . . . only those limits that you put on yourself will exist, but if your imagination and will being strong, the doors of this place, with all of its secrets and dimensions, being open to you! And not only to you but to all the living beings. Thanks to this place, your world having the opportunity to evolve positively, maybe you seeing them only in little pieces, but there still being possibilities, for this place exists, and now you knowing for sure."

Asanaro smiled and shuddered, overwhelmed with happiness. He slowly began to understand why he was there: to know and see more clearly the importance of clarity in the Astral State. Slowly he understood that every human being, in its essence, could be as free as he was now, and whatever happened to Hypatia and all of the dreamers from that or any other era did not matter. The Bamso would always exist for them, greater than any library, than any creation of the Empire, of any Caesar, of any religion or negative superstition.

Asanaro was immersed in what was being born inside of him, in what he was feeling, and Omboni gently rested his Astral hand on the Apprentice's shoulder, and chuckled his usual chuckle.

"Hehehe ... bit by bit ... bit by bit ... Now we can follow our path further along and you will understand that what we see will be real for your time-river, but at the same time being only an example, for the essence of the truth no one being able to damage, persecute, forbid, or erase."

Asanaro smiled again and, almost unintentionally, began staring at a young man, who came running from the far sidewalk, his arms full of parchments, his face full of happiness. His energy radiated, more pronounced than anyone else who shared the street with him. On a closer look, Asanaro could see his eyes shine in a special way.

"Hehehe ... remembering who that being?" the Astral Guide asked the Apprentice.

"Of course! It's Mangazar!"

"Hehehe ... yes, being the same, and guess where he is going, so happy and sure ..."

"Don't tell me ... I'm thinking that he must be ... going to see Hypatia!" said Asanaro, infected with Mangazar's happiness.

"You saying well, Apprentice of the Astral, wanting to see what happens?"

"Of course!" answered Asanaro.

Apprentice and Guide quickly rose a little off the ground, their feet hanging, with the gentle feeling of flying just above ground. They followed close behind the enthusiastic Mangazar. For the Astral Travelers, the people who crossed their path were of no concern, for they passed right through them, quickly coming to an entrance to the Great Library, entering the building and moving through some dark hallways, always just behind the young man. They finally arrived in a large hall that they had not seen before.

She was in the back. The young man halted his rushed steps, took a deep breath, and began moving toward her as gently as he could, as if he did not want to intrude or interrupt her work. Hypatia was carefully organizing the various writings that sat on a large desk, grouping and raising them gently with her delicate hands, putting them inside of little holes in the great walls of the library. The Travelers of Time quietly watched what was happening.

The agitated man cleared his throat gently, and Hypatia turned to see who was there. She smiled and spoke in a charming voice.

"What brings you here, Mangazar? Weren't you working this morning with your good friend Celio?"

"Well, yes," said the young man, "but I needed to come here and . . ." Before he could think of more words, she tried to alleviate the awkwardness, speaking politely.

"I understand . . . you are here to leave a new document that you have discovered or bought from the merchants this afternoon, aren't you?"

"Yes . . ." answered Mangazar, a little hesitant.

"Well that's fantastic! You know they are always welcome. You are a great researcher and historian, and I assume that, as usual, you're bringing something very interesting. I will call Akena to help you organize and classify it. What do you think?"

"No!" The word flew out of Mangazar's mouth, and Hypatia looked at him strangely. Then he added nervously, trying to better express himself, "No . . . I didn't mean to say no, I'm sorry . . . I'm just a little nervous, and I think that it would be great if Akena could help me, he is always so kind, but . . . I really wanted to speak with you," and he took the already disorganized papers he carried out from under his arm, putting them down on the table. Several parchments fell to the floor, and the beautiful Hypatia immediately came closer to help him pick them up, an understanding expression on her face.

The young man, still nervous, put some of the papers on the table, and as he knelt to reach the rest while she stood to place the ones she had picked up, their faces touched. He perceived how her hair, her beautiful brown hair, touched his face; the young man shivered as both of them tried to shrug off what had happened, though they both enjoyed it very much.

With the documents now safely on the table, and while pretending to look at them in an attempt to distract them both from the whole situation, Mangazar began speaking with a great effort.

"I really wanted to read you something that I've written . . . a poem, it's only a poem, and I wanted to know your opinion."

"Well, go ahead, please," she answered quickly. "I've heard that you are a great poet, though you've devoted yourself more to history and research."

"Yes, Hypatia, I am just a novice poet, and to be honest, no one lives from poetry . . . though I'd love to do it more . . . but I know I'm no great poet."

"Well, come on, read me what you have brought. Go ahead . . ." she added, understanding.

The young Mangazar searched among the papers, until he found a small piece that was nearly lost among all of the large documents. He took it, a little shaky, and trying to steady his voice he began speaking.

"Here it is, I found it . . . it's no great thing, and it's a bit far from the rules of poetry . . ."

"Please, Mangazar, I don't care about that, just read it. I promise to listen carefully."

The young man, whose energy was emanating great emotion, began reading the poem, stammering at first but soon steadying his voice as he became consumed in the words and thoughts he had developed. He read:

Wherever I go, I go with you.

Wherever I am thirsty,
I drink from the same waters;
wherever I walk,

I find a path;
wherever I look,
I find a horizon.
For wherever I go, I go with you.

Wherever I need air,
I simply breathe;
wherever I lay,
I find rest and joy;
wherever I need to hear,
there are beautiful sounds.
I am certain of that,
for . . .
wherever I go, I go with you.

The sunset
to me seems always sublime and tranquil;
the storm and the winds
look to me like old acquaintances;
the immensity and the darkness
of the seas, they are not hidden from me,
but a shield;
for I am certain . . .
that wherever I go, I go with you.

Mangazar fell deeply silent, tenderly watching the sweet Hypatia. There was a lapse where there seemed to be no sound at all. Hypatia, discreet and quiet, spoke.

"It's very beautiful, very beautiful . . . You've stirred in me a strange nostalgia. Tell me, what have you meant? Please tell me, is it knowledge? Wisdom? That which goes so deeply with you, and helps you to overcome all in such a profound way ... ?" Her voice faded and she could no longer speak.

They gazed at one another, and for a few moments felt that nothing else was necessary; not words, not that whole place so full of history.

Mangazar could only say, "No, my lady, no ... who else could I mean but ... you ... only you ..."

They held each other with as much strength and tenderness as they could, and their lips united in a passionate kiss, filled with a subtle and extraordinary energy. Their auras shone beyond usual, like the northern lights, and their magnetic forces showed the most brilliant colors.

The Voyagers of Time smiled as they watched that affectionate scene. Omboni chuckled and spoke to the Apprentice. "Hehehe ... Asanaro, being the moment for us, as they would say in your world, to give them some privacy," and, as he made a little gesture, the Apprentice followed him away from the tender episode. They left the room to continue their adventures in the great Astral World. Behind them, mysterious universal forces united two beings, beyond destiny and the sway of the current of times.

IV.

Beings of Blindness

Again Guide and Apprentice, as if by magic, for that
is the Art of Dreams, found themselves in the streets
of Old Alexandria with its buildings, shops, animals,
and the noise of the crowds. They walked quietly, as if they were
simply another pair among all of those people, who seemed
to come from many, many different places on the Earth of
that time.

The sun was setting on the horizon, and the people in the
streets were hurrying home, before the night caught them.
Meanwhile, the two Astral Travelers discussed what they had
seen and learned, the Apprentice asking questions of his enigmatic Guide.

"Omboni, where are we going now? I'm thinking, because
we're still here, that you want me to see something more,
don't you?"

"Hehehe...Come on. In your own words, enjoy the show...You will know what you must know, each thing in its moment."

"I'm curious," said Asanaro, "if Hypatia and Mangazar are so attracted to one another, why has neither of them shown it before? Because, from what I could see, they both have feelings that they've kept inside for a long time ... at least that's how it seemed."

"Hehehe ... well, I will explain the situation a little. Hypatia being a woman somewhat older than Mangazar, and in this stage of the time-river, that being an impediment for they being together. Besides, she also being his teacher ... hehehe ..."

"Well, I figured it was something like that," replied the Apprentice.

The Astral Being quickly replied, "There also being a second factor. She having great responsibility before the library that she runs, and as you may have noticed, the work of supporting knowledge, teaching, and what is different, having brought her many enemies. This city, in this time, being a place of many tensions and conspiracies, and, as usual, the most defenseless being those like Hypatia. She being kind and careful, for she knows what she is venturing, and she not wanting to involve another in that risk. On the other hand, he respects and admires her in a very particular way, and that respect and admiration making him fear being rejected. However, the strength of the energies that being manifest between Hypatia and Mangazar having overcome them both, defeating their fears, neither being able now to hide what they feel. Great strength in the dimension of the woman and the man."

The Apprentice thought for a moment before breaking the silence.

"I'm glad it worked out this way. After all, as Alsam says, you only live once!" Both travelers laughed as they walked through the streets of that city, slowly darkening with the shades of dusk.

Soon, without intention, they found themselves at the entrance to an enormous palace; two guards wore nasty, suspicious looks. The Apprentice cast an amazed glance at Omboni, who returned the gaze but without the emotion. At a gentle gesture they walked into the palace, as if nothing had happened.

Once inside, Omboni said, "Mmm ... well ... I know you wanting to know where we being. Do not get anxious, for you might not like this place."

Meanwhile, the Apprentice wandered around, studying this new place. It looked extremely luxurious, but at the same time the energy contained inside was deeply sinister. There were two great halls, very well adorned, with murals on the walls and statues of all sizes. A few people were walking around, apparently servants, for they carried dishes laden with food of the most exquisite variety.

"This place gives me a bad feeling," Asanaro affirmed. "Maybe it's too luxurious ... I don't know ..."

"Mmm ... remember," answered the Astral Being, "that every place holds a magnetic record of those who have used it, and this place being charged with the force of much aggressiveness, negativity, and tension. Despite the fact that this being a projection from the past, still it keeping those details, the full record of its solid times, the living and the energies emanated. Now you will see why we coming to this place."

In that moment they found themselves in a new room, as luxurious as the previous ones. Many servants walked about as five men sat for what looked like a private feast. The table was laden with delicacies, whole roast birds, grilled, decorated suckling pigs, and an assortment of vegetables. The service was in gold and silver, and the tablecloth had delicately embroidered golden borders, all very ostentatious. On one of the walls hung an enormous cross encrusted with precious gems, the diamonds and rubies shining in settings of gold. At the middle of the table sat a cheerless old man, with beady eyes and thin lips. He was dressed strangely, his clothes as elaborate and extravagant as that palace; their extremity set him apart from the four others who sat with him at the overloaded table. As the travelers entered, the dour man was speaking to the others, who seemed to be his guests.

"I am sick, Lords! I am sick of these pagans! We must take definitive and final measures against them. How long must we endure their boasts of knowledge ... Only God knows! And God is jealous and vindictive, and we are his representatives ... we are his weapon! Why must we stand like fools before the people, before this group of intellectual, arrogant pagans who think they know everything?!"

All of them nodded in assent, and one of them asked, "But what must we do, my Lord Cyril? You are the Bishop, you are the only one who can know what is right. Besides, how can we control them? There are many people who support them."

"We are the Law, we are God, we are the Empire. And these people must be exterminated, sent to hell where they belong ..." He paused for a moment before adding, with a sinister look, "Kill the bitch and the trouble ends ..."

"What do you mean?" asked another.

"You know perfectly well what I mean: I mean Hypatia. I am sick of her popularity, for there are far too many who admire her, and that is bad for us. If we intend to govern forever, in our way, Hypatia must cease to exist."

The looks on the other men's faces became clouded, and the atmosphere grew even more ominous and tense than it already was. The Time Travelers followed the scene carefully, and the Apprentice of the Astral, fearing for Hypatia, became especially attentive to the conversation, for he had begun to appreciate her in a very special way, though they both belonged to apparently different worlds and times.

Cyril, Bishop of Alexandria, spoke again.

"It has been a century since the Empire changed its destiny; if it had not done so, then its power would have inevitably come to an end. Now our religion controls, and it will continue to control the destiny of the Empire—we are its perpetuation! But if we allow people like that *woman*," emphasizing that word with a special hate, "to continue existing, with her den of perdition, and her damned library, we will be in danger. If the pagans win, we lose, and she is a damned bitch! Who does she think she is . . . she is only a woman!"

He paused a moment before continuing.

"We must govern in all ways; the people cannot have access to knowledge, for then tomorrow they will again be our enemies. The people must know only how to fear God, and therefore us, his only representatives on Earth. Submission is all that they must understand from religion, and whoever dares to teach the opposite is our enemy, and enemy of the new Empire, the Reign of God! If they do not fear, if they have access to dangerous knowledge, they will not be obedient. How will we control them then? It is time to take it all. The Church is the Empire, and we must govern forever!"

Asanaro could not control himself anymore, and burst out, "This miserable old man is really a dangerous, sectarian fanatic!"

Omboni answered quickly. "Mmm . . . calm down, Apprentice of Time. You must continue listening, not upset, for otherwise you will lose this opportunity for listening and learning, and in that case this twisted character that you see here would win, after all."

"I'm sorry, it's just that this guy is so sinister, so horrible, like the Emperor we saw on our previous journey."

"Yesss, Asanaro, they belong to the same temporal-fluid, and both being fed from the same current of negative and morbid thoughts that will govern most of your dimension. But keep quiet."

Those foul guests enjoyed a large draught of wine, then ate just one bite of each dish, contemptuously leaving the rest. A boy entered through the front door, a servant, carrying more exquisite dishes to the men gathered there. He walked with his head bent and placed the tray at the side of the Bishop, who cast a strange look at the little boy; he bent his head even farther. Cyril then made a gesture with his hand, sending the boy from the room.

"This guy gives off pretty awful vibes," the Apprentice of the Astral added, "he wants everyone to be his submissive little slave. Who does he think he is . . . !?"

"Mmm . . . not needing to say what being obvious, and I insist, not becoming upset because of it. Wrongdoing being a plentiful custom on your planet. You must grow accustomed to seeing it, for the more conscious you become, the more obvious it being to you. Now let's continue listening."

As the guests continued their conversation one of them, servile and twisted, with curly hair and eyes like the Bishop, spoke.

"Highest Prince, Holy Bishop, my Lord, as usual you are right, that woman is a whore. I am sure she is one of the foulest sinners. I know from a reputable source that not only does she teach her daily pagan lessons, but that she also has many secret students; I am sure they are all blasphemers and fornicators. Some of my men have even informed me that she entices and forces her students to drink her dirty and evil . . . I can't say it . . ."

"Go ahead, Peter, my faithful servant. Say it! . . . Say it!" ordered the Bishop.

"My Lord, I have been told that she forces her students to . . . drink her filthy menstrual blood! The woman's shame itself, that aberrant symbol of their sins and perdition!"

The four others looked disgusted, especially Cyril, who demonstrated not only his sanctimoniousness but also an expression of contradictory morbidity in his eyes. He spoke again, quickly.

"Please, Peter, continue . . . continue . . ."

"Well, my beloved Prince, it is very possible that, besides organizing orgies and all of those dirty things pagans do, she might also be a . . . a daughter of Lesbos!"

The four others gave a shriek of disgust. Another of the pernicious guests, tormented and made pale by what he was hearing, added, "That is enough! We must act against this abominable woman! Just repeating that word . . . *woman* . . . I am terrified! They are all dirty . . . whores! They are sin personified, and this prostitute Hypatia, represents them all, as well as those libertine pagans from Greece. They must be banished, just as before they banished that degenerate Socrates. God willing, we will never hear from him again. We must finish them and their muses, we must continue the wise steps that holy Constantine began a century ago and cleanse the Empire of these sinners. I am sure that our dearest Emperor will support us. The Empire requires submission and absolute chastity... It does not need people who want to think but people who unquestioningly obey."

Cyril continued.

"My fellows, my brothers, we must be wise in our actions. The Emperor supports us—you well know that I have direct contact with him—but we must be discreet. The writings say it already: We must be clever as snakes, yet seem as doves to the people..."

They all laughed, and the Bishop spoke again.

"Listen to me. The Emperor does not wish for more troubles, more rioting, but he does desire a definitive end to all of the pagans—they are enemies of Christianity! And therefore enemies of the Empire. It is also true that Hypatia has become popular among many people as unsavory as herself, but as I said before, kill that bitch and it all ends... She is the symbol for all of those people, and she must die. By exterminating her, all of her followers must fear us, so we must set an example, strong enough to leave no doubt that we can definitely convert the rest into our servants, to the good and faithful of our Church. We must have total control."

There was a short pause, and then Peter, faithful servant of the Bishop, twisted his face and said, "Then let's kill that sinner, my Lord. Nothing stops us."

Cyril answered him quickly.

"Not so fast ... not so fast. She must die, but it must not be a death only of her body but of her spirit as well. I want her absolute and complete death, but without injuring our public reputation. As you know, it is not enough to be the Caesar's woman, one must also look it. First I shall inform the Emperor in a discreet way, so that he may know the evidence; it of course goes with saying that this information must not leave this room, and whatever I request from you, you must deal with your subordinates as if it were coming of your own initiative, never from me. My position as Bishop must not be compromised, for the pagans must fear me yet have the best image of me possible ... I am pious, and my image must remain flawless! I wish to be adored as they adore that sinner Hypatia; I want that admiration, and even more ..." He sighed. "Have you all understood, my brothers?"

The fellows looked furtively at one another, trying to show that they fully understood the Bishop, while urging him to continue so they might truly understand him.

"Lords, my faithful allies," the Bishop continued, "I know you do not quite understand how to attain what I have in mind. You have heard me well: I want the soul of Hypatia! Do you understand me?"

No one answered, and he repeated, "I want the soul of Hypatia! That means that I will first eradicate her in life, then she will die in life, and then I will erase all memory of her, all of her books and her teachings forever! I will wipe her off the face of the Earth ... She will die forever, and I ... I will win eternal life! I will be worshipped among the saints!" The Bishop was feverish, his eyes popping and his jaw opened wide.

He tried to calm himself, adding, "To solidify my plan and completely control Alexandria, you must pay attention . . . First, you must send all of your men to work, monks, priests, and all others who are faithful to our Church."

One answered, as the rest nodded in assent. "Of course, Excellency, whatever you say. Please, command us."

"Well, Lords, I wish to organize a campaign of rumors against Hypatia. I wish all of her blasphemies to be openly spoken about among the people, her degenerateness, that she is a miserable and impure daughter of Lesbos, that she teaches in secrecy and that she does it against the Empire, that she bewitches her students and fornicates with them, that she leads gruesome ceremonies with her filthy menstrual blood, that she keeps blasphemous and seditious books, that she has friends among the enemies of Alexandria and the Emperor . . . I wish all of the possible rumors to be spread, we haven't got much time . . . we haven't got much time . . ."

The eldest of the visitors now spoke.

"I understand, your Excellency, but we must consider that she has some influential friends, such as Orestes, Prefect of our city. And her father, Theon, has also been important to this city . . ."

The Bishop responded fiercely.

"And that is exactly what makes her dangerous—I want no more influences in the city but mine. Orestes is an easily manipulated coward, he depends on Rome and will fear me, washing his hands of it as soon as he sees me decided. That is why this campaign against Hypatia is so important, for we must discredit her! Rumors will be our allies, and will tell us the right moment to exterminate her; when it comes, we will erase the remains of her memory, and her students will die or convert to us." He added, scornfully, "And as for the people, they are no problem, for they are fearful and do not think, and they will submit quickly. I control them with rumors and fear..."

Everyone in the room was covered with a dark aura and a pallid energy, showing the low quality of those beings. The conversation continued as they developed the twisted plans of Cyril, and after a while their macabre dinner concluded, the guests said farewell and left the place, each hurrying to organize his servants. Peter, the one closest to Cyril, stayed longer, and once alone he spoke to his Lord.

"Your Excellency, I wanted to speak with you further in private. I have some other information that will interest you."

"Go ahead," answered Cyril, "I am listening. Tell me, what can be so important?"

"My Prince, since your holy uncle Theophilius began the extermination of these heretics, many of their books were burnt; many pagan authors were erased from the face of the Earth so that you might reign quietly and serve the Emperor as he deserves. But I have heard, through my informers, that this whore, Hypatia, keeps many books that speak heretically of Our Lord. I have been informed that one of her assistants, a young man named Mangazar, has writings that he has obtained from some of those damned Jewish and Eastern people that tell information of the life of King Christ, information that might make the people doubt, that would damage us. I was certain you would be interested in this information."

"You have done well to tell me, my faithful servant, and you have also done well by doing so privately: Keep it that way. Now, tell me, what else have you heard?"

"Well, my Lord," continued Peter, "I am certain that those

books are in the hands of Hypatia; she must be keeping them hidden. And that is not all. There is an arrogant man who was expelled from Rome, who I have heard is creating an infernal machine that does not require the impulse of horses or men, to move it; it needs only the power of the devil. My Lord, these people are all blasphemous ... they must all die ... Grant me a part of the task, and allow me to set a bonfire to all of these heresies ..."

After a pause, the Bishop answered.

"It's all right, my faithful servant ... it's all right ... The proper moment to vent the wrath of God upon these unfaithful will come ... But first, continue with your investigation and put your men to work on these rumors. I will let you know when our master strike is ready to fall ... Oh, and if you uncover any more information about these heretical documents or that demonic machine, bring it to me ..."

With that, the Travelers of Time, invisible guests in a corner of that room, began speaking to each other.

"Mmm ... well, young Visitor of Time, being the time for us to leave this place. You having heard enough to know the situation and the thinking of these people for yourself."

"Yes, Omboni, this is far too negative, and in a way I wish I'd never heard it. I'm concerned about poor Hypatia; these people are willing to do anything for power ..."

"That being it, Asanaro ... being the power-being, the materialism-power, the ambition-power ... neither mattering what clothes they might wear, nor the way in which they are named; the essence being the same throughout the time-river, they all being humans ... And remember that these events being part of the same time-river from which you, too, come ..."

"I understand," answered the Apprentice, "but I'm worried about Hypatia now; she is in the middle of everything."

"Do not worry for her. Now it being time for us to go, for we have to make some other visits, which being more pleasant!"

"Then let's go!" said Asanaro, relieved.

Peter and the Bishop said farewell to each other. A servant led Peter to the exit, and the Bishop was left alone with another very young servant, who came inside the room. Cyril closed the doors behind him.

The Travelers of the Astral found themselves walking on the streets of Alexandria, where it was already day, yet the time for them had passed in the blink of an eye. All of those scenes appeared to the Apprentice one after the other, connected in a sequence outside of the logical linking of events that is normal on Earth; but after experiencing so many things Asanaro cared no more, only wanting to continue knowing, learning from the teaching of Omboni and the examples to which he guided him.

Guide and Apprentice strolled among the Alexandrians of that day, like simple, absent figures, yet conscious of the events taking place. They advanced quietly, neither seen nor heard by any in the city, which at that hour of dawn was bursting with life and activity. The streets were full of people carrying out their daily lives, like any other city in the world. The expressions of the people, their energies and their ways, were no different from beings of any other time, already forgotten in the mirages projected by the memories of humanity. In the distance Asanaro could hear the soft sound of drums and stringed instruments that wafted from some corner of the city, where people of all times enjoyed the comfort of music.

The shops were full of movement, the merchants fully engrossed in their usual work: selling and bargaining. The great variety of food and other items that could be bought called Asanaro's attention, reminding him of the markets of his own time where he would often go, if only to see what was there. The spices, the variety of dried fruits, grains, and other foods gave the place a distinctive aroma that reminded him of home. But the people and their clothes were very different, their robes varied, it seemed, based on the rank of the wearer, and their texture varied from that of rough cloth to extraordinarily fine embroidered and exotic fabrics. Alexandria seemed prosperous and cosmopolitan, full of different races and beliefs, just as the Eastern silks mixed with the European marble, and the fine crystals made in that city. Even the architecture and the shape of the buildings expressed that union, somewhere between Egyptian and Greek, as if the city had tried to compose a new song, with notes of the East played on instruments of the West.

The Apprentice was enjoying himself, taking in the whole city, long forgotten in time. He was beginning to relax after the unpleasant scenes he had just witnessed. As he walked with the Astral Being, the two of them analyzed what they were living.

"It's strange," said the Apprentice, "walking down these streets, watching these people, these buildings that don't exist anymore, but when I look at them they seem so real, familiar, even . . . Everything looks new, as if this were only another city from the Earth . . . It's strange."

"Hehehe . . . well, Asanaro, being true, these should not look strange, for being your world, your people, and your time-river; it always seeming familiar to you. As a matter of fact, what this city trying to do, or, more accurately, what some people of this city trying to do, being still being attempted in your time, the one you belong to, but of course they being the same time-river. The forces here united being always present in the flowing of human beings. What wisdom, what ignorance . . ."

The Apprentice was thoughtful for a few minutes, as they continued to quietly walk through the streets of the city. Then he spoke again.

"But really, I don't quite understand you. On one hand, I'm clear that this city, its people and it circumstances do not exist anymore, but then how can they be related to my time and space?"

"Mmm . . . must see things from a different angle than the one you have always seen and listened from. That being why you are here, and when saying here I mean not this particular place but the one called Bamso, the great state of understanding in the depths of the Astral. This state teaching you that if you look at Earth—and I say Earth in the sense of your human race—and begin moving away slowly, you begin seeing it in a completely different way. If every day you doing the same job, as in your cities, meaning that you work only to want the sixth or seventh day to recover and again return to the same work, you having but few chances to see things outside that angle that your job gives to you. If your labor being construction, that being your reference to see the world. If your labor being on the farm, that being your reference. If considering yourself an erudite and great know-it-all, that being your point of view, no one being able to change it . . . but being it real?

"Oh, you Traveler of Life! The Galaxy being great, the Universe being immense, the skies spread not only in that blue color that vaults your world ... Go away from your world, and see it again! For there you seeing yourself.

"The time-river being like the water emanated, that erupts from a great spring," continued Omboni. "Each molecule relates with every other, being linked, influenced, whether bound or released. If that fluid has become stagnant and fetid ... it inevitably affecting you. Thus what you seeing here in this forgotten city from your past disturbs you, makes you angry, or perhaps you like it, and it seeming familiar ... For you, she, and all the ones of your species belong to the same time-river, with its same errors, contradictions, wars, fanaticism, and, in conclusion, with its same ... its identical fear, so much feeeaaar ..."

The Apprentice was so captivated by the Astral Guide's explanation that the background of people and streets was lost, as if by magic, and he could pay attention only to the words of Omboni, as he continued.

"Asanaro, from a certain point of view this city being symbolic in your world, as contradictory as it being, as indifferent and cruel. What will come to pass here will not please you, being like a terrible nightmare from your mind, but being necessary for you to know it; in a way you wish to know it, otherwise being impossible for you to match this frequency from the Astral."

On hearing these words the Apprentice thought of Hypatia and became sad, as Omboni continued to speak.

"The time-rivers, when being watched from afar, take a special form and obey a certain pattern, still incomprehensible to you. If you grow to see the form of that fluid, you being able to explain many circumstances of your human-world, just as you could decipher and search within the Astral of the future. If you understand your time-fluid, you will discover a great part of yourself and your attitudes. Something of this city existing in you, too."

The Apprentice was left even more thoughtful at the words of the wise Astral Being. He thought to ask Omboni to clarify what he had just said, but he realized that for the moment it would be useless for him to try to understand, that it would be better to wait and, just as Alsam had said, to go step by step. They continued their walk down the streets of Alexandria, which suddenly had returned. So they walked, though the noise of the crowds, made up of people from everywhere in the world, amid the camels, the carts, and the children, who as usual played and ran barefoot. Seconds later, seconds that flew past, they were in the port of that city, and it had all the activity of a modern port: large ships and small vessels, buildings, carts loaded with goods, the penetrating smell . . . It was like watching the activity of any port on Earth, only that the ships had masts and sails and there were no noises of modern machines; instead they heard the shouts of the people in charge, the noise of the carts, but behind that the same sea, the same birds in the sky. The scene was very entertaining for Asanaro, who had always enjoyed ports. Already at the shore, looking out at the sea, he spoke to his Guide.

"Omboni, this place is beautiful . . . To be honest, it's just like any port on Earth, with only a few minor differences."

"Mmm . . . what seeing you different?"

"Well . . ." And after a moment of doubt, Asanaro continued, "the ships have sails, the carts are pulled by animals, and . . . there are people loading things . . . are they slaves?"

"Mmm ... well," said the Astral Being, "but what being the difference with your time and space? The ships, in essence, being the same; the carts, in essence, being the same, at least in their objective; and the slaves being the same ..."

"But how? In my time there is no more slavery."

"Being completely sure, young traveler? What difference you seeing between the one who loads here and the one who loads in a port of your time?"

"Well, that here he is a slave! He's not free ..."

"Freedom, what you call freedom, if you not using it, being the same as not possessing it. If you being a servant, if you being called slave because you cannot change your destiny, well then I ask you: Can the free ones from your world change their destinies? Can they go beyond what the rest tell them, beyond what the currents of their time-river have determined for them?"

As they were speaking, near where the ships were being unloaded a group of well-dressed men were leaving one of the ships berthed at the old dock. They carried many scrolls and parchments and were ceremoniously bidding farewell to the man who seemed to be captain of the ship. After exchanging some words they crossed a weak gangway to the pier, where some other fancily dressed people awaited them, helping them to carry the rolls. The group walked directly past the travelers.

"What's happening?" asked Asanaro.

"Well, in a certain way it being something they trying to do again in your world. This city, Alexandria, as I said before, belonging to a stage that being transformed, following the chains of circumstances and conflicts of the energies of minds.

"The time-fluids have had different shades, according to the

mentality of human beings," continued Omboni, "and the stage
we see still enjoys the influence of those who longed to know
and were curious in the immensities of the Earth, the Universe,
and Nature. They have made mistakes, but also, many of them
being able to visit the world of dreams, being able to grasp more
than one idea. To keep that memory of their dream they determined, here in this city, that every book, every document, every
work written by humans should be kept in their library, their
'dream keeper.' Each ship that comes here must lend the writings they have, to be copied and kept in the library. The more
restless minds also dreamt, as you, and thought that if they kept
a small piece of the dreams of each of the thinkers in this world,
this would influence the minds of the future inhabitants of this
planet, and by influencing them it would help them to dream, to
investigate, to create, and in a certain way to be a bit more free
from the negative determinism that flowed from the past, from
the past of the time-river.

"Hypatia being, especially, a being full of dreams, full of
energy and curiosity, and wishing that thirst for knowledge to
continue into the future. That being why she has asked for these
scrolls."

The Apprentice was thoughtful again and gazed toward the
blue sea, trying to find an answer within himself to all that he
was living and what was yet left to be seen. He was so accustomed to that experience that, for a moment, he had forgotten
who he was on Earth, in his body, and he felt comfortable with
his new self, moving through places and times. He didn't even
think about waking up. He felt himself a kind of vagabond,
detached from things, connected only to the Bamso, connected
so he could learn and discover the vision of which Omboni

spoke. He wanted to understand what a time-river really was, and, in turn, who he really was.

The sun shone high in the sky, he blinked, and time passed at his will, touched by forces far distant from the nature of common things. It was nearly dusk, and the noise in the port calmed while the star languished on the horizon, only a few seconds having passed for him. He heard the soft voice of Omboni, saying, "Mmm . . . well, Asanaro, let's follow your thoughts . . ."

"What . . . ?"

"Yesssssssss . . . Let's only follow your thoughts. You wish to see again Hypatia, so let's visit her. Our trip not ending yet . . ."

DEATH AND LIFE

Both travelers, who were facing the ocean, turned to go to the library in search of Hypatia, and as they turned, in a fraction of a second they were in front of that excellent building. Again, in the blink of an eye, they found themselves inside the great central hall, which was lit by many lamps as dusk was falling over Alexandria like a soft mantle. A few people were talking, and there was Hypatia, distinguishable from afar by her elegance and composure, dressed in a soft linen gown that fell fine and gracefully on her. She was speaking jovially with an old man; the travelers came closer to hear the conversation, and when they were only a few steps away Asanaro immediately recognized the man, for it was Horace, the first person they had seen working in the halls of the library.

"How goes your work?" Hypatia asked kindly.

"Very well, for here I have found everything I was looking

for: all the books of Archimedes and the writings of Heron about gears and the use of steam! To be honest, it is all more extraordinary than I could have ever expected."

"Of course, Horace ... have you explored his work the Automaton?"

"That was one of the very first things I did! The idea of building a mechanical being, one that moves on its own, is extraordinary, but I find myself more fascinated by his collection of writings about the application of the energy of steam to the shops, particularly those that were perfected by his students. I will soon have some results with my work, for I have been speaking with some artisans, and I am sure that we will be able to build the machine I have been designing. If it works in this scaled-down model, the first thing I will do will be to encourage a shipbuilder's interest, to build it larger and install it in a vessel. Can you imagine, Hypatia, a ship that does not depend on the whims of the winds or the currents ... it could travel around the world!"

"That would be excellent, Horace. I can see that you are still as enthusiastic as the first day you came to Alexandria. But if you're wandering around saying that the world is round, people won't trust you very much."

"It's true, Hypatia. In these days one must be very careful with what one says, for there are things that one too quickly assumes everyone else knows. But, anyway, each day that I have spent searching among the parchments, I have discovered new surprises, and I feel satisfied, for there have been many before me who have investigated these same questions. You have surprised me as well, and your fame, well, before I even met you, and now I know that it wasn't at all exaggerated. As a matter of fact, and since we're speaking about ships, I've been thinking a lot about one of the inventions that you helped to develop, the astrolabe."

"I can see that you're interested in sailing, and everything related to it . . ."

"That's it, my Lady, there are so many mysteries in the sea. If we can build a ship that is aided by an automaton, a machine, and even better, if we give that machine a good system to discover its position on the Earth . . . we could even reach Atlantis! Beyond the columns of Hercules! In fact, I have discovered here several writings that speak of a continent on the other side of the Open Sea of the West," and he added, with a touch of irony, "though I'm not telling anyone . . ."

Hypatia smiled.

"Horace, I like your enthusiasm, and on occasion I have had similar thoughts; great things could be done . . ." After a pause, she continued, with a hint of melancholy in her voice, "but I also fear that if ever your machine worked that well, and men were able to reach all the unknown points on the Earth, wouldn't they also bring with them all of their diseases, their wars and cruelties . . . ? Perhaps those places we do not know are best left alone, without us, Horace, without our conflicts."

They both went silent for a few moments, until the old man added, as low as he could, "And especially without characters such as Cyril . . ."

They laughed together at that, releasing their tension over the subject.

"Well, it's true," Hypatia spoke again, "especially without Cyril and his fanatical followers. Can you imagine, Horace, to discover Atlantis and then, because of us, Cyril arriving on that wonderful island?"

The old man replied quickly, "Everything good would end, my Lady, poor Atlantis! It would be sacked, dismantled, and later Cyril would stand in front of the people and tell the people, with his shrill, awful voice, 'Repent, sinners! Either you believe with me or you are against me! Either you convert into my servants or you are all pagans, heretics, and will know the wrath of God!' Those zealots have always been the same . . ."

They both laughed again, and as they did the young Mangazar came into the hall, hurrying directly toward them. A little agitated, he greeted them both.

"My Lady, Hypatia, it is a pleasure to find you, and Horace, how have you been?"

Both of them greeted him affectionately and exchanged a few more pleasantries. Soon the old man, sensing that it would be a good idea to leave them alone, said, "Well, my Lady, it is time for me to go, for one of the artisans has promised me an answer regarding my scale models, and I must speak with him before nightfall. Farewell, and all of my respects, Hypatia. Take care, Mangazar."

Having said this, the old man left the great room, even brighter now that more oil lamps had been lit to accompany the fading light of dusk. They were now alone, and Mangazar voiced how upset he was.

"My Lady . . . how can I express the deep feeling I have that turns my concern for you into a torment . . . I fear for you, I am very distressed."

"Please, Mangazar, do not be so dramatic . . . what makes you so sad? I know you love the Greek tragedies, but do not follow them so literally," Hypatia replied in a soothing tone.

"My most beautiful Lady, you are the most extraordinary person I have ever known, but you have isolated yourself too much from reality. I am in the streets every day, and poetry gives me vision, especially to see the beauty you possess, but I can also recognize the filth in this world. In the streets there is too much hatred and violence. They speak too often of you, too many rumors have been spread, designed to discredit you, and in more than one argument I have intervened to defend you against those wretched and ignorant fools, but it is growing worse every day. You cannot isolate yourself in this place, or in your books ... you know how dangerous it is to continue teaching and writing publicly ... Rome is in chaos, and the riots will extend ... and when there are riots, freedom is always the first victim, and you and your teachings represent that ..."

"Please, Mangazar, do not come to me now with these protectionist ways of a traditional good man ... I've had enough of that from my father. I am free, and no man, not even you for whom I feel something so special, will tell me what to do with my own life. My studies are a part of me, I cannot abandon them ... and merely thinking that that fanatical Christian will get what he wants through his threats ... it makes me furious! In the end it is always men wanting to control the situation, through their religions, their wars, or their love ... !"

The young man lowered his eyes and, after a pause, he answered in a broken voice, "You can't think that the royal governor will help you ... I know of your friendship with him, but you are unimportant to him ... He is faithful to the Empire, and the Empire rules through religion, not through its governors."

Hypatia answered him quickly, "But ... what is happening to you? Don't tell me that now you are jealous of Orestes," and, adding in a sharp voice, "look, Mangazar, if I have accepted you, I have done so honestly, and if I were at all interested in someone other than you, you would be the first to know ... so please, don't come before me with these ludicrous expressions of jealousy!"

"I'm sorry ... I'm sorry ... that was not my intention, only to care for you. I fear that in any moment a riot could begin, and that you will be one of its victims. Cyril is too influential, and his followers are blind, they are fanatics ... they believe them-selves sole owners of the truth, chosen by God, and in the face of that there is nothing we can do."

"You are wrong! We can do many things ... we can con-tinue studying, keeping our books, creating. You can write, for that is the best way to show the Bishop that there are still many people who can think for themselves, that there is still light in the hearts of human beings, and that no matter what he says to the contrary, the Earth is round, not cross-shaped!"

"Please, my Lady, don't even think of repeating this in front of others, for it will only inspire more viciousness from the Bishop and his followers. There is much that needs to remain hidden, that is better left unknown."

"You are too apprehensive and too passionate. Relax a little."

Mangazar paused for a moment before responding.

"I cannot ... my heart belongs to you, and I can do nothing but think about you and your safety. I did not want to compro-mise you, but I also have several documents that would greatly upset Cyril, and I am afraid he has found out about them."

"How is that, Mangazar?"

"You know of my studies in history, and that I also col-
lect rare documents. To make a long story short, a while ago
some papyri came into my possession—and I am certain of their
authenticity—that speak about the life of Jesus of Nazareth.
These documents come from old India and give interesting
information about his life there, especially from the mountains
of the Land of Eternal Snows. In those writings the story told
by the Church is openly contradicted, and there are things told
there that the Church has not been able to explain. If they discover their existence, both you and I will be in danger. The
writings also prove absolutely that Christianity is clearly an
Eastern belief, with characteristics very similar to other Eastern
beliefs the world has known."

Hypatia responded immediately, clearly upset.

"And why hadn't you mentioned this before? Did you not
trust me?"

"Please, my Lady, do not be upset with me. If I hadn't mentioned this before, it was to protect you from even more conspiracies, for there are enough of them already. Now I can only
think of your welfare, I don't care about those writings anymore . . . I will burn them! I care for nothing but you."

"You do not flatter me by saying those things, Mangazar.
What you have discovered, as well as what has been discovered
or written by so many other thinkers, philosophers, and poets,
should be preserved, for it belongs to all human beings, not to
you, or to me, and less to the Bishop or the Emperor himself
with his Church and all that garbage. I am aware that I am not
the proprietor of truth, but I am even more aware that they
are less so. That is why you must keep your writings, and for

the same reason I must continue, firm in my teachings and my studies."

Again Mangazar emanated a great sadness, and, nearly begging, added, "My Lady, please hear me. Let's leave all of this behind—people are deaf, they do not want to hear or see beyond their own fanaticism, they are happy being blind, ignorant. They are lazy cowards. You have proven it well: They are happy believing that gods make miracles for them, that they should fear and bow before them. No one would want a Jesus who was as human as they, nor to know that all who claim to represent him are nothing but opportunists. For the people, thinking for themselves means an effort, a sacrifice; it is much easier for them to leave everything in the hands of someone else, like Cyril, to tell them what to do and forbid the rest, to control their brains and their hearts and guarantee them paradise in exchange for their coins. You wish the happiness of the human being? Here and now that is impossible; none of them want to fight. There are so few who want to do something, and they are already frightened and will not defend you—I have seen them already. You have read the story of the world of Berros the Babylonian—what is happening here has happened too many times, and the dreamers are always the most damaged . . .

"My Lady, my beautiful Lady," Mangazar continued, "let's leave Alexandria, let's run away, far beyond the limits of the Empire, far from the Emperor, his Church, and all of the Cyrils that could every be part of it. Let's run to where there are no fanatics flagellating themselves and others, where we can be free . . . Let's go away from Alexandria forever . . ."

"Oh Mangazar! Where is that place . . . ? Where? If it existed, I'd go with you happily . . ."

Hypatia and Mangazar held each other, their eyes filled with tears. They radiated a strong energy of happiness at being together, though it was mixed with nostalgia for something far away, far beyond the situation brought on them by the whirls and the flows of the time-river.

Silent up to then, the Astral Travelers began speaking again.

"What's going to happen, Omboni? Hypatia should leave; this city is rife with conspiracies against her. Besides, from what we've seen of the maniacal Cyril, it's obviously better for her to be somewhere else."

"Mmm . . . being true," answered Omboni, "but think that we having seen, knowing what they have not, what they can only suppose, and she keeping the hope that sanity and respect will prevail."

"And will it be like that?" the Apprentice asked fearfully. "Will sanity prevail?"

"What having happened you must see for yourself, and taking from it your own conclusions. Now, come with me."

Both travelers left that place, walking quietly. Behind them stood the two lovers, their energies colorful and bright, invisibly illuminating that ancient and lonely room.

Omboni and Asanaro walked back out into the streets of old Alexandria. It was already night and there were few people out; most of them used those dark hours to stay quietly in their homes, to sleep, and then awake with the powerful Egyptian sun so as to make the most of the day.

"Where are we going now?" asked the Apprentice of the Astral.

"Mmm . . . to solve what you wish to know. Being already time for you to see what you must see, for us to continue with your lessons in other places and other times. Now simply follow me. You have not noticed, but for Alexandria having passed a few days, and the new night being very significant. We must make another of our unpleasant visits for you to continue understanding."

"Well, then, let's get going," replied the Apprentice, a little restless.

They continued walking until they found themselves again in front of the large palace of Cyril, Bishop of Alexandria. They passed by the guards and entered the building, coming into one of the sumptuous inner chambers. There sat the Bishop with his ever-willing servant, Peter. They were speaking privately, though their secrets could escape neither the ears of the Visitors of Time nor being captured in the Great Universal Record.

"My beloved Prince, Holy Cyril," Peter was speaking, "everything is settled, just as you have commanded it."

"Very well done, Peter. You are a great Christian and a noble servant of the Holy Mother Church; you will be well rewarded. But tell me, are the men ready for their evangelical labor?"

"Of course, my beloved, Your Holiness. Four hundred and forty-four men are ready to do your bidding, my Lord. Two hundred more will be waiting nearby, close to the residence of the blasphemer. They will assure that no one can come close or help in any way, while the larger group will go straight for the sorceress and will send her straight into the perpetual flames of hell, just as you have ordained."

The Bishop sat thoughtful for a few seconds, his eyes shining with dark malice.

"No, Peter," he spoke slowly, "do not make it so quick . . . take her to the Church near to her house; the parish priest is faithfully devoted to us. Strip her of her clothes and make her choose her destiny: the cross, or hell. Make her repent her sins and her arrogance, make her recognize that the only salvation is in God, his Church, and his Empire. She will be fearful of dying, for after all she is no more than a woman . . . Later, when she embraces the cross, bring her to me . . ." He paused, took a deep breath, and, full of hate, added, "I want her before me, crying and repenting at my feet. I will forgive her . . . Of course, to measure the sincerity of her repentance she shall be flagellated, then infibulated . . . and then, surely, she shall torment her own body . . ."

Peter replied quickly, "My Prince, you are merciful and wise, and you are a true Vicar of Christ. But what will happen if the harlot is disdainful and does not wish to convert to a servant of God?"

The Bishop opened his eyes wider. "Let her serve as an example for all to know what happens if they do not unite with the Church . . . the Empire of the Holy Mother Church. I will erase her from human memory, burn her books, and bring down what remains of that disgusting library where all the pagans gather . . . Neither she nor any of those pagans will be remembered, and in that way I will complete the work begun by Nostrum Numen Constantine. Hypatia must die, whether forgotten in one of our nunneries or skinned by you . . ." He then added, with even more scorn, "Oh! And if you must skin her, do it with shells, for is that not the symbol of her pagan goddess? What could be better than for her to die by that symbol of the original sin shared by all women!"

The Apprentice, who stood with his Guide in a corner of the room, all of a sudden understood whom and what they were speaking about, for somehow he did not want to understand that all of this hatred was directed at Hypatia.

He said to Omboni, "This psychopath wants to abuse her! Murder her! We must do something!"

The Astral Being looked at him with understanding, and he placed his ethereal hand on Asanaro's shoulder.

"What you seeing being only a recording. What was being no longer, being only a ghost . . . Being nothing we can do."

"But Omboni," insisted the Apprentice, still agitated, "this is unfair, this despicable fool is just terrible! Why do we have to let him do whatever he wants? We have to do something. Let's tell Mangazar, there must be a way . . ."

The Astral Being answered, as always very compassionate.

"You must calm yourself and see the depth of the things. These facts being only part of the continuity formed by a time-river, of which I have spoken to you often. Being nothing we can do, only you must understand that what has happened here being only part of this great current that has a body larger than each particular fact. The attitude of Cyril not being his attitude but the attitude of a great part of his time-fluid, and what he plans being a consequence of the era . . . One way or another, it being inevitable. For you, there being no other way to learn."

"But you have proven to me that nothing is impossible . . . Then we can change these events!"

"Mmm . . . from a certain viewpoint, being true," answered Omboni, "we can transform these facts, you can change them by rejecting them in your mind; but by doing so you being only converting the raw reality of the Great Record into a simple dream. In that dream, Hypatia would be as safe and protected as you wished, but that would not change the physically recorded facts; it would only change them within your internal image. Once returned to your bodily dimension, you would see that even when you having a dream as you wished it, the dream not being real. Is that what you want?"

"No, Omboni . . ." answered Asanaro sadly.

"You must overcome your feelings, Apprentice of Time, for they also tie you to the river where human beings meet, and being so, you lose the real vision of life and yourself."

"It's all right," answered the now resigned Apprentice, "let's move forward and witness what shall be."

With a blink they were again in the city streets, leaping across hours. The Star-Sun had already risen over the city.

That morning there was something different in the air. The people seemed rushed, and there were fewer of them than usual. The rumors had spread and taken the whole city; the tension and nervousness were more apparent than ever. Both travelers walked quietly, confident of their immunity, knowing themselves outside that dimension and projection of the past.

Some of the shops were closed, which was strange, for they had never seen them closed at this hour before. The Apprentice was restless as he walked, as if he was mixing with the events of this old Alexandria, taking them as his own. Finally Omboni spoke to him.

"Mmm . . . well, Asanaro, we being almost at the completion of this stage in our journey, and you must being strong, keeping

your attention on the reality. Just like being. Just like being in
your time-river, with all of its rawness."

The Apprentice looked at him and sensed that nothing good
was about to happen, though he was prepared for it all.

In that moment they found themselves very near the house
of Hypatia, and Mangazar appeared just behind them, running,
his face distorted and obviously distressed. He ran past Asanaro's
side, and when the Apprentice saw him, he looked at Omboni
with surprise. His mind could see beyond the mind of the young
man in love and understood that he was running to save Hypatia from the danger that pursued her; his mind projected only
the image of her, only wanting to embrace her that morning, to
be able to protect her from whatever threatened, for he had just
woken from a nightmare.

In those seconds Asanaro wished he could have told the
young man what he knew, and that he was involved, in a certain
way, in that nightmare. He was about to yell instinctively, to
hurry that young man in his mad race to rescue her: He wanted
to believe that Mangazar could hear him.

Mangazar took a breath, as if holding himself in time. In
front of him, about a block away, was Hypatia's carriage, with
her inside. With his eyes the young man traveled to the beautiful lady; she turned, attracted by an invisible force, and they saw
each other without distance. How long a second can be! How
eternal a minute! Both somehow knew that this was the last
time they would see each other.

In a terrible instant a man dressed in the habit of a monk
passed in front of Mangazar, and stopping, threw him violently to the ground. Four men quickly came from nearby and

without compassion beat Mangazar all over his head and body. Everything happened quickly, and as Asanaro hurried his steps to come closer, the men who had attacked young Mangazar were gone; he lay motionless in the middle of the street. No one came to help; the few people in the street quickly hid. Only the travelers of time came forward to find him lying there. Omboni, who continued walking steadily, spoke to his Apprentice, who simply stood, astonished, staring at Mangazar.

"You must continue, Asanaro. Being injured and uncon-scious, but he will not die. Follow me."

While the Apprentice turned his eyes away from the young man lying there on the street, he found himself next to the Astral Being, very close now to the house of Hypatia. He could see her in her carriage a few feet away: She looked as beautiful and splendid as ever. For a second he thought that the ancient Greek sculptors must have been inspired by someone like her, the reality of their ideal of beauty and refinement. Her eyes were uselessly searching for the figure of Mangazar, lost in the distance. At her side, directing the horses was Akena, her beloved assistant.

But her thoughts were immediately interrupted. From the surrounding shadows, from the stores and the streets, came a crowd of men dressed in the traditional habits of Christian monks of the era, mad beings of blindness. Their faces were distorted and there were shadows underneath their eyes, betray-ing their insanity and severe lack of sleep. Many of them passed directly through the visitors of time, who were still before the scene. The whole crowd rushed toward the carriage Hypatia's carraige. The Apprentice gestured as if trying to go there and protect her, but Omboni again put his hand over Asanaro's Astral shoulder and the Apprentice knew that there was nothing he could do, that he wasn't meant to do anything more in that time and place than simply observe.

The crowd was almost upon the carriage now, surrounding it completely, holding the horses and looking upon the beautiful woman with an indescribable hatred, and at the same time with great fear. Among the men close to the carriage was Peter, Cyril's ever-willing servant. In the distance a few people who knew Hypatia saw the whole scene and ran away, hiding their faces. The neighbors, who had come to their windows, now closed them and quickly locked themselves inside their houses.

Hypatia knew immediately that her fate was sealed, and she stood completely still, not for one minute losing her composure. Akena stood up almost immediately, in a desperate attempt to move them out of the situation, whipping the men who held the horses while yelling at the animals to move. All was useless, and the throng of cowardly assailants threw themselves on the carriage, savagely beating old Akena and violently dragging Hypatia out of it.

The Travelers of Time watched the scene, following its every detail. The Apprentice was aghast, but at the same time he knew that he had to keep a certain coolness in order to remain able to watch such a horrible event.

Several monks from that horde of criminals dragged the woman by her hair, while another group sang Christian songs and spat out prayers, adding a ghastly sanctimoniousness to the already appalling scene. Another group raised a great cross, screaming like madmen, making the Astral Apprentice wonder if they weren't the same ones who crucified Jesus, they, his vaunted faithful followers. He wondered for a second at how contradictory life on Earth is, how those who adore the cross as a symbol of sacrifice and crime against their prophet so quickly use it to justify their own crimes.

The monks began yelling, "Take her to Holy Ground! Take her to the Caesarium!"

The mob dragged the defenseless woman toward a nearby building, a church. Hypatia was already badly beaten and partially unconscious as they dragged her through the street. In the church, which rose up above her like a grim scaffold, she was cast brutally in front of the altar, mute witness to those terrible facts. Led by Peter, several of the monks threw themselves upon the helpless woman and violently tore her clothes, leaving her completely naked and forcing her to kneel against the wall before her cowardly executioners.

The beautiful daughter of Theon came slightly back into consciousness and made no complaint, no lament, and shed no tear. The monks were astonished at the beauty of her naked body, and in the back of the crowd some flagellated themselves with whips for their sinful desires; others drew back, and most of them carried in their eyes a combination of hatred, admiration, and fear before that beauty, before the woman.

Peter stepped in front of her, while two of his servants held her by her arms, and a third by her hair. The rest watched the scene, praying while they screamed. With a deranged, insane voice, he began shrieking at her.

"Repent, Sinner! You are treading on holy ground! The time of your final judgment has come to you; prostrate yourself before God! Repent, daughter of sin, whore, you who tempted Adam and have led the Holy Man down into perdition! You, whose seductive words make him go away from his Church, repent, for inside you live Sodom and Gomorrah, you are the damned, the woman! You have carried this sin from the beginning of time, and you have been marked and punished by God with the pain of childbirth and the flagellation of your own menstruation, sign of your sin, sign of your inferiority. You must submit yourself to the word of God and his Vicars on Earth. You must acknowledge our Prince Cyril as your only salvation. Repent, Sinner! Your only salvation is to acknowledge our Bishop, and submit yourself to the nunnery!

"Your whole body is the sign of sin: Shame on it! Shame, Sinner, or you will die and you will know Hell!!!"

Hypatia, barely conscious, raised her head with dignity beyond comparison, unknown to the cruelty and ignorance of those men. She only said, "Your Empire, your superstition, your belief, and your ignorance are the worst of all hells . . . if I shall die, I am certain that anyplace will be better than the Earth that you are poisoning."

At these words, Peter, with a premeditated coldness, raised his murderous arm in which he held a great shell, and killed her, cutting her throat. The blood welled up red and alive, dressing her delicate body in a fine shroud. In the mind of Hypatia there was no fear or anger, only a sensation of relief, like the sleep that comes at the end of a long day, as that precious, vital liquid gushed from her.

The crowd of assassins came in that moment to her and skinned her, taking the flesh down to the bones. The blood invaded the floor of the church and spilled on the gold relics and the altar. The group of monks seemed to be celebrating a vile ceremony, taken from a nightmare, and the place matched their thoughts of persecution, hatred, and intolerance that frenzied them. Every one of the men in that huge crowd wanted to take a piece of Hypatia's flesh. They slipped and fell on the blood and organs that were spilled across the floor. Many of them shrieked unintelligibly, while others, their hands dyed with the red, flagellated themselves with large, many-pointed whips as they continued to pray.

Peter, chief of the murderers, screeched with a distorted voice, "Burn her! Burn her! Spread her and let her serve as a lesson!"

A group of them picked up the remains of what was once the beautiful body of Hypatia and began burning it. Some grabbed the pieces of her flesh and went to spread them throughout the city, as their Master and Lord, Cyril the Bishop, had commanded, to serve as an example to all those who dared to rise up against the Holy Mother Church, for all to know that the pagans were doomed and that, from that day onward, there would be only one Empire, one Church, one God ... and, of course, they his only and legitimate representatives.

The Travelers of Time watched from a corner of the macabre scaffold in doleful silence. Asanaro was dumbfounded, violently disturbed—it had all happened so fast, passing in just a few minutes. The fact that he could not help her stuck in his mind, even though he had desperately wanted to, even when it trespassed the logic of travel in the Time of Dreams. Suddenly he saw Hypatia again, as a mirage, standing behind one of the columns and quickly hiding behind it. Amazed, he searched for her with his eyes, and at the same time he saw in the entrance the reflection of another feminine figure. Immediately he called to Omboni.

"I've seen her! She's alive! She's alive!"

"Mmm . . . Apprentice of the World of Dreams . . ." answered the Astral Being in a very understanding tone, "you still having much to learn."

"But I saw her, I'm sure! And someone else is there, too!"

"No, Asanaro . . . From the point of view of your world she having died, but from a higher point of view she being still alive, and that being what you see. Come, follow me."

They walked a few steps and reached the rear of one of the columns, and there was Hypatia, with all of her usual beauty, but now she looked more radiant than ever. She stood in front of them both, and the Apprentice stepped back, for he thought she was looking at them.

"Do not worry," Omboni told him, "for she not being able to see you. Calm down, Apprentice . . . She being in a process of change . . . we could call it the 'awakening of the dream,' and in that process her vibrational state being more like ours, and for that she seems to be looking at you. She having died, for the Earth, Asanaro, but now being born into a new dimension, and there the flows of your world do not rule, neither ignorance, and even less the ignorance of any religion–superstition, no matter how fashionable."

They both watched happily as the woman or new being that they saw walked, quietly investigating a different place.

"But she . . . where is she, really . . . ? And who is that other shape?" asked the Apprentice. "If this is a projection, I'm getting very confused . . ."

"Look around you," answered Omboni.

Asanaro did just that, and he discovered that there was no more crowd of assassins, no macabre churches . . . not anything.

They were in a new place, a quiet and colorful field through

which the new Hypatia walked, without any worries. There were beautiful trees, and from behind one of them appeared what seemed to be a beautiful young girl. Immediately the Apprentice asked, "What has happened, Omboni . . . ? What happened? But if those cretins killed her . . . they cut her throat . . . Poor Hypatia, she was murdered, she was covered in blood, and we couldn't do anything . . . and now . . . What are we doing here? Who is she?"

Asanaro felt as if he were fainting, falling, pulled by an invisible rope tied to his back. He knew that it was the end of that journey . . . he was falling . . . and he sensed that he was going to wake up, that in a way he needed to wake up. He seemed to be falling through a great abyss.

He thought it better that way, that he had seen too much for one night. He was descending, helplessly . . .

TIME OF
BIRTH

I.

If There Were No Limits on the Mind . . .

The Apprentice was again violently experiencing the coldness of the body and all the discomforts of gravity. In the beginning he was decentered, confused; slowly his thoughts turned toward himself. Even before he began to move any part of his terrestrial body, like flashes of lightning in the storm of consciousness, within seconds he was taking all of the images and sensations he had lived in that strange and long night and making them part of himself. He felt something he never expected to feel in his entire life, an overwhelming and intense feeling of sorrow combined with joy, of strength and stifling, of nostalgia and lucidity; he felt like an overwhelmed little child.

He cried and cried, with the freedom and relief of a newborn child, without wanting to contain himself . . . He moaned and he cried, with the joy and pain mixed in only one word. The tears welled up in the dawn of consciousness, and he knew that he would never be the same, that there was no way back. Bit by bit his tears turned into sobs, and then quietness came, and with it the understanding of all that he had lived and discovered. He smiled to himself in his half-consciousness, thinking of the great path he had walked, and at the same time he grew saddened at the strength of the truths he had discovered.

Between the previous dimension and the complete awakening there passed an indeterminate time.

He had to return to the world of his dimension; he had to go back to feeling the weight of flesh, the coming and going of air through his lungs, the strange numbing of the muscles, and the low rumble of his bowels. He was back, and he could do nothing to return to the point where the projection of his mind had taken him, though for a few seconds he wished to.

He was completely lucid within the square-dimension, but he tried to remain tranquil, and before moving he began the exercises that Alsam had taught him so he would not lose any memory, image, or teachings from that very special journey he had taken ... to not lose the precious thread that united him every night to the Universe, to the marvelous Cosmos.

The morning had advanced and Asanaro was leaving his shelter much later than usual; he arose slowly, silent, reserved. The deep vision of the Great Record and of knowing distressed him, and he continued to feel some of that mix of sadness and happiness, akin to seeing something unpleasant, undesired, but which he had always sensed. But truth relieves. He could not stop thinking of Omboni, of the places he had visited with him, and of how his vision of many things, which he thought were one determined way, had changed. Strange and surprising is life!

His mind was full of images, his ears still echoed with the voices of the past. The world of dreams was so real for him now, as real as the reality from the dimension of the way to the Earth. He organized his things slowly and then stood up. The sensations of his clothes, the sun, the air, were no longer the same as they had been before. Everything seemed different.

In the depths of his mind he thought about Alsam, about what he might be doing at that moment. He wanted to tell his Guide what had happened that night, tell him about his impressions and of the great teaching into which he had been so strongly initiated.

Asanaro rushed out of his tent; he did not see anyone around. He walked quickly to the small field near the camp, where his Guide usually spent his days working on his strange designs. Asanaro was surprised to find that Alsam was not there, and felt lonely, more lonely than ever before. There was a gentle breeze and the sky was of an intense blue, adorned with beautiful white clouds that seemed to be made of cotton. He went inside the circle, made a kind of greeting, gathering his hands very slowly and quietly to center himself and relax his mind, then sat down cross-legged with his eyes closed. He stayed there, still, for a moment. He opened his eyes again and noticed that the place was not the same as it had been. The circle was now surrounded by various small new diagrams, like writing from another world, unlike anything from the Earth. Each figure was delicately ornamented with small stones, sticks, and leaves. He sat there for a while, observing Alsam's work, wondering what it all meant, though he already knew the answer. Simply looking at those strange figures he felt rested, and it crossed his mind that all of it might be there to help him.

After a while he rose and made the same greeting; he felt much better. He ran toward the side of one of the mountaintops that created the small valley where they camped. Once there, he saw, about half a mile up the slope, a small human figure, and he had no doubt that it was Alsam, quietly sitting on one of the boulders; it could be no one else but him. He seemed to be painted in sharp contrast to the background of mountains and cliffs. Without thinking, Asanaro began climbing.

After some time walking, already warm and breathing heavily, he arrived at the rock where the extraordinary teacher was still sitting. The place looked familiar to the Apprentice's memory. He greeted his teacher.

"Alsam! I have been looking for you!" He then added, a bit more thoughtful, "I have so much to tell you . . ."

The Guide smiled and made space on the plateau formed by the rock. The view from there was spectacular; it calmed the senses.

Alsam replied to the Apprentice, "Well, now tell me, Asanaro, how have your travels been? I get the impression that you've had a long night."

The Apprentice's gaze became dejected and melancholic.

Alsam added, "The truth is heavy, but our own truth is even heavier. You still have much to walk."

"Why do you say that?" asked the Apprentice.

"Your preparation for the vision of the Astral World will always bring you great surprises, and they will always be strong. If you do not understand that, you might take them in a negative way, and then you will have only increased your fears; thus the door to that great dimension will close to you again. But if you take everything in a positive way, you will see that everything was simple, and its intensity was only a varnish, its essence beyond the images."

After a short pause the Apprentice began speaking, telling his Guide about his strange journey in the world of dreams, including as many details as possible. He also discussed how intense it had been for him. He would occasionally interrupt his narration to ask, "But I don't understand . . . how can there be so much evil and malice on Earth?"

Alsam would only shake his head.

And Asanaro would continue recounting his adventure, at least what he could keep in his head. His Guide listened attentively. The hours passed as they went over the details of that long Astral Journey, and at the end, the Apprentice asked again, "Can the past be something so terrible? Honestly, it wasn't what I had expected from that stage of history."

"What has been . . . is. Stages only divide the mind, not the facts," answered Alsam.

"Humans possess a high impressionability while they are in this dimension. Everything you have heard in your life-Earth you have assumed as certain, for your inside, as that of every human being, is essentially pure. However, you must know that minds, through time, have plotted too many negative things, forming false beliefs, unnecessary images, incorrect values, all based on stories through which they can easily control the thoughts and minds of the people. You, too, have been one of those people, and that is why to see straightforward truth hurts you to the point that you almost fail to understand it.

"When certain beings who have ruled over your world have managed to dirty enough people, these people become easily controllable and can be dragged into unconsciousness and fanaticism. Worst of all is that their minds begin to be controllable even within the Astral. What they call dreams are also bound, turning only to nightmares or undefined stages of images, and that is why it is said that they'll never see past the ends of their noses. If you have succeeded in overcoming that state, imposed by a skeptical and controlled media, you have taken a great step toward being able to see the reality in the dimension of the Bamso, but you must be willing to accept its rawness and learn to overcome it.

"Where you have been taken, if you had not been prepared, you would only have suffered a great shock before the hard and direct truth ... which your cultural-me does not like, that programmed thing. If it persists and is strong, it will automatically twist what you have seen, for it will not allow you to encounter the truth. If yours were like that, you would have reacted with anger, telling yourself, 'This is all fantasy, this is fake ... this can't be ... I know it's not this way.... I know ...' "

"If your 'pure-me' is prepared," Alsam continued, "and your 'cultural-me' has been overcome, whatever you have seen and what you will see will seem normal, already learned. If it is that way, you will be able to continue exploring further and further in the Bamso, and remember: There, there is neither time, nor space, nor impossibilities, nor anything hidden, only the limits that you have acquired through your Earthly contact.

"Do you wish me to continue widening your field?"

The Apprentice nodded, and Alsam continued.

"The written history, the one you think you know, is only

a fable, a tale arranged by conveniences. Excuse me for my example, but it is like the case of the politician who buys the journalists for them to hide his filth and write instead stupidities about other fools, distracting the people from reality while the politician hides the fact that he is shamelessly stealing from them. Meanwhile the people are fascinated by tales told with cheap gossip or simply by bizarre facts . . . That is the True History of the World. The few who have tried to speak the truth have been criticized, persecuted, and stifled. So if you want to know the true history of humankind, you must enter the Bamso with no prejudices and see things for yourself, no matter how painful or raw they might be."

After a silence, the Apprentice spoke.

"I don't know, Alsam, but people have certain beliefs that are supposed to make them better people, and make everyone else better, too . . . I don't understand."

The Guide responded with a soft, sad smile, "As your vision becomes clearer, you will understand that the world belongs to only one river, just as you have heard and seen in the Bamso. People might have their particular belief of religion, they might even divide the time of the world into years before and after the beginning of their faith, but human beings have been cruel, they have been foolish, and they have been evil and good both before and after. Belief is a wardrobe, nothing more—it is not a body! Mind has always been mind, with all of its sophistries."

Asanaro listened attentively while within he walked through the different scenes of his long trip through the Astral.

"But . . ." he asked, "why so much cruelty, so much persecution, so little understanding, and so much hatred? Can only hatred and division set the pace of the life of men on Earth?"

Alsam answered quietly, "To be honest, neither hatred nor division are necessary, but they must coexist with what you feel as right…" And then he continued, "What has been shown to you in the Great Record is true, but don't take it too personally, otherwise you will be caught in that stage. Among humans, 'men,' many centuries ago, began a war that they have not yet ended, and so long as it goes on you will continue to see its consequences, only wearing different clothes. There will continue to be fanaticism, there will continue to be hatred, and there will continue to be division. It is necessary for you to see the raw reality, but you must also remain calm before it."

Asanaro was looking to the valleys and horizon, trying to understand. After a while he said, "Too many injustices are done… and the worst of it is that most of the people, from what I saw, with their ignorance, their fear, and their mass mentality, as you say, do nothing to change or evolve… The image of Hypatia is still stuck in my head, as I've told you. Nobody helped her, after everything she gave—no one in that city did anything to defend her, only Mangazar and Akena. The worst is having watched all of that and having been able to do nothing."

"Asanaro, it was not for you to do anything. You will do something for her, however, if you really learn from what happened…"

"Why so much hatred toward her? Was it just because she was a woman … ?"

"In a certain way, Asanaro. All that negative energy that was vented against her is part of what you have named as a time-river: It is simply the weight of the culture. Those ignorant people who sent her to be murdered, just as those who actually carried it out, acted as simple pawns of a tradition. As I told you before, a war was begun by 'man' many eons ago . . . if there has ever been any record of that war, it was lost there in Alexandria. The conflict is also part of what you are currently living, just as it is part of what Hypatia lived in her era. All humans sense that unconsciously; while that conflict continues, the river of time will follow its own course.

"Before what you have had the chance to know, before this time, 'man' took control of belief, and with it 'power' and 'divinity,' and he has been fighting ever since that long-past epoch for control of the situation. Just as you have seen, and though these are strong words, religion does not exist. I insist— it is only a suit made at the measure of all, a form of power for the clever, and an expensive crutch for those who do not wish to think. In one way or another, all those who wear this suit remain the same. That is one reason why what you have seen has repeated itself so many times on Earth, in the most diverse parts of the continuum of history. On the other hand, 'woman' is the one who lost that war, and who remains latent. Thus she has been charged by 'man' with the weight of all his guilt; he has turned the essence of her naturalness into something filthy and unintelligible. Analyze any belief of the Earth, and you will see the ones that govern will always consider, directly or indirectly, 'man' as superior, whether he is God, Buddha, or any prophet. It is the weight of the flowing of time, not the weight of reality. Have you noticed that all of the most famous prophets are men? This is only an example. . . .

"Behind this eternal man-woman conflict are hidden the biggest persecutions on Earth, division and hatred, as I mentioned before. Wherever there are fanatics, and wherever there are rumors of war, ask first how their women are treated, and you will have the answer to their attitude. While harmony and equality fail to overcome this conflict ... tragic events will continue to happen.

"This explains that those tragic events you witnessed were only the logical consequence of the trajectory followed by the men. They could not allow that advancement, the development of science and knowledge, and even less could they allow it to be led by their worst enemy, the woman. You will travel again soon, even farther beyond ... and you will see how these facts are repeated. You will be able to understand me better, and through your own vision."

The Apprentice sat for a moment, doubtful and silent. A gentle breeze trickled past them, and he tried to understand everything. He knew there was much he would understand bit by bit.

He then asked again, "What happened was unfair ... I wonder what happened to Cyril ... was he left unpunished?"

"Yes, from a certain point of view he was left unpunished," replied Alsam. "And not only that, he was later canonized by the Church. Now he must be adored as a Great Saint ... that is normal."

The Apprentice looked at him in astonishment and quickly responded.

"But how!? That's outrageous ... !" He paused, and then asked again, curious, "But how do you know that?"

Alsam smiled.

"I don't need to know. I only need to know the human mentality, and the result is invariable. The greatest heroes are praised for their crimes. Power always finds a way to justify itself and justify its actions as well . . . that does not change."

Again, the Apprentice asked, "But then Cyril was punished for his crimes?"

"Come on, Asanaro, don't blind yourself with that idea. If it helps as a consolation, what you saw shows that Hypatia, in her martyrdom, died quickly in the prime of her life. Cyril had long to live with the burden of his crimes and injustices . . . how do you think he slept each night? How do you think he was tormented by his own thoughts? Do you think he lived quietly, ever enjoyed something clean and pure? Have you ever considered that as he murdered, as everyone who murders, who persecute those who do not think as they do, those narrow-minded superstitious fanatics, those who organize persecution . . . do they live quietly? Can they even get to sleep?

"Understand that the energy of every mind has alarms to tell them of errors in their actions. When the person hates, he believes himself hated by everyone; when the person cheats, he believes himself cheated by everyone . . . That was the life and the payment of Cyril; his grief was to live with his own darkness. That is the life of all his kind, and that is not a life.

"How do you think Cyril's death was?" continued Alsam. "Do you think it was peaceful? Perhaps those who write the history will say that he died with a 'holy' smile on his lips, but I am certain that in his mind he had to suffer all the harm, the persecutions, the crimes, and injustices that he had committed. The society created by 'man' can be arranged in his way, can arrange appearances as well, but that is all that belongs to them . . . Reality does not belong to them; nor does the Astral, dreams, the Universe, or life after death; not even the Earth belongs to them.

"Where they do not rule, all the stupidities, persecutions, and crimes they can commit are compensated for. It is true, many of them try to claim power in what they call the 'beyond,' but we can be happy that the beyond does not let itself be manipulated by anyone, and that there is beyond the reach of foolish people with their peddling of political favors or their manipulation of public opinion. No matter how many medals, great titles, golden crowns, or cassocks full of diamonds they wear, no matter how many palaces, churches, and luxurious temples they might build, they cannot buy what cannot belong to them: They will never be able to purchase the energies that they do not understand. They might boast that they are messengers, emissaries, the one and only chosen representatives of their God or Gods, and commit any atrocity using those names as a shield, but that means nothing: Only the ignorant masses get scared and let themselves be influenced according to their own needs and laziness.

"No one, not even you or I, has power in the beyond. If you have been granted the possibility of entering into the world of dreams, take it simply and learn with humility what you must learn. You are only a guest."

Asanaro felt relieved, and sensed that he was understanding more.

"It's just that everything was so sad . . ." he said, "too sad. That library, the work they were carrying out . . . all of it must have ended, and on the whim of some high-ranking fanatics . . . I try to understand, but I don't . . ."

"It's true, Asanaro, though unfortunate, and the losses for mankind no one can measure. However, in a certain way it was inevitable, for you cannot go beyond your time-river in such an open and public way without expecting opposition. Discretion is necessary, for every action brings a reaction, and the reaction of human beings in the face of what they do not understand is always the same, and it always has the same cause: fear.

"If human beings were to awaken, can you imagine how much they might advance? Even with all of the problems and interests that have gotten in the way, there has been the possibility for so many positive advancements ... Alexandria's Great Library was a timid experiment, gathering the best of West and East under an open mentality, but it was destroyed ... The 'today' pays the consequences for the failure of that union. Can you imagine what would have happened if humanity hadn't so mutilated its own brain more than fifteen hundred years ago, that truly massive lobotomy that you experienced? Can you imagine East and West united? Yet from that stage on, every scientific advance was persecuted with even more hatred ... It has been fifteen hundred years of delay ... a very dark era, from which, slowly, the world has been recovering, though many continuations are being lived in many parts of the Earth, too many. Ignorance and division last, and they carry hatred within.

"Can you imagine," continued Alsam, "what might have happened if the steam engine you were telling me about had been developed in that age, fourteen centuries before it eventually was? If humans, and especially those who consider themselves powerful, had really supported it, men could have been traveling in space long ago; now they could be visiting other galaxies! They could have overcome starvation, destitution, and devastation on Earth ... or investigated the Astral Travels. They could be researching the energy of the body and the magnetic fields of the mind ... Imagine that, instead of dedicating so much time to dividing the planet, creating so many useless borders, they could work together! Can you imagine if all humanity could have understood, from long ago, that one's own belief is simply a personal option and must not be a fanatical, sectarian, and prejudiced imposition, imposed massively only to allow for control, materialism, and the justification of the actions of power ... ?

"If there were no limits on the mind ... humans would stop being entities, and they could really be called beings ...

"To those who cannot see these things sound now like science fiction fantasies ... but that is the weight of their culture ... of the time-river. The scent of the dark era still lingers ... it is still present ... but it does not matter. Take your lesson, overcome it, and learn to evolve."

Asanaro listened attentively as his Guide continued.

"Now, raise your energy to its maximum, for what has been shown to you has been for you to wake up, once and for all, and with a good slap in the face ... a painful slap, but necessary. You are a stone thrown into the river ... the waves you will produce are countless! Now you carry a new vision, and you must be gladdened by it; do not become sad ... sadness is only another limit! Nothing is unfair or fair in the time-flow that the Bamso has shown to you: Everything is knitted together in the same fabric, and it is only a lesson to polish yourself and come closer to your own crystal-clear spring. Smile at life, because today you have awoken wiser, more free, more understanding, and more conscious, and, best of all, with a much greater thirst to know and evolve."

As Alsam spoke, the Apprentice felt his spirit increase and he began to see things in a wider way, realizing that, after all, life had its own way of teaching, and that he had to learn how to understand it. Whatever unfair thing he may have seen or lived was only a small part in the incalculable processes of a great time-river, as Omboni had said and Alsam now confirmed. He had to begin to see things in their universal way, just like the valleys seen from that rock on high: as a whole ... the mountain slopes, the cliffs, the forests, the river, as well as the hardness and aridity of the stones, as well as life, dreams, and death.

He knew that he had begun a steep road toward understanding what surrounded him, and how much it was part of himself; it was the only road to fully understand who he truly was.

II.

Bon Voyage!

After a good conversation between Guide and Apprentice, they came down from the rock into the camp to prepare their food. A few logs served as a table and some others as chairs, and some branches humbly helped as brooms to sweep the place before they prepared their meal.

They spoke merrily, relaxing, and Asanaro told his Guide about some of the other details he had lived in the Astral World, details that came back into his memory as the day continued.

After a while he was completely relaxed and comfortable. Slowly the Apprentice understood better how everything is part of a necessary process, and that fate would afford him visits to superior and more pleasant worlds.

The meal was ready, consisting mostly of a variety of greens and vegetables, perfect for a pair of diners who shared a taste for natural things. Alsam always had a joke reserved for their conversation, and they laughed together as they ate. The Guide had always said that joy within food had the same effect as cooking it over a natural fire, that it always gained a special taste, no matter how simple the ingredients. Nothing compared to it, none of the fancy dishes of a city restaurant with all of its luxury and artificiality could compare to a meal like that, cooked over a wood fire, with great humor and the air of the mountains.

When sunset came, expectation came to the Apprentice. The night and the stars that cluttered those clear skies of the Universe were an invitation to new discoveries. The bonfire that united Guide and Apprentice before sleep, the diverse subjects of the Apprentice's advancements and achievements became the subtle answer to his wish to launch himself into the galaxy and its mysteries. Watching the flames, their twisting and dancing, smelling their gentle odor, unmistakable and alluring, playing with his imagination to form weak figures of each flame at the center of the bonfire, was the best exercise for Asanaro before going to sleep.

Alsam, getting up to go to bed, smiled and, making a singular gesture with his hands, said, "The night is already ripe . . . it is time to project ourselves . . . Bon Voyage, Asanaro!"

The Apprentice looked at him, smiling, too, and asked, though he already sensed the answer, "And why not a simple good night?"

"Ahaa! You already know . . . If I were an ordinary person, I would say 'good night.' But I know that you are determined to awake for the Bamso. For you there will never again be a 'good night' or a 'sleep well'; these two sentences tell your mind: 'Close your eyes, try to make your body rest so you can continue the system tomorrow, and the day after, and eternally'; they tell you,

'Don't be conscious while you dream or while you are awake, for dreams do not exist, and you cannot be different ... just have a good night and rest well, for it is the best you can take from life; don't bother to imagine anything else.' For you, all that is over.

"From now on, as you have already lived, you will only wish to be told: Bon voyage! and good takeoff!"

Asanaro smiled and nodded. Alsam added, "The world of dreams is something wonderful. Humans can limit and persecute other humans in many ways, but the world of dreams is forbidden to those who are excited by power and materialism. It is another state, into which none who get rich or boast of their authority, their titles or rank can enter; their thoughts and ideas have no meaning in the world of dreams. For them one must say, 'I hope they rest,' for even that they cannot do without swallowing a handful of pills or drugs, and not even these things can truly make them rest. All those who possess 'power,' who abuse, pay dearly for it. They may like to step on others and pretend themselves great, but life is wise, and in its wisdom it takes from them the greatest gift: the conscious dream. For ordinary people there is a distant possibility; they must overcome their fear and their mass mentality, their mediocrity and their taste for being mentally manipulated, their habit of being driven, for that also forbids to them the entrance to the wonderful world of the Astral; for them, good night is enough.

"For you, Asanaro," continued Alsam, "the work is only beginning, the path is long, and that is what makes it wonderful, for it possesses neither goals, nor power, nor riches, and no one on Earth even recognizes it ... this makes it even greater, even more noble. Thus from now on, each time someone tells you good-bye, long for them to tell you instead 'Bon voyage!' for those who have the consciousness of dreams do not sleep while the rest sleep, do not rest while the others rest ... On the contrary, they live while the rest die, reach the top while the rest are lost, enjoy where the others fear and do not see. That is the great secret that you possess now, Asanaro, and do not teach it, for no one deserves it."

The Apprentice was thoughtful for a few moments; he knew that Alsam spoke directly and that for many people his way might seem shocking. He did not want to be left with a question, however, so he asked, "But ... maybe people could wake up a little and have a bit more consciousness in their dreams ..."

Alsam's answer was sharp and came quickly.

"People, Asanaro, are as ignorant as they are foolish. If you wander around offering something, the first question they will ask will be 'What are you trying to pull?' or 'What are you pretending to do?' wondering if you are trying to trick them. Their minds are focused on making a profit, on being crafty, and they are controlled by a fear of change, whatever form it may take ... they think, 'it could never be good,' and it is according to that concept that they would judge you. That is why I have removed myself from that world, why it does not interest me or worry me. To me they are only a swarming throng controlled by an association of wily people who tell them what to think, how to act, and when to do both. But you are always concerned about the people, none of whom would thank you, Asanaro ... that surprises me ..."

The Apprentice was left feeling insecure, but in reality he had reached the same conclusion; he felt no desire to go deeper into the subject, for he knew clearly how Alsam thought.

"Well, Apprentice," Alsam added, "this is a moment for speaking of positive things, for you to leave and take the best sensations to your Astral stage. Enjoy the fire, the stars, the mountain air ... they are the best food for the mind, and for the Great Bamso."

They stood a few moments there, around the bonfire, whose flames and shine still fascinated Asanaro. After a while, the time being right, his Guide said farewell: "Now, Apprentice of Dreams, bon voyage!"

"Bon voyage, Alsam ... !"

III.

The Old Designs
of the Desert

The night passed quietly, and there the Apprentice remained, sitting by the fire. The flames reached toward the sky, singularly long and brilliant, and as he followed them up they seemed to reach the stars. He felt a sudden impulse to touch them, so he did; slowly he passed his hand over the flames, tentatively at first, then thrusting his hand into the fire. Nothing happened—he felt only a little warmth, and no more.

"I'm in the world of dreams... it looks so real... but I know it is... It is real!" he thought.

In that instant everything seemed to glow and the night had its own sensation, which for him seemed clear, as if he could feel the night. All transformed itself in less than a second, everything shone, and in his astonishment at the shape that place was taking, he heard a familiar voice behind him.

"Hehehe ... this time-place being pleasing, Asanaro ..."

The Apprentice turned immediately, and was greeted by a pleasant surprise.

"Omboni! But if it's you . . . ! It's you! You've come here to get me. Where are we going now? I hope you won't leave me again in the middle . . . Huh?!"

As Asanaro spoke the Astral Being turned, made a gesture, and harmoniously extended his hands to center the Apprentice's attention to the majestic horizon, and before Asanaro's eyes he saw that they were in a great and lonely desert, in the lost dry hillsides of cliffs from another world. Omboni spoke.

"Ahaaa . . . I having brought you already! You being beyond time, as they say. And in the Superior Projection of the Bamso, there being no need for you to walk all the way. I having only called you where necessary, in order for you to understand."

Asanaro was amazed at the immensity and loneliness of the desert. Behind him the flames still reached high up into the sky. Omboni continued, "Hehehe . . . well, Asanaro, where thinking we being?"

"Well," the Apprentice relied doubtfully, "I really don't know. In a desert? I suppose . . ."

"Mmm . . . if you wishing to know where-when we being, put less attention in me and more in what surrounds us; remember your mind being like your batu-ma . . ."

"What?" asked Asanaro.

"Hehehe . . . relax and you will understand . . . to translate myself to your mental sparkle, I explaining in your inherited dialect: batu-ma meaning that your mind is what you would call a directional antenna, for that being what it is used to, and from habit becoming. Your antenna catches only one frequency at a time, and only if your mind being tuned correctly can it catch

more than one frequency at a time. You having already begun
your teaching, but that means nothing in the path. That being
why, many times, when I speak to you, you only receive me, and
what being around passes unnoticed. That being why the ones
from your species getting so little in the state of dreams, their
antennae being too directional, and poorly focused... You,
with me, having seen more, for I have helped you, but later it
being time for you, when you must learn to focus your mind,
your antennae, which must being multiform if you wanting the
great vision of the Astral; you must walk wide. Understanding
me now?"

"Well, I think I do ..." answered the doubtful Asanaro.

"Hehehe ... first you must say you understand, later understanding. Now do not focus only on me, and you will know
where-when you are."

The Apprentice of the Astral relaxed and looked toward
Omboni, but without focusing on him; instead he gave his
attention to all that was around him, and as he relaxed he saw
more and, without looking directly, noticed that the surroundings began to change. First, the great bonfire appeared again,
which reminded him of the one at the camp the night before.
Then he seemed to see someone seated close to the fire. Immediately he saw some bushes and realized that the entire place was
not a barren desert. A few ethereal figures appeared close to the
fire, dressed in long gowns like those of desert caravan traders,
and slowly they became more and more real, until they were as
real as any living being. To Asanaro's surprise he suddenly recognized one of them, and said, "Omboni, the people I see here
seem familiar ... Yes, I know! That's Mangazar. But what is he
doing here? And where-when are we?"

"Hehehe ... do you see?" replied the Astral Being, "you being beginning to see on your own, without my help. But I will help you anyway. Yes, you being right, it being Mangazar, and we having followed his time-path, for you having some questions being left from previous encounters and travels we have taken together; these have to be solved, do they not?"

"Yes, Omboni, the journey where I met Hypatia and Mangazar has remained with me. That trip was hard, and I'd like to resolve it and finish the lesson ... I think there's something missing."

"Hehehe ... if you feel it, you, being of the species that doubts, being like it being, and being better for you to resolve what orbits within your head like a planet around a sun. Your restlessness will take us on stronger and stranger journeys, but first let's complete this one. Our place-time being projected only a few years after last we saw Mangazar, and we being far from the city of Hypatia. Now pay attention, and let us come closer so we might hear."

They turned together toward the fire and, before Asanaro's eyes, the scene became clearer. The fire lacked the proportions he had seen; the flames were normal and the fire less broad. There were several men settling the camp and moving things from one place to another, perhaps a group of porters for the caravan, which also included a large group of camels. The place itself seemed to be a small oasis within those great desertlike steppes, populated only by small bushes and occasional scrub brush.

There sat Mangazar by the fire. His faced showed the passing of a few years, yet more than the years it seemed that he carried the weight of the past, and of having witnessed many painful things. He was absorbed in his thoughts, distracted by the dance of the flames, when two older men approached him: one was tall with gray, disheveled hair, and the other was shorter and dark skinned.

The Astral Apprentice followed the scene from nearby. The shorter of the two men lay his hand affectionately on Mangazar's shoulder, and both men joined him in watching the fire. Asanaro's attention increased and he was even more amazed when he realized that those two men were Horace and Akena. They were there, safe and sound, though the years had left their mark. Old Akena, Hypatia's faithful servant, was nearly the same as before, yet now his cheek bore a great scar, which Asanaro supposed was a consequence of the actions of Cyril's monks.

The scene was now more interesting to the Apprentice, who sat down as if he were just another member of the group listening to that conversation lost in time.

Akena spoke first.

"My Lord, Mangazar, do not torture yourself anymore. I am certain that my Lady, my noble Lady would not have wanted you to dwell on her with so much grief."

"I'm sorry, Akena, I can't help it," replied Mangazar. "I can't help thinking of her each sunset, and every night of my life. The fact that I could have saved her will always weigh on my conscience, that I could have done something else, something more, I could have been by her side earlier, or better, I could have died with her . . . I don't know . . ."

"No, do not say that. She wouldn't have wanted it; she would never have wanted you to face the same fate that she did."

Horace, a quiet and wise man, spoke up then.

"Come on, Mangazar, gladden your spirit! Hypatia would be

happy to know that you are well, and that you have saved many of her books. You must do many things in this life, things to keep alive the ideals that moved her. If you let yourself go to the sadness and the grief, then Cyril will have won his war against knowledge and freedom; but if you hold on to your mind, your freedom, and your imagination, he, with all his ignorance, will never win."

There was a pause, after which Mangazar said, "What I'll never understand is how people can let themselves be so fooled. No one, not even Orestes, was able to face Cyril, and thus he did whatever he wanted. He murdered Hypatia, we know, everyone knows, and no one has been able to do anything about it. Sometimes I think it would have been better to go straight to Cyril and murder him, as he did to Hypatia."

"No," replied Horace, "that is not the answer, and you know that. Cyril and those who think as he does are experts in war, and we are not, Mangazar. We study, we think and admire life, and we know no other way of seeing things . . . that is our weakness, yet at the same time it is our strength. If you had gone and killed him, you'd have been just another fanatic like him."

"It's true," said Mangazar, "but it's just that in addition to all of this, that cretin destroyed all that remained of the Library, burning and stealing at his whim. It's such a small portion that we've rescued . . ."

"It was inevitable," responded Horace. "I haven't been able to finish my project, either. I know my machine would have worked, but it doesn't matter, for I'll build it anyway. And that is what you must do, Mangazar, finish the work you have started, for that is the best way to cherish the memory of Hypatia, even though Cyril has proposed to erase her from history."

The night was clear, and the fire warmed the conversation of the three men, now lonely pilgrims of the desert.

"At least twenty camels loaded with cloth . . ." said Akena, smiling, "I mean, with papers, all having passed unnoticed out of Alexandria. Let those people stay there with their rioting, for the memory of my Lady will live and what we have saved is enough, and well . . . we have saved ourselves; we wouldn't have lasted much longer in that city. And you have saved those original writings you were studying . . ."

"But that's nothing compared to the Library," added Mangazar, "there is so much that has been lost . . ."

"Come on, come on man!" replied Horace, "I am older and I keep my spirit high—you have saved the original writings about the Saint of Issa! The Bishop took only copies—I bet that fool boasted as he burned them or locked them in the basement of some dark monastery. With all of life's irony, maybe they wound up in Constantinople or Rome, just as you had wished!

"Mangazar," continued Horace, "the load on these twenty camels is enough for the minds of human searchers. Our friends in the outskirts of Jerusalem will know how to take care of what we are giving them, and they will copy and preserve these writings: They will survive! When people wish to learn more, they will know where to look . . . otherwise they will follow ignorant men like Cyril and the Church that the new Empire announced, with or without parchments. After all, knowledge is a gift that humans give to themselves, and if they are not ready for that gift, there is nothing we can do about it. What we have saved is enough, and we can still accomplish much, especially you, the youngest of us three, the one who was closest to Hypatia, the one who should have the most courage."

"That's true," answered Mangazar, his voice now more relieved, "my happiness has been greater than the sadness that takes me sometimes. I knew, I lived it, and that is enough ... each time I think of her, from now on, I will think of how happy I was, and nothing else; the truth is I should leave sadness to evil and twisted hearts like Cyril's. Everything that has happened has happened for a reason ... It seems that we need to suffer, need to have powerful experiences. This whole situation has made me think ... it has made me value, and see deeper into things. Before I trusted in those I shouldn't have, like Celio, who ended up selling us to the Bishop for a handful of coins, a position within the Empire, and, according to him, to save his own skin. In a short time so many things have happened to me, but in a way I feel they have happened for a reason, and that somehow we are being directed, maybe even watched ... and that, in some way, we are part of a great task, of a great teaching. Perhaps even the suffering is only a lesson. Perhaps suffering is the only way of ennobling ourselves, maybe it is our master, and if it is necessary for people as ignorant as Cyril and his followers to exist in order to cause us suffering, we must accept it as part of our lesson, but also as an incentive to look toward the truth with more determination and devotion than ever, without prejudice, and without the superstitions created by religions.

"I would have liked very much to have taken this journey with Hypatia ..." continued Mangazar, "but if nothing had happened, we never would have done it. Really, what happens to us, the surprises that life gives to us, are too much. One thing has led to another, and what happened there has served as a lesson to us all, especially to me. Because of her sacrifice much of the knowledge that was kept in the place she so loved has been saved; her death saved us from total destruction, and despite the attempt to stain and erase her memory, it has instead been recorded for eternity. Sometimes I see our world entering into darkness, but this is necessary if the sun is to rise again tomorrow, and for human beings to finally have their moment of truth, of liberation and comprehension of all beings."

The three lonely men smiled, transmitting a sensation of relief, and though the weight of memory hung heavy on them, their eyes shone with the vigor of restless searchers. While they sat in tranquil silence, Asanaro followed the scene carefully and in his own way understood and sympathized with those three people who appreciated knowledge as much as they had appreciated Hypatia, who had inspired them all in different ways.

Akena intervened again, now more joyful.

"My Lord, Mangazar, for a few days now I've meant to show you something; now that we are more relaxed and on our journey, I'd like you to see it."

Akena went quickly to the cargo, and from a saddlebag he took a relatively small parchment. He hurried back to the others, and once there he said, "Well, this is what I wanted to show you. It is a copy that I made personally of the speeches of an old philosopher from two centuries ago. You've probably heard of him; his name was Celsus. He speaks brilliantly and I have saved this text from the fire that surely awaited it in Alexandria. Listen to me, for what is written here is related to everything that has happened. It would have delighted me to have read it to Cyril's face."

Akena began carefully unfolding the papyrus, searching the text for pieces appropriate to the occasion. He carefully came closer to the fire, and as his companions watched him attentively he began to read aloud the words of the philosopher. They mostly concerned the machinations and conspiracies created by the religious as they attempted to impress and trick the people, about how what was written in the Gospels had been manipulated, changed, and extrapolated, and how the menace of the divine was a common way for people to dominate, control, and lead the masses.

The three men looked at one another and smiled. Horace said, "Do you see, Mangazar? Celsus was a great man—we are two centuries after his time and what he said is still as current as it was then. There will always be thinkers, like Hypatia or him, to lend a little clarity to our sad humanity. They may be persecuted and erased from history, but there will always be one ... always ..."

"That's certain," answered Mangazar, "and now it is our turn. In Alexandria I began something that I will now finish, even if it may only be for you and me. I can imagine how much these writings I have found and saved about the Saint of Issa would encourage the curiosity of a philosopher such as Celsus. Many people should know the truth of what they are made to believe. The Empire imposes its ideas on them, but they are only at their convenience, and the people swallow them whole. These places make me wonder what the real life of Jesus of Nazareth was like, in whose name so many crimes have been committed and who knows how many more to come. I would have liked to have known who he really was, how he thought, without the adornments of time ... he must have been someone special, for he was equally persecuted and misunderstood, which says quite a bit about him."

"Mangazar," Akena asked, "are you still thinking of traveling to the East? It's a long, hard journey."

"Yes, Akena, after Jerusalem I wish to continue north, to see old Palmyra; from there, as I've mentioned before, I would like to take the road to the East, until I reach the mountains of old India, past where Alexander went. My notes and the documents I have read speak about the valleys of a place called Kashmir, and about the Land of Eternal Snows, where I believe more secrets are hidden about the Saint of Issa. I want to see those places, know them, and discover their mysteries. Nothing calls me back to Alexandria, or any city under the influence of people like Cyril; I have learned my lesson and I sense that the Old Empire is turning into something more dark and sinister, intolerant, and more dangerous . . . at least for those who think."

"You are right," added Horace, "nothing binds me, either, and if you do not mind, I will join you in your pilgrimage. Perhaps there, far to the East, we can build my machine!" His eyes sparkled. "I have heard, too, that there are towns beyond India that have developed a system to thrust things beyond the skies! Imagine a force like that united with my machine—why, perhaps we could visit the Moon!"

Mangazar and Akena laughed heartily, and soon they transmitted that feeling to Horace, who joined in their laughter even though he had spoken in utter sincerity. The laughter of the men, the bonfire, and the silence of the place felt both mysterious and comforting.

At that moment Omboni addressed Asanaro, who was laughing with the men as if he were one of them, a new pilgrim added to the caravan.

"Hehehe . . . it being time to leave, Asanaro. They have settled their course, which being already their line in the time-river. Now you must follow your own."

The Apprentice paused and turned toward Omboni without answering. After a moment, he said, "All right, Omboni. I was already thinking that I was part of the group . . . I've always liked expeditions . . ."

"Yesss . . . your energy being very volatile. They, too, having been travelers, they three will pass through many places, but now being your time for walking . . ."

"Where-when are we going?"

"Hehehe . . . you already asking as Astral Being . . . Where-when you wanting to go?"

"Well," answered the Apprentice, "I was thinking about Mangazar's restlessness over those writings on the life of the one he called the Saint of Issa. I've always had that same curiosity, for as long as I can remember."

"Your curiosity being part of your time-river, it being normal. When you speak, your time speaks . . . when you speaking, your time will no longer speak."

"What do you mean, Omboni?"

"Hehehe . . . you will understand. Now you must overcome your restlessness, but beforehand I will ask you unnecessarily: Being you ready to see, and not to interpret? Do not answer. This travel being strong for you, being strong encountering your time-fluid.

"For now, relax, become happy, and follow me. There being yet many surprises!"

IV.

Amlom

They began walking together through a path in that desert landscape. Everything seemed normal, nothing out of the ordinary, and slowly a new day was approaching. The Astral Travelers were conversing, like two mysterious beings invisible to the world; at times they seemed to walk while at others they appeared to slide, dragging their feet through the air.

Asanaro asked, "But Omboni, explain one thing to me. In tonight's projection. why haven't I come to this time-place in the same way as usual? Because we're really in the Bamso, in the Universal Record, outside of my time . . ."

"Ahaaaa . . . you like all explained! That having no end. But since you like, I will speak. Your mind being a batu-ma, remember? It directs and focuses, but I help you and guide you along the road. If you have a question about the journey, the process . . .

we having had to take the whole road, as in the beginning, and I having been able to show you what this state we are in now being, how to enter and reach it. You have understood that this stage not existing from the eye of your time-river, being its past and its projection in space, years from the necessary light-ray. You have already seen that one can travel into space with thought, having a speed faster than the light-ray. All that road you have already traveled, already understood. And then you reach the necessary distance and find the channel of space that connects to the where-when we wanting to reach. All that you have appreciated, understood . . . ?"

"Well . . . yes," said the Apprentice, "I remember our first travels, the ways we took, but why aren't they necessary now? That is my question."

"I have already explained. The road being within your mind, and for her it not being necessary to walk the whole path again. That being why I have called you directly to this place, and you have come. Not always being the same, your state and lucidity, you might think it being a dream and forget, but now you being lucid and will remember. The whole road not having been necessary, only you being. In your words, I could call that an Astral Blink. The mind being faster than you; it projects you faster than you reach to understand, for you having been influenced by your time-river, and for that sometimes you only dream, and not the truth, and not yourself . . ."

"Astral Blink?" the Apprentice asked.

"Hehehe . . . yesssss . . . Hehehe . . . In your dimension your mind composing time continuously, as when uniting an image from one blink to another. In this world, your Bamso, mind should become accustomed to move within time and space from one blink to the next ... and form them as a continuity. The Astral being infinite; you having many things yet to learn. The important being that you enjoy this dimension, that being the best lesson."

"Yes ... sometimes I enjoy this so much. It seems so real ... more than the life in my body ... I'm not even sure if I'm here or not, and when I'm there I'm not sure of it either ..."

Suddenly Asanaro stopped, for he thought he saw something out of the corner of his eye, like a fast-moving shadow, strange and whitish.

"Hehehe ..." Omboni chuckled. "Only see, and you will see, Asanaro. You always visiting, and not seeing."

They were still walking, or, rather, gliding through the ridges and cols of this lonely place, and the Apprentice was becoming more aware of the surroundings, searching out that strange thing he had seen before, but as they moved only nature unfolded before him, with all its beauty and simplicity. Bit by bit the vegetation grew more dense and trees began to appear. The view became a form of rest for the Astral Apprentice.

Again that ephemeral shadow flitted by, then vanished quickly in the bushes.

"Omboni, did you see it?" asked Asanaro. "Did you see that shadow? It's strange, and it seems to be following us. This whole situation feels familiar ..."

The Astral Being did not pay much attention to him, only answering, "Mmm ... must being an Amlom."

"What?" asked the surprised Apprentice of Time. "An Amlom? What's that?" He looked around them, searching out that bizarre mix between shade and light.

"Hehehe ... being a playful being, good natured ... It come

with messages, or only out of curiosity. There being many Amlom, but few of them contact, for they do not like your species, finding them boring and serious!"

At that moment Asanaro opened wide his Astral Eyes, for just a few feet in front of them, from behind some stout olive trees appeared the most beautiful white horse he had ever seen. It was playing with its head and pawing the ground, as if calling their attention. It was a beautiful being, and it wore an expression like that of a naughty boy.

Asanaro was shocked and stammered out, "Do you see that, Omboni? Do you see it! He's greeting us! But how can that be? We're invisible in this state ... I don't understand ... But, Omboni, say something ... It's the ... A ... Am ... Amlom, or whatever you said."

Omboni stood silent, smiling. Then to the further amazement of the Apprentice the horse gently turned its head, and nuzzling its side with its lips, great wings grew out from it. With the wings spread out the horse looked like the Pegasus from the old myths, elegant and graceful. Asanaro was so fascinated he could barely speak, repeating only, very quietly, "Omboni, tell me ... is it an Amlom?"

Omboni's smile was even wider now.

"Hehehe ... Nooo, Asanaro ... no, he not being an Amlom ... She being an Amlom!"

If the Apprentice had been surprised before, now he was stupefied, for out from behind the Pegasus appeared a new Being. She was the most beautiful creature that he had ever seen: a beautiful girl with a smiling face and anxious, bright eyes, brimming over with innocent joy. That Being, that young girl, looked straight at him as she stood there, caressing the Pegasus, hugging him and playing with his long white hair. Those two figures, from a dimension or world unknown to Asanaro, looked radiant and distinctive. The girl wore a soft dress of green, like the smooth color of a forest after the rain. Her face was delicate, tender, and expressive. He felt that he had seen her before, though he did not know where.

Still astonished, he could barely mutter, "Bu ... bu ... but, who are they ... ?"

"Hehehe ... being-are only a blink in the dimension ..." was Omboni's cryptic answer.

"But ... I don't understand ..."

"Ahaaa ... for that not understanding, you Being from the Species that Doubts, saying too much, 'I don't understand, I don't understand, I don't understand' ..."

"But ..." replied the Apprentice, "if we're in the Great Universal Record, nothing from the Record can see us; it's only a projection, so how can she see me? And ... and, she's smiling at me!"

"Hehehe ... In your world teaching that for everything there being a rule ..." Omboni continued, mimicking the Apprentice, "'If we being in the Great Record, we must follow this rule ...' which does not help here-Astral-now!"

The strange girl gently lifted herself onto the Pegasus, laying her head on the long and elegant neck of the white animal. She seemed to be speaking with him, and the Pegasus moved his head graciously, spreading his wings lightly, apparently approving of what she was telling him. Asanaro was hypnotized by what he saw.

"It seems ..." he mumbled, "it seems ... that she's inviting me to join her ... I never thought we'd see anything like this ... I know I've seen her before!"

Omboni replied, "Hehehe ... yesss ... she invites you ... hohoho ... the small vision invites you ..."

The Apprentice replied, "But what should I do?"

To which Omboni immediately answered, "Why do you always ask when you having already resolved ... Being your mind ... go with her ..."

Asanaro's Astral Heart began beating faster, and for the first time he realized that he could have such a thing, an Astral Heart, with the same sensations of a heart beating in the flesh. Now he was sure he didn't want to wake up, he couldn't believe what was happening. "It's a dream," he thought for a second, and then told himself, "Yes, I know it's a dream, but it's conscious, and real ... and even more solid, more definite, and more sensible than reality!"

The Pegasus and the young girl astride it came a few steps closer. She was smiling, looking tenderly at the Apprentice. He, too, stepped forward, and extended his arm to her. He felt the soft touch of the gentle hand of the Being. He felt her to be subtle, essential, enough for all sensations, and at the same time it all seemed familiar.

It was like blinking. He only opened his eyes and saw the roof of his tent; he was back in the world. He closed his eyes again, making a desperate attempt to return to the last instant, and he could feel being in the air, flying with the Amlom on the Pegasus, among the mountains, but it vanished quickly. He opened his eyes again, hoping to wake up in the Astral, but he was uselessly still in his tent. The reconnection with his body was sudden, the weight and the invariable sensation of wearing wet and heavy clothes. He soon discovered a new pain in his neck, which seemed to come from having slept in an awkward position. There was nothing to do now but relax and wake up not brusquely but slowly, dedicating a few quiet minutes to the exercises necessary to refresh the memory of dreams.

However, this time they did not work as Asanaro would have liked; he remembered many details about the pilgrims and their caravan, and about Omboni, but when coming back to his meeting with the mysterious Being and her Pegasus, everything was blurry. He felt that he had lived something in his dreams that was very out of the ordinary, even a sensation of happiness or illusion; in truth, he couldn't even explain it to himself.

Half an hour later he rose as usual. The field had the pure, unmistakable scent of dawn, which combined with the smell of the fire that Alsam had already made to prepare breakfast. The combination was perfect, and it fed him inside.

Almost instantly Alsam appeared, full of energy. Asanaro could tell that he had already been awake for a while.

"Suam Odaonai, Asanaro! I can tell you've taken your Astral practices seriously. Every morning, you're stuck in your sheets!" The two had a good laugh at this, for even before beginning these practices the Apprentice had gained a reputation for enjoying his sleep.

"I'm sorry," answered the smiling Apprentice, "the truth is that I am taking it seriously. But I wouldn't miss breakfast!"

They laughed again, long and hard. Soon they sat and had their breakfast, their spirits high, for happiness was always on the menu those days.

As they ate, Alsam said to the Apprentice, "Your energy is strong. I don't even need to ask how your studies in the Astral World have been going."

"It's true," answered Asanaro. "I feel especially happy today, I don't know . . . it was a good night, restful and constructive. I feel like I have two lives, and I don't know anymore which one is greater or more interesting."

"That is good," answered the Guide, "you are waking up. Enjoy whatever you live, in one dimension or the other . . . That is what's most important."

They both continued eating quietly.

"There's one thing that's bothering me this morning," said the Apprentice. "There's a part of my dream that is still very present and conscious, but the rest of it has been erased. It was something different than what I've lived so far, and I don't know how to remember it."

"Patience," answered Alsam, "patience. Usually when you enter higher states in the Astral, you'll notice that certain stages are relatively easy to center or remember, but others will slip away from you, and that is because they are too direct or too strong, and also because you're about to be shown something new for which you are not totally prepared. If you are patient and continue with your exercises, you will find that those new stages or visits will repeat themselves, and you will understand them better and live them more fully."

"There's one simple question that I haven't asked you yet, Alsam."

"Tell me . . ."

"Who or what is Omboni? And who are those beings that have been appearing lately, who don't correspond to the record

I might have in my memory of Earth ... ? And, especially ...
who is that she Being?"

"That is a great question, Asanaro ... and, generally, great
questions lead us to other questions, not to definite answers.
The core of that reality you will have to discover for yourself.
The Astral is yours and answers to your call ... the more you
awaken in the Astral, the more the clear and fine essence of what
you do not yet understand will come closer to you. If you want
my best advice, I will tell you to make the most of these few
days, Asanaro. Relax, and live your experiences to the utmost.
Each moment in the Astral is unrepeatable."

V.

A Road to the Universe

The day passed, and the Apprentice had hardly noticed. Time was losing its old meaning, and reality began to take on the character of dreams, only that in dreams the sensations were stronger and clearer. The sun rose to its zenith and began to descend, continuing its never-ending blinking between day and night, between one world and the other.

That afternoon passed more quickly than any before, as teacher and student walked and talked in the hills near their refuge.

At one point Alsam said, "It is not much longer before the rest of the students will gather and come here."

"You're right! I'd forgotten about that . . . but, you know," added Asanaro, "the truth is, now that you mention it, I don't really want them to come yet. I've progressed in such a strange way here, in this isolation, that I really don't want them to come and interrupt us."

The Guide was thoughtful for a few moments, then answered, "It is normal, for you have formed a field of energy that is yours, for yourself, so much so that you don't want anyone to interrupt you. That field of concentration allows you to advance in the consciousness of dreams, and unconsciously you are aware that as soon as you are interrupted, your concentration will no longer be the same. But don't let it upset you, for there will come a time in which you will be able to do your work no matter what the circumstances, and you will not need this loneliness. Everything changes . . . get used to it."

They continued to walk quietly, and while the Apprentice thought about everything his Guide had said, Alsam spoke about many ways to center memory in the Astral World across various circumstances.

The day had been a good one yet it seemed to languish on. The sky shone an intense, extraordinary blue particular to the remotest places of the world, and from time to time they could see a long cloud hanging in the sky.

Between short expeditions to the surroundings and their daily labors and activities, the days passed, and despite Asanaro's dedication to his exercises, the results weren't impressive; only a couple of semi-lucid encounters with dreams, which weren't enough to satisfy him, for he had become accustomed to the stronger sensations that the Bamso produced in all its states.

He continued his practices regardless, not letting himself be intimidated by the parenthesis that seemed to be enclosing his control of consciousness in dreams, though he was beginning to feel the pangs of restlessness. He feared that he might never have

those experiences again, and the fact that his classmates were to
arrive soon only added to his tension.

Those final days grew long for Asanaro, without any new
encounters, for when he achieved consciousness in the Astral
he felt like a child with a new toy and wished only to return to
that feeling.

Soon enough, the date for the arrival of his fellow students was
upon them. For the Apprentice it meant that there was little time
left to develop his Astral Consciousness; he knew that those open
spaces, the nature and the solitude, were an irreplaceable element
in the exercises of conscious projection. When he thought about
how everyone else would be joining them, and then there would
only be a few days before they returned to the city and its routine,
Asanaro lost his quietude and his nightly lucidity diminished. To
his mind the city meant limitation, and recalling the electrical
wires and poles made him nervous. Even though he could smile
at this, knowing that everything was relative to the mind and his
own will, the practice was more complex than the theory.

The seventeenth day had come and there was barely time
left to complete that stage. It was one of his last nights and
Asanaro's restlessness had only increased. The darkness advanced
and he could not fall asleep, despite trying several relaxation
exercises. He got up and went outside, where he saw the small
glow of the bonfire left from dinner. Without the moon it was
very dark, but a vast sea of stars spread itself across the vault of
the sky, broken only at its borders by the shadows of the mountains, their silence intermittently hidden by the soft litany blowing through the trees.

He thought that Alsam must be asleep, so, following his compulsion, he walked noiselessly toward the field where his Guide's
schemes lay. He felt both fear and respect for that place, and for a
moment he doubted whether or not it was a good idea; besides,
why did he want to go there anyway? Yet while he thought,
without realizing it he was already on his way there, silent, grop-
ing his way through the dark, climbing the small slope, passing
through the bushes, and recognizing a shadow in the middle of
the great circle. His heart jumped . . . he stood stock-still, but as
he sharpened his sight he saw that it was Alsam himself.

There he stood, working on his figures, looking upward at
the starry skies, then moving toward one of the edges of the
circle, forming a new figure out of sticks, with the help of small
stones. He stood there for a moment, still, in meditation. Then
the Guide returned to the center of the circle, looked upward
again, then down to the horizon, as if he were searching for
something or measuring something immeasurable to common
eyes. He took a group of sticks from the circle's center, which
he seemed to have gathered there before, and moving to another
point on the circle continued with that singular endeavor.

Asanaro was surprised, and was unsure of whether he should
interrupt his teacher, continue watching, or leave without saying a word, if any or all could be taken as lacking respect. He
crouched, silent and doubtful, and at nearly the same time heard
the voice of Alsam.

"I see you cannot sleep, let alone practice."

The Apprentice felt found-out, and as he quickly stood up
he hit his head on a tree branch.

"Ouch! I mean, I'm sorry Alsam . . . I don't mean to bother
you . . ."

"Bother ...? Bother ...? Come on, come on ... come closer and enjoy the stars."

Asanaro respectfully entered the circle. Alsam spoke again, looking at the great way of the Galaxy.

"It is not always so easy to go to sleep. Whenever that happens, if you have the chance, don't waste it, and watch the Universe instead."

The Apprentice replied, "It's really beautiful, and comforting ... Every time I look up on a night like this one, I feel so small and insignificant ..."

"Well, Apprentice, we are ... however, our insignificance is also part of the greatness you see up there, and in that way, we cease being small or big."

The night was filled with a quiet conducive to meditating and clearing the mind. Asanaro, a little timid, said, "Well ... the truth is I didn't want to interrupt what you were doing ... I don't know, it looks to me like a secret ..."

"No ... no ..." answered Alsam. "No, Apprentice, what I was doing may be incomprehensible to you, but not secret. Have you not yet seen enough in your projections to the Bamso? Only ignorant or closed-minded people want to cross out as hidden or secret what they don't understand. You should move beyond that ... the Universe is not a secret, but because of our limited way of thinking it becomes impossible to understand. That isn't the Universe's fault ... on the contrary, it offers itself openly.

"For many ignorant people who have governed the history of human beings, what some scientists thought to discover and explore was a sinister secret. Based on that argument they could justify their persecutions, as you have already seen in the times of Hypatia: She was neither the first nor the last victim of that mentality, and many have followed her to that fatal destination. If you think about it, it is the same as what happened to investigators like Michael Servetus, who dared to scientifically explore the human body; or Galileo Galilei, who was forced to choose between apologizing for his discoveries or dying; or Johannes Kepler, who was also persecuted for his astronomical discoveries, which were contrary to the dogmas of those who governed at the time. Closer in the flow of time you have the case of William Reich, who dared to investigate energy and its relation to the body and mind of humans, and beyond ... he, too, paid a high price for his restlessness. The list of persecutions is countless. New ideas and those who hold them are always considered dangerous. In the past they were considered hidden, secret, and heretical, and were eliminated; nowadays it is the same, only the methods are more refined. If you want to eliminate someone, you simply call the newspapers, and they do the job that before was done by the executioner or the stake. From there on the trial is easy. 'Secret' is a word for the ignorant, not for you, Asanaro.

"If someone wants to be a surgeon," Alsam continued, "she must memorize an entire system. First she must be admitted, via tests and other systems, to the place where she will be taught, aside from getting enough 'materialism' to pay for the studies themselves. Later on, after enduring many years of sacrifice, hours upon hours of hard work, she gains her degree, only now having to specialize in surgery, for which she needs a mentor, a Guide in that field who will explain everything to her in minute detail, who she can watch at work, performing operations, and she will have to be quiet and humble before her Surgeon-Guide if she really wants to learn the finer details of the field. It is a long process and requires a great constancy. For a normal person this whole path and the knowledge it leads to could be seen as something secret or hidden, but if you look at it with an open mind, you will see that it is not. As in all sciences and arts, if someone wants to learn, they must make some sacrifices, dedicate a significant effort, and have outstanding discipline . . . and all this makes mediocre, ignorant, and envious people catalog those who are able to project themselves beyond the mass as strange.

"Everything you have learned in the physical and mental spheres is not a secret: It is an art. For those who are not able to do what you have done or to have your discipline, this Art will be a secret, but this is not the fault of the Art, only of the narrow and limited mind.

"And beware, Apprentice," continued Alsam, "of speaking about the Art of the Bamso with those who are not prepared, for you will only win their envy and, after that, their incomprehension and anger, as if you were a scientist bearing new discoveries in the dark ages of the Inquisition."

There was a silence, then the Apprentice said, "You are right, Alsam. Sometimes I am too superficial, but I want to change that and learn. I don't know why, but I just thought of something I heard Omboni say in the Astral, that I'm also part of the time-river . . ."

"That's true," answered the Guide. "You are not apart from the weight of the mentality that exists in all the people. Now you are more aware, and you are more willing to listen, which is a huge step that only a few take. Most of the people allow themselves to be dragged by the force of the time-river that pulls them, and they accept too easily what they inherit from the past. There are but a few who innovate and experiment for themselves. People classify themselves, they are dragged without an already established design. That is the weight of the time-river. They go to war, they kill, without ever knowing why or what for. Yet they never even ask, or even consider it strange. They only consider good what is given to them as good and bad what is given them as bad. It is in that scheme of thinking that gods are raised up when it's appropriate, dressed up with the appropriate look . . . in the end you'll realize that it was just a small group of cunning people who decided to protect their own interests, to use the things of which we have spoken over these past days so they could govern thousands of millions of people. From a certain point of view those millions approve of it, for they do not want to think for themselves, and if any do, they are the best guardians and accusers at the service of those who control them.

"You come from that world, and it is inevitable that you now participate in the time-river, but now at least you are conscious, and that is a great responsibility. If you know how to keep your balance, you can flow in any water, for you will know your own nature."

In the heights of the sky a shooting star burned quickly, and Asanaro meditated over what he heard, from the solid and known things of Earth to the impalpable infinite yet to be known, and he valued even more what he had learned. He gazed long into the heights and around him until, finally, he asked, "Alsam, I don't want to be too intrusive, but what are you doing with all of these figures? I've never seen anything like them before... you've never made anything like them in the city."

The Guide stood silent for a moment, watching the stars. After a while, he spoke.

"Remember... for you, years ago, when you were only a beginner, new to the Osseous Art, in the first classes each movement seemed a whole mystery to you, like a lost piece of a great puzzle. Over time, as you have been advancing and have gained a basic mastery over the movements, you have come to understand the meaning of the loose pieces, you have given them a form, and they are accomplishing an objective. To you they have become a language, which for someone who does not know it, who is not able to see beyond, seems mysterious and a secret. You have had your moment of learning, of listening, and of practicing what you've learned... and that same moment, that same progression, you have been experiencing in the Astral World... and just as in the Art, as you advance you become more aware of how much you can accomplish, but even more aware of how little you actually know.

"You ask me about what you see here," continued the Guide.

"For you they are only designs, just as for someone who does not know it, your Art is only a complex gymnastics or a strange defense. In the same way, what you appreciate around you is not, or are not, strange and indecipherable figures . . . it is a road . . . a road to the Universe . . . Today you do not understand it, for you are just beginning to walk . . . . with time this road will tell you things that you never imagined, and you will again discover how great your knowledge could be, and at the same time you will be aware of how small it is. As soon as you decipher this path, you will also be able to travel to higher worlds within the Astral. Be patient, Apprentice, and your time will come."

Alsam stood and walked toward one of the figures on the periphery of the circle, and the Apprentice watched him with curiosity. He seemed to be looking for something, and almost immediately he came back to the center. Asanaro was anxious to know what was happening, but he remained silent. The Guide gestured for him to sit, and they both did so. Then he said, in a quiet yet profound way, "Well, Apprentice, you have begun your path in the Bamso. Slowly you begin to appreciate the flows from whence you come, and begin to understand how they have been directed in both past and present. You have begun to walk your own road, and you have discovered that today, new flows begin to refresh you. Once the doors of the Bamso open, they never close again, and you can never go back to who you were. Before you were a piece of wood being carried by currents you didn't even know existed; now you begin to be the owner of yourself, and because of that, the owner of your dreams."

The Guide took a small object from his sleeve and showed it to the Apprentice: It was a flat, wooden oval no bigger than his thumb. He gave it to Asanaro, who took it carefully. Looking closely at it, the Apprentice saw how finely carved it was. On one side it had careful figures like the ones Alsam had made around the circle in that field. On the reverse there were others, different and more complex. The Apprentice held it tightly, with two hands, sensing that it was important.

Then Alsam continued, "Keep it carefully ... what you knew here, is there written. Every time you feel, carry it with you: It is the Great Symbol of what you have learned, and of what you are, yourself."

Asanaro was thoughtful, and he did not know how to thank his Guide, even though he did not fully understand what he had received. He sat silent.

Yet many questions still circled in his mind. Now more than ever, he wondered from where-when came the teachings of his mysterious and extraordinary Guide, but he did not dare to ask.

Alsam looked upward, toward the stars and the infinite tunnel that forms the Universe, and answered, "You will know ... you will know ..."

The night was extraordinary. The Guide explained in detail many of the teachings of the infinite Astral World, and about the Mind. For Asanaro the hours flew past, and it was nearly dawn when they said their farewells and each went to rest in his own shelter.

The next morning Asanaro woke ... later than usual. The day was cloudy.

VI.

The Last Voyage

I t was their last afternoon alone, already the eighteenth day since Asanaro had made that sudden decision to come there, where he had encountered so many amazing surprises. All was quiet.

An unusual fog had settled in and covered the whole area around those fields, as well as the camp. That afternoon Alsam continued with his teachings, though hurrying a little through many things. He showed his Apprentice in detail how to use the small oval-shaped piece of wood; he also explained its purpose, its form, and how it would help him in the path he had already begun. The afternoon was shorter than usual, and the fog grew denser, until the tents were barely visible from the fire. The fog lifted a little after sunset, the air grew fresher, and both Guide and Apprentice, rather tired, went to sleep earlier than usual.

Asanaro, in his refuge and through his meditations, entertained himself by listening to the sound of the wind, which prowled through the silence like a sweet and melancholy flute. The sound sent his imagination to faraway places, places even more isolated than where he now was, where forgotten hermits of elder days might have experienced the strange world of consciousness in dreams. After a moment he felt himself falling asleep.

At nearly the same time he felt a compulsion to get up, but he found himself heavy and numb. He wondered what time it was, and if, as usual, he would be the last one up. He sat up slowly but he could see nothing, and a question crossed his still-sleepy mind: Was he awake, or still sleeping? He tried to open his eyes but couldn't, or were they already open and it was simply too dark? He was still confused and tried to clear his vision, but he could not.

All of a sudden, like a spark, he realized that he was still sleeping, and he was experiencing sensations from beyond the barrier of dreams. Slowly everything became clearer, and he stood up to see his physical body was there, lying down beneath him. It was strange to see his own body, actually a bit disappointing. He thought, "It's much better to see yourself from the inside, where you don't look so bad, the same as with your voice . . . it never sounds bad to its owner, but when we hear it played back it always sounds awful, hollow, and disappointing."

He turned his gaze and centered his mind in; for the moment it was better to forget that he had a body. He passed through his tent as if it were nothing, only a phantasmagorical veil that melts on contact.

Already outside, trying to subtly direct his thoughts, he began his meditations to increase the energy of his projections and consciousness. He knew that if he did not take that opportunity, the consciousness he was living would turn to a normal state of dreams, undefined, like a ship without a helm.

The fog was still dense, and only by wishing it he levitated a few inches off the ground and went into that fog, ready for anything, with no fear at all. There was none of the sensation of weight that a body possesses, none of the small pains of muscles or bones, nor was it necessary to blink. His throat wasn't dry and he did not need the unceasing flow of saliva or even oxygen: There was neither the need to breathe nor the subtle beating of blood through the veins and the whole physical body. He felt no cold or heat, only the tender sensation of being received, of satisfaction, which no one who has not been conscious in the world of the Bamso can understand. What was beyond? That was not the question; in fact, there was no answer at all, only going into that mist, from the diffuse himself into the diffuse.

Unworried, he looked to his side. From the shapeless suspended humidity, a figure slowly took form, a silhouette that walked toward him, followed by hues, colors, an aura, and a Being: it was Omboni. Asanaro smiled.

The Astral Being laughed.

"Hehehe ... we have a journey awaiting us, you know ... you knowing sensation."

"Yes!" replied Asanaro. "It's a great time to continue our lesson. I feel strong, renewed!"

"Ahaaa ... the rest having done you well, Traveler of the Bamso. Now you understand that this subtle world possessing cycles, not always you accede, only when it being time, only rested. Now it being time, now it being strong. You having to complete what you have started, having to clear the time-river that you carry, for in another way there will be no more advance.

You must know what your thoughts having been, what the weight of the road of time having been, the one you having carried in your batu-ma. Today being good sensation to travel . . . Follow me, we will finish what others having walked."

At an impulse he raised his head to look at the open sky: The stars seemed alive and close. It was like a blink, for when he lowered his gaze everything had changed.

Now the moist fog had turned into a hot sandstorm, as dense and dry. He had to control his own consciousness, making an effort to not let himself go at the feeling of the wind, the sand, and the heat. He knew that if he gave in, those sensations would become a reality for him, the shock of which would send him back to his body, and perhaps it would be a long time before his next opportunity to return. Omboni was by his side, and the Apprentice could not help but ask, "Where-when have you brought me?"

"Hehehe . . . where-when being where-when you want to solve . . . I do not bring you, only come with you . . . there being many time-places more interesting than this one, but for you and the weight of the time-river that you carry, this where-when you must solve. Advance, and you will see for yourself . . ."

After a moment the sandstorm cleared, and they saw the wide steppes of the desert. In front of them there was a group of camels, part of a complete caravan with many men and women wearing adornments and jewelry. They were dressed like Bedouin, in the old fashion of the Middle East. Some covered themselves with many robes to protect themselves from the heat of the desert and its enveloping sands.

The Astral visitors came closer to the caravan, joining the

pilgrims as if members of the group. Asanaro watched with fascination, feeling pity for those poor, laden animals, and curious at how docile they seemed. Their line was long and they carried many things, all very carefully wrapped. Most of the people walked silently. Suddenly a thought crossed Asanaro's mind: Wasn't this the great caravan of Mangazar and his friends, fleeing Alexandria? Omboni interrupted his thoughts and said, "Mmm ... nooo ... Apprentice of Dreams ... already Mangazar having been left behind for you ... behind four hundred sun-turns, after the now!"

"What ... ? Do you mean that we are four hundred years ... before the time of our last journey? But where are we?"

"Well, simple, Asanaro, in your words being so, we have jumped to a place close to the one in which we being the last time. But this being a different caravan ... with the same direction, heading East on your planet ... with different passengers, four hundred of your years before. We being further in the space of your world, being able to see the echo of this scene."

"Then, translating, if I've understood, we are close to the year zero in that era of my world!" said the Apprentice, trying to clarify his own thoughts.

"Hehehe ... well, yes, if so arranged you counting ... for this time knowing nothing of zero ... Hehehe ..."

"But who in this caravan has made us come here?" asked the Apprentice.

"Mmm ... remember this here being the projection of the Great Record, here travels someone who searches, known to you and your time-river."

They continued walking together with the caravan as the

Apprentice tried not to miss a single detail. The Astral Guide came closer to one of the camels, which was being pulled by a man wearing thick clothes just like the other pilgrims.

Asanaro came closer. The man uncovered his head and they could see that he was very young, still a teenager in fact, well built and not very tall. His skin was tanned dark by the strong sun of the East, his nose was thick and well defined, and his eyes were black, very black, and lively: His gaze was full of the imagination and singular happiness of youth. His hair was black, and tied back it hung to his shoulders; he had an incipient beard, typical of his age. Asanaro wondered why they were stopping to look at this kid. Intrigued, he asked, "Who is it, Omboni?"

"Ahaaaaa . . . being-was someone who searches. Open your mind, listen and you will know . . ."

In that moment, a man came back from far ahead. He looked older, with clear eyes and a hawk's nose.

"Secure that animal's load!" the man snapped. "Come on, Ieschuah Bar Iehuda! If you want to reach even the outskirts of old Seleucia, you must secure the camels! We are just beginning our journey, and . . . if the cargo doesn't reach our destination, then neither do you!"

The name sounded familiar to Asanaro. He searched his thoughts.

The older man continued checking the camels and was lost in the back of the caravan, though he could be heard through all of it, shouting orders at everyone.

"Secure the load, check everything! If you've lost anything, I'll make sure you wish to the gods you were born a slave or a woman!"

The Apprentice was still trying to figure out where he knew that name from.

"Mmmm..." Omboni intervened, "say what you thinking first ... being right."

Then the Apprentice said, "Ieschuah ... Ieschuah ... Ies ... Jes ... Jesus ... ?! Jesus. It's Jesus! Jesus! But how! Where are we, really? And if he's Jesus, then what is he doing in this caravan, and where is he going?"

"Hehehe ... as always, you not listening in detail. Pay attention, the Bamso requires lucidity, and to rid yourself of the inheritance of the torrent-thought."

Asanaro looked back at Omboni with curiosity, while keeping pace with the group marching through the solitude.

"But ... give me a hint. If he is Jesus, the one Jesus that I'm thinking about, he shouldn't be in any caravan going anywhere, least of all to the East ... he should be in Jerusalem, or Bethlehem, or something, any town in Israel, learning to be a carpenter or something like that. And what do you mean by the inheritance of I don't know what?"

"Mmm ... you see, Traveler of Time, you speak with the inheritance of thought, what speaking not being you, being what you inherited from your time-river, which being the torrent-thought. That being why you get confused."

"I'm still not clear ..." said Asanaro.

"Then clear yourself!" answered Omboni. "Or else you'll go back to unconsciousness. If you wanting to continue, then accept what you see, do not analyze it with your ..."

"Yes, yes, my torrent-thought ... it's just ... that ..." the Apprentice said, hesitating. "All right! He is Jesus, and he's

traveling to the East; this is a bit different from the image I had
of him . . . I don't know, I thought that he was blonder, thinner,
taller, but well . . . and besides, on the other hand, there's a lapse
in his life that's unknown . . . and no one has ever proven that
he was blond . . ."

"Hehehe . . . knowing the beings of your Earth, I correcting
you: there being a lapse in his life which it not being good to
talk about. There being always a difference between the myth
and the reality. If you want to learn, understand from the already
learned . . . That being good advice."

Asanaro still didn't fully believe that the person walking a few
feet from him leading some camels could be Jesus, the prophet
of the writings, the one that so much of the world called the
Son of God.

"Yesss, Apprentice of Time," Omboni said, "being your
inherited thoughts the ones that bringing you here, they lead
and they carry. Not for any Being have you come to this period
of time echoed; you being curious, you having things to clarify
that you do not understand, how they being inherited and how
trespassed. He being Jesus, the one your time speaks of, neither
before nor after, but your time—for you—being the eternity of
truth . . . yet the truth being that your time being only a shining
phantasm . . . you will see more."

"It's all right, Omboni," answered the Apprentice. "I know
I must open my mind; you have shown me enough times that
things aren't usually what they seem to be. It's just that it's
easier to take them that way before intending to know their
depths without prejudice, in an open way. It's true what you
say, I'm happy to be here . . . well, or happy to be visiting this
projection from the past. I've always been curious to know

about the life of Jesus, the one who's moved the world so much . . ."

The Guide of Time smiled as if to himself, as if he intended to say something to Asanaro but then stopped to say it in a different way, in the state of the Apprentice's mind.

"Mmm . . . to understand his life . . . forget what having moved the world, the world being always moved . . . not always for the reasons that you think. Now follow me, watch, and discover what you have to discover."

As they spoke, in the blink of an eye all the images before them vanished; the same caravan had jumped in time, and appeared near the ending of its journey. Greener valleys opened before them, and they could feel in the air the freshness of nearby waters. In the distance an Eastern city was rising, perhaps a mandatory way station for all traders in those years. The caravan, with its camels and people, looked happy at the sight of the city; the road was less barren, more inhabited, and people with their animals were walking along the same road, kindly greeting the new visitors. Children came from the surroundings, running joyfully by the tired camels.

The Travelers of Time were again with the young man. The older man, who seemed to be the director of the caravan, was with him, and the two of them spoke kindly to each other.

"Tell me, Ieschuah, are you planning to stay here in Seleucia? These are good towns for barter; I could introduce you to the heads of several caravans, for you've been a good assistant, and the road back from here to the cities of the Roman sea is much requested."

"No, Jacob, thank you for all your help, but my destination lies even farther . . . I want to continue to travel far beyond these valleys! Beyond the mountains . . . even beyond the Pass of Khyber, in the far East, to the lands of Sindh! I need to clarify many things about myself . . . I could not explain." The young man spoke with enthusiasm, yet fluidly.

"You and your crazy ideas . . . Always the same! You know that the road past Seleucia grows more and more dangerous. I don't understand your eagerness to travel, and not make some good money along the way! If you like traveling, then get into trade and commerce, young man, and forget all your crazy ideas! Religion hasn't saved our people from the Romans. And besides, maybe our people don't really need to be saved after all . . . hahahaha . . ."

The older man laughed hard, holding his belly. He looked tough and clever, and his voice was rough, like any good merchant of any era, from any place on Earth, but at the same time he was kind with that strange pilgrim. Once his laughter had ceased, he continued speaking, seeing the determination in the eyes of the young man.

"Do you know, Ieschuah? I think you're nice, and it's rare that I think that anyone is nice! You've got conviction, and I like that—only a few people have conviction nowadays. I've got conviction, you know . . . ? Yes! Conviction for good and legitimate gold coins, hahaha . . ." He laughed again before continuing, "I like you, kid, but listen to me: Religion is the hope and consolation of fools. I know you think I'm a tough man, maybe even a little ignorant, but I am no fool! I've seen many things in my life, I've seen how our people have been humiliated by those Romans so many times, but I do like their gold, and they pay

well. Let them sell me as a slave! After all, those bastards know
how to live well. There are many puritanical sorts who say they
hate the Romans, looking for salvation in God, but they're all a
bunch of cynical hypocrites, and they give lessons on morality
with one hand while the other gladly takes the Roman gold,
and that's what keeps them great, and safe from the Empire.

"Ieschuah, I don't believe in God. In my life and all my travels I've seen many different towns, too many gods, and in the
end every one of them understands one language: gold!"

"Jacob," replied the pilgrim, "I know what you're talking
about. I am young, but I've also seen what you have, and that is
why I've taken this journey, for I search for the correct answer,
to come closer to the truth."

The man answered, gesturing widely with his hands, "What
correct answer? Camel's dung! Let the desert storms take me!
There is no correct answer, Nazarene! Don't waste your youth,
do something practical with your life—don't waste it looking for
answers and craziness, there is no God of Israel nor any god anywhere, they're just old wives' tales to scare the fools! I'm telling
you, I know only one God that the whole world respects: gold!"

The young man walked quietly on, looking with bright eyes
at the buildings of the city as they slowly appeared before them.
Jacob added in a half-growl, "I've been watching you, and I can
see that you're as stubborn as a mule. Be careful, Ieschuah, the
profession of prophet has never been well paid, unless you're a
prophet in the court of the Caesar, and Rome is far away from
here. I've known many who preached, Nazarene, and all of those
I've kept track of ended up in one of two ways: saying their
prayers before the executioner, or before the gold that squeezes
the people."

The young man smiled and looked at him with compassion. "I know there are more ways . . . that is why I have to go on."

The man shook his head and made short gestures with his hands. As he calmed himself down, he added, "All right . . . all right! I know you won't change your mind. You should have stayed in your hometown and helped your father, your mother, and your brothers, like the writings tell us . . . not run away from them! But you are stubborn . . . I am worried about you, Iesch-uah, you're not the type of prophet who ends up counting their gold behind their gods, which wouldn't be so bad. But, well . . . poor prophet . . . the sands follow the winds! And the inevitable is inevitable, hahaha . . ." He placed his hands roughly on the young man's shoulders.

"Well . . . well, Nazarene, anyway, you'd never make me a good assistant . . . you think too much. Look, tomorrow, once we're in the city, I'll introduce you to some old friends of mine, traders, some of whom belong to the tribes of the Kusana of the Far East. They are very interested in opening a definite and more secure route between the old Kingdoms of the East and the Roman Sea, and they owe me some favors. They can take you where you want to go, beyond the summits of the Cau-casus, to the lands bathed by the river, son of Brahma, even to the mysterious Mountains of Bod!" He continued then, more serious, "But if you do become a prophet, pray for me and my goods."

The young man smiled, and answered Jacob, taking both his arms.

"I will always do so, I will always keep you present . . . I know you are a good person."

Suddenly the man seemed to wake up, and yelled out, "Aha-hahahaha . . . Let the desert swallow me! I'm a trader! When I die, something will save me, Nazarene! If it's your prayers, all the better. I insist, I like you, and you are from my land. But I also have friends who light their fires to Auramazda in my name, and some others who put their share in with Mithras, or with Osiris, even some of them I've saved pray and burn incense in my name before the Buddha, the God of King Ashoka . . . My old man taught me never to put all my dates in one basket . . . Hahahaha . . ." and he laughed loud, clutching his belly with his hands.

The Travelers of Time were softly gliding along with the caravan, and they listened carefully to the conversation between trader and pilgrim. Asanaro watched in detail all that was happening, or, more precisely, what was recorded in that state of the past. The determination, quietness, and energy of the young man, who would later be recognized as a savior and great Being, called his attention, and he thought as he listened that the truth was that Jesus had always had great conviction, as Jacob said. He looked very decided for one so young, radiating a determination that ceases before no barrier, something only a few have possessed.

"Mmm . . ." Omboni interrupted his thoughts, "youth in the body of the square-dimension and decision in the mind of the eighth being strong combination, Apprentice of Time."

"What will happen to him?" asked Asanaro. "Will his life end as history says . . . ? Will he find what he's looking for?"

The Astral Being answered, "Achieving or not achieving, only he having known . . . His road being hard, the roads of those

who search with sincerity always being hard ... its achievements or goals being immeasurable by the measures of your
world. Its success can be failure, and its failure success; the useless can be real and the real a waste of time. Apprentice of Time,
now you sleep ... for your world and you being useless ... for
you, you learning ... Where being your achievement and not
achievement ... ?"

After a pause, Omboni continued, "Mmm ... but you wondering if his life having the ending as your history says ... better
seeing for yourself ... hehehe ..."

The Apprentice was doubtful at Omboni's words, and the
vision of the caravan became blurry, vanishing like a mirage, the
same way it had formed.

He heard the voice of Omboni again, but his vision was confused: It was difficult for him to see, no matter how hard he
tried. Only a moment seemed to have passed, an Astral Blink,
and without realizing it he was in a new place. There were white
mountains, snowy and majestic, which reminded him of travels
he had taken in his bodily life. Suddenly he lost again the vision
of those landscapes that surrounded him as he felt a strong wind
blow huge amounts of snow whirling past his head.

He centered his mind in the consciousness of what he was
living, so as not to be swept away and taken back to his physical casing by the sensations he was perceiving; that was the last
thing he wanted. The best he could do was to speak, and revive
his consciousness.

"Omboni, where are we? I know this is a projection of time,

I know my body is safe and far away, I know I possess a body and
mind that is projected by the pure-wish, I know I am aware and
that my tendency is unconsciousness, to let myself get carried
away by apparent impressions ... Tell me, Omboni? Where are
we? Where-when does this projection of time-space belong to?
I am aware of my dreams! I am aware!"

Through the solitude of the mountains and the thickness
of the blustering winds laden with snow, he heard the familiar
voice of the Astral Being.

"Hehehe ... come on, Asanaro! I being here side by side
with your energy, I haven't stopped being-am ... Relax your
thoughts! Follow me, so we may continue our travels."

Rapidly the storm became silent, an innocuous bluster of
wind, and the majesty of the mountains reappeared. The great
expanses of snow reflected an incredible amount of light, but
it didn't bother him; on the contrary, it was refreshing to the
sensations of the Astral Traveler. Slowly, and without knowing
whether he had even been on Earth, they began flying together.
From above the vistas were marvelous. They brushed past the
highest summits, followed by great abysses where no living being
could be seen. The greatness and strength of the Earth could be
seen in all its essential power, and Asanaro laughed, enjoying its
beauty. He remembered the words of Alsam, "The best sensations are given us ..." He did not even want to ask any questions
of the Astral Being, wanting only to enjoy what he was living.
That sensation of flying freely was always unsurpassable, regardless of the time, place, or planet.

Thousands of feet below there were small valleys, thin creeks
where the snow gave way to the heat of the Earth. There was

barely any vegetation, but it was the brown color, with its varied hues spread out over rock and stone, that caught the attention of the Apprentice.

From those heights, the mountains spread out endlessly below them, and the colors uncovered by the snow were innumerably diverse, yet all in harmony with the dryness of the lands. Far away he could distinguish a couple of paths, winding delicately through the sharp slopes beneath the summits. The Astral Traveler wondered where they were, and if his vision matched the same projection in time, or if they had simply jumped to another moment and place without noticing, as had happened so often before. In that thought he heard the voice of Omboni.

"Mmm . . . Asanaro, close your eyes, then open them . . ."

"How . . . ?" he asked, thinking that he did not have his physical eyes to close.

"Simply do."

The Apprentice of Time, with no further thought, closed his eyes, and when he opened them the scene had changed again. He was no longer in the heights but on the slope of a great mountain, which seemed to be one of the mountains they had seen from above. The question was inevitable.

"Where-when are we, Omboni?"

"The eternal question . . . walk and you will see. You must learn to better control the sensation of state-time, and then not asking, for not always-dream being I by your side."

"But . . . what do you mean . . . ?"

"Mmm . . . it does not matter, Asanaro . . . now the important thing being for you to see and learn. That being important.

Watch carefully, these being mountains from ancient worlds . . . only their traces remain. It being the time of the one you called Jesus, but a few turns to the sun having happened since we last saw him, and he has lived and walked a distance to this place."

Omboni was quietly walking along a small path in the lonely mountainside, while the Apprentice wondered where they were going and who they would meet this time. It seemed strange to him how easily they walked in those places, without feeling cold or discomfort, and without the fear of falling from those enormous cliffs. As they advanced, the path grew narrower.

The view, even from the ground, was still impressive, and as they continued walking, the path was almost a thin thread drawn on the soil between the great wall formed by the mountains and the sheer drop below.

Asanaro, by some unconscious reflex, looked upward . . . and felt chills. There was someone sitting on the edge of a high boulder more than a hundred feet above them. He couldn't help but stop and examine the scene, and to his surprise there was not one but three figures sitting on the rock, unworried at the risk, the cold, and the solitude. The Apprentice was stunned, and he tried to clarify his vision even more. Soon he was able to see that the three figures were women, who, very curiously, were smiling, watching him. One of them dangled her legs from the height of her granite seat, while another lay her head on her partner's shoulder, and the third held her legs to her chest, resting her delicate chin on her knees. Asanaro was fascinated, frozen, and for some reason he thought he recognized the last young girl. Suddenly he heard Omboni's voice.

"Hehehe . . . let's go Apprentice, we have a task . . . we must follow our path . . ."

"But who are they? How can they see us?" asked the Apprentice of Time.

"They being Amlom . . . being travelers, and volatile, do you not remember? All the Travelers of Time being visited, sooner or later, by an Amlom, hehehe . . . Your time and energy will come. The Time of the Bamso can cover many states in one of your instants, but you being not yet prepared to understand.

The Apprentice was doubtful, and he felt again the feeling that his Astral Heart, if he really had one, was beating harder than usual. He asked, "But why her? Why is she watching me . . . ? Who is she?"

"Mmm . . ." whispered Omboni, "she being the element air . . . Hehehe . . ."

"What? Can't I talk to her?"

"Hehehe . . . you can do everything and nothing at the same time. This being a world of many dimension-times for you to understand: being too many worlds, yet you can create any projection you wish or any projection you wanting to know . . . but not yet prepared for having two Astral Bodies at a time. You must choose if we continue our route in the nearness of the year zero, or if you being going up there with her."

Asanaro's gaze was fixed on the beautiful Being that he seemed to know, felt he had seen before. The delicate young girl stood up on the corner of the rock where she had been sitting, just on the edge of the cliff, an ethereal breeze making her long hair fan out the aura playing softly along. She opened her arms and smiled with her eyes closed.

"Mmm . . . Astral Apprentices, always being the same! Hehehe . . . Listen, Astral foolish face, you, as always, now choosing!"

Asanaro could finally tune Omboni again.

"It's just that . . . It's just that she's so special . . . I've never felt anything like this . . . It seems that all the sensations of Earth's dimension are multiplied and embellished."

"Mmm . . . all right, Dream Catcher. I see that the lessons of the Record not being so interesting as before . . . In a way, that being good . . . you looking for new worlds in the Bamso, and they being infinite . . . But remember, for you to understand you must understand from where you coming. You not being that one who woke up every day in being-city! We still having many tasks remaining . . ."

"All right, Omboni . . . you know I want to learn, but allow me to go with the Amlom . . ."

"You go . . . I not allowing or disallowing, you being. Many nights remain, Asanaro, many journeys ahead, and there being time for this part of the Universal Record. Hehehe . . . I having a great flight-plan for you . . . You seeing this time, seeing your time, the time of the world before your time-river, even before the two continents . . . and then, being a great flight-plan of your world-future! If you knowing the time-river, knowing its waves and its shapes, you can know how the river being ahead . . . Mmm . . . but you deserving rest in the dimension of the Superior World, go now with the Amlom . . . she will take you to her dimension. Now do! Feeeeel . . ."

The Apprentice felt he had already heard some part of what Omboni was saying, but in that moment he just looked at him thankfully, thoughtfully, and smiled. He knew he would see Omboni again, though he couldn't be certain when.

"Hehehe . . ." Omboni chuckled, "remember Apprentice, the Time after Dreams being the Dream of Time! Hehehe . . ." He made a quick gesture with his head, and winked at Asanaro with his Astral eye, giving him the signal to leave.

The beautiful Amlom was still sitting there in the heights, enjoying the sensation of that imaginary wind in her ethereal and vaporous body. Asanaro looked upward and wanted to fly to where she was, but, curiously, he could not. He looked to his side, but Omboni had already vanished.

He decided to climb up in the style of the Earthly dimension, step by step, and so he did. With great effort he grasped each rock, slowly moving higher, wondering why he couldn't fly. It crossed his mind that he might be too excited. He continued climbing, slowly. Suddenly he felt a soft hand touch his left shoulder from behind. Without seeing it he knew it was feminine, and in a blink, without a thought he looked, and to his surprise there was the Amlom, riding her beautiful white Pegasus, suspended in the air. She extended her arm without a word. The Apprentice took it, and without even knowing how he was already riding the Pegasus, flying with that extraordinary Being.

They flew beyond the clouds, beyond the dimension of the Records, to those states that caressed the stars and their eight luminescences.

VII.

Being the Dream
of Time . . .

The Star-Sun was born with the turning of the planet. Slowly its rays reached the first summits, then the mountainsides, and, finally, the lonely tent of the Apprentice of the Bamso. The Earthly nature continued in its inscrutable cycle, as always, beyond the dictates of man.

The little birds began their morning songs while the sun completed yet another birth between the peaks. The creek bubbled crystal clear as the waters cascaded down from the summits, along the slopes, and down to the valleys. The morning was exceptionally clear, transparent, without a cloud in the sky. The heat seeped into Asanaro's tent without compassion. Moments before waking, he could be heard saying, "Amlom . . . Amlom . . ."

Suddenly the Apprentice returned to the Earthly dimension,

with all of its discomforts and limitations. It had been a strange night. All of it remained clear in his mind: Omboni, his words, and especially the vision of the Amlom and the extraordinary places they had visited, as well as the moments they had spent together. He kept these in the profound secrecy of himself, not even trying to look for an explanation.

That morning's awakening was full of happiness and vibration. He felt as if he were still in the Astral World; even though the normal sensations of the body were solid and concrete, he could now appreciate them in a different way . . . perhaps, simply, like one more state . . . one of many, as ephemeral and circumstantial as any other.

After slowly regaining himself and doing his exercises, he got up to look for Alsam; he wanted to talk to him, tell him many things. Once outside his tent he looked around, but Alsam was nowhere to be found. Asanaro remembered the field where Alsam was always working on his figures. He went quickly there, but when he arrived he stopped in his tracks and his jaw dropped at what he saw.

There was nothing . . . the circle was gone, the figures around it had vanished; there was no trace of any of it. It was as if the winds had come and erased all of it . . . it couldn't be, he couldn't believe it. He went back down, behind the bushes, where Alsam had built his tent. He opened the trees, and there was nothing there, either. His heart jumped. "It can't be," he told himself, "it can't be . . ." Then he remembered that he had never actually walked Alsam to his tent, for Alsam had always said farewell first and disappeared behind those thick bushes, so he had assumed his Guide had built his shelter there. He did not know how he could have ignored that detail. The idea crossed Asanaro's mind that Alsam could have pitched his tent farther up, closer to the rock ledge below the summit where they had sometimes talked. So he ran there, searching, and after a scrambling ascent he arrived, drenched in sweat. There was nothing to be found there, and nothing in the surroundings.

He felt as if everything was rushing at him, and he was very confused. Could he still be sleeping, and that moment part of a conscious dream, different from what he was used to? No, it was impossible. He sat on the edge of the rocks and looked down at the valley, which seemed more alone than ever.

After a while he could distinguish far away a group of people wearing backpacks. He said to himself, "I'm such a fool! I thought I was going crazy, or the dimensions had gotten tangled..." and laughed at himself. "Knowing Alsam, he's packed up everything, taken his tent, and gone to greet the students in the valley; they're coming today; that must be them. I'm sure he doesn't want them to know we've already been here so many days... and I was starting to think crazy thoughts... hahaha...!"

As quickly as he had climbed the rocks he was hurrying down now to greet the group, where he was certain he would find Alsam. Of course he wouldn't leave his students on their own.

In a few moments he had reached the valley, and the group was approaching quickly. A couple hundred feet past the camp he found himself face-to-face with the line of hikers. He saw Rudolph and Jessica first, and asked them immediately, "Where's Alsam...? Isn't he back? I've been looking for him!"

Jessica looked surprised, and said, "He's not coming with us..."

Without waiting for her to finish speaking Asanaro ran to ask the rest of the group. Their looks and answers were all the same. At last Hernan, who was sweating and complaining because of the heat, said, "But why are you asking for him if he's not coming?"

"What do you mean he's not coming . . . ?" Asanaro asked desperately.

The whole group was gathering together, repeating the answer he had already heard from Hernan. Another student named Joseph added, "Alsam left three weeks ago. He closed the school for the whole summer. Just three days after the last class, the class you were in, he called us all for a meeting. It caught us by surprise. Since you didn't show up, we figured we wouldn't see you again until after the summer."

The Apprentice immediately fell to the ground. The students thought he was simply tired from the walk he must have taken some time before. Joseph sensed that Asanaro did not really under-stand what had happened, so he sat by his side and explained.

"He had us all there for that meeting; we tried to let you know, but at your house they said you were away on your own vacation, backpacking. Alsam said he had to travel abroad, something he hadn't planned but was necessary. You know how reserved he is . . . he wouldn't give us any more details. So he gave us the whole summer off . . . and to be honest, we're all a little worried that he might not be coming back."

The entire group was gathered there, talking as they put down their heavy backpacks. Vanessa, who had been walking with Joseph, said, "We just got together on our own and decided that we should come anyway . . . Why weren't you waiting for us down there?"

Asanaro was thoughtful. Everything seemed so strange, and questions circled inside his head.

"Well . . . I just moved forward a bit."

As he spoke he got up and ran to his tent, while the rest began to settle their camp. Rushing inside his little shelter, he searched among his things and took the knit bag in which he had decided to keep the small oval piece of wood that Alsam had given him only two nights ago . . . and there it was, intact and unblemished. He wondered if it was really Alsam who had given it to him . . . but he wasn't sure of anything anymore. The whole world was spinning around him. Yet one thought stuck in his mind, about the whole time he had spent in that lonely place. Had it all been some sort of conscious dream, but in life? In the end the foods he took from the peasants as a present for Alsam could have been a present for himself. It was inexplicable, and at the same time, he understood.

Asanaro left his tent and began walking toward the mountainside. No one in the group noticed; they were entertained settling their tents and talking among themselves. Slowly he began to ascend, toward the rising ledge where Alsam supposedly had sat and watched the mountains in those now mysterious days. As he sat there he felt more comfortable, enjoying the vista of the valleys, abysses, and the sky, a soft smile on his lips.

After eighteen days he felt he had emptied himself of many prejudices; he also felt strangely happy and fulfilled, though with many more questions than answers. He thought, speaking to himself, and closing that chapter of his life, "Where do dreams begin, and where does reality begin? Aren't they part of the same knitting . . . ? Really, who am I . . . ?"

In that moment he thought about the space . . . the flowing of time, and the dimensions of consciousness he had crossed—it was something that would be beyond explanation for him for a long time, as long as he still did not fully control the Art of the Bamso, the Art of Dreams.

These questions continued revolving in his mind for days and days, but he saved for himself those strange facts that blurred between projection and consciousness. He would wait until he saw Alsam again, and even though it might never happen in the dimension of the Earth, he now held the key to the place where they could meet whenever they wished, the same key that, in the future, might open again for him the hermetic gates of the Great Bamso, where he might resolve all of the adventures and journeys that remained unfinished.

Just a few words were imprinted in his mind, words that sounded like a message from another world:

The Time after the Dream
being the Dream of Time

Mmm . . .

First Part Completed on:
Tuesday, Third Day
Seventh Month
Circle to the Sun, Time of the Bamsei
Northern Hemisphere
Earth

To be continued ...

FURTHER INFORMATION

Asanaro, author of this book and teacher of the Arts described within, teaches at and supervises the Mmulargan School, a center for the Boabom Arts. These Arts are grounded in the understanding that body and mind form a perfect unity, essential and complete.

Within the Mmulargan School, three basic Arts are taught:

- Seamm-Jasani, or the Art for Eternal Youth, which is developed through fluid movements, meditation, and relaxation
- Traditional Boabom, or the Osseous Art of defense and meditation of the Inner Path
- Yaanbao, or the Art of Elements, which develops a complete cycle of coordinations, defense, and relaxation by using elements of various sizes and shapes as an extension of the movement

For further information about the Mmulargan School, visit:

www.boabom.org
E-mail: boabom@boabom.org

The principal Boabom School in the United States is located in Boston, Massachusetts. It offers regular classes through the primary development of these Arts, as well as special seminars and intensive courses. For more information on the Boston School of Boabom, please visit:

www.bostonboabom.com

Classes are also being taught in New York City. For more information, please visit:

www.boabom-nyc.com

BOABOM ®

ABOUT THE AUTHOR

Asanaro has dedicated more than twenty-five years to the study and transmission of the Boabom Arts, a path with roots in pre-Buddhist Tibet. The teachings of Boabom are transmitted in various ways, including breathing techniques, relaxation, defense, meditation, and philosophy.

Asanaro has taught around the world, offering courses, workshops, and seminars as well as developing schools in South America, Europe, and the United States. He has also been instrumental in the founding and creation of many different centers and associations for alternative arts and medicine.

He is the author of *The Secret Art of Seamm Jasani: 58 Movements for Eternal Youth from Ancient Tibet*, a practical course book in Seamm-Jasani; *The Secret Art of Boabom: Awaken Inner Power Through Defense Meditation from Ancient Tibet*, an introduction to Boabom; and *Bamso II: The Legend of the Mmulmmat*, the tale of a lost world in the ancient mountains of Tibet (The Valley of the Warm Breeze), describing the mythical origins of the Boabom teachings. Asanaro currently resides in the United States.

For further information about Asanaro, visit:

www.asanaro.com

If you wish to contact the author, ask a question, or make a comment, please e-mail him:

asanaro@boabom.org

Asanaro is currently sponsoring the Tibetan Altruism Association, an organization based in Lhasa with the goal of fighting poverty through improving education and health services in Tibet. You can find out more about the Tibetan Altruism Association at:

www.tibetaltruism.org